PIPE DREAMS

Also by JACQUES POITRAS

JACQUES POITRAS

PIPE DREAMS

THE FIGHT FOR CANADA'S ENERGY FUTURE

VIKING

VIKING

an imprint of Penguin Canada, a division of Penguin Random House Canada Limited

Canada • USA • UK • Ireland • Australia • New Zealand • India • South Africa • China

First published 2018

www.penguinrandomhouse.ca

LIBRARY AND ARCHIVES CANADA CATALOGUING IN PUBLICATION

Poitras, Jacques, 1968-, author
Pipe dreams : the fight for Canada's energy future / Jacques Poitras.

Issued in print and electronic formats.
ISBN 978-0-7352-3335-5 (hardcover).—ISBN 978-0-7352-3336-2 (electronic)

I. Petroleum industry and trade—Political aspects—Canada. 2. Petroleum pipelines—Political
aspects—Canada. 3. Petroleum pipelines—Social aspects—Canada. 4. Environmentalism—Canada.
5. Global warming—Political aspects—Canada. 6. Energy industries—Canada--Forecasting. I. Title.

HD9574.C22P57 2018   338.2'72820971   C2018-902406-2
                                                     C2018-902407-0

Jacket and interior design by Andrew Roberts
Jacket image by VisionsofAmerica/Joe Sohm/Getty Images

Printed and bound in Canada

10 9 8 7 6 5 4 3 2 1

Penguin
Random House
VIKING CANADA

For Giselle

From the beginning he had seen the railway as a device to unite the nation—to tie the settled East to the new country beyond the Shield. Now in the very first year of its construction the railway had become a divisive force, antagonizing the very people it was supposed to link together.

—Pierre Berton, *The Last Spike*

CONTENTS

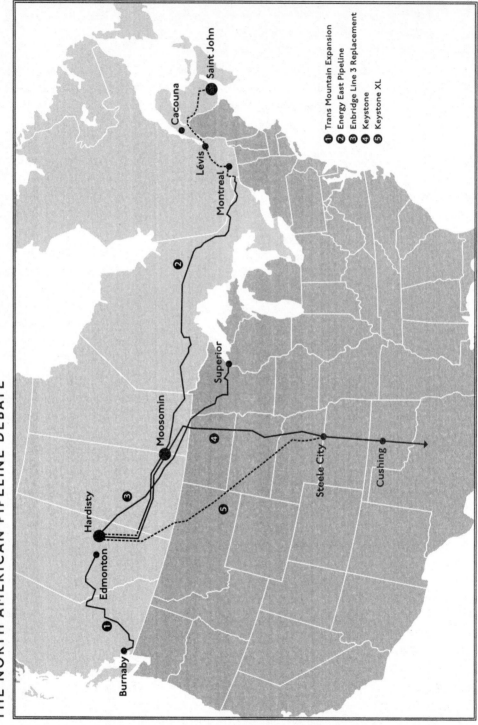

THE NORTH AMERICAN PIPELINE DEBATE

1 Trans Mountain Expansion
2 Energy East Pipeline
3 Enbridge Line 3 Replacement
4 Keystone
5 Keystone XL

Saint John
Cacouna
Lévis
Montreal
Superior
Moosomin
Hardisty
Edmonton
Burnaby
Steele City
Cushing

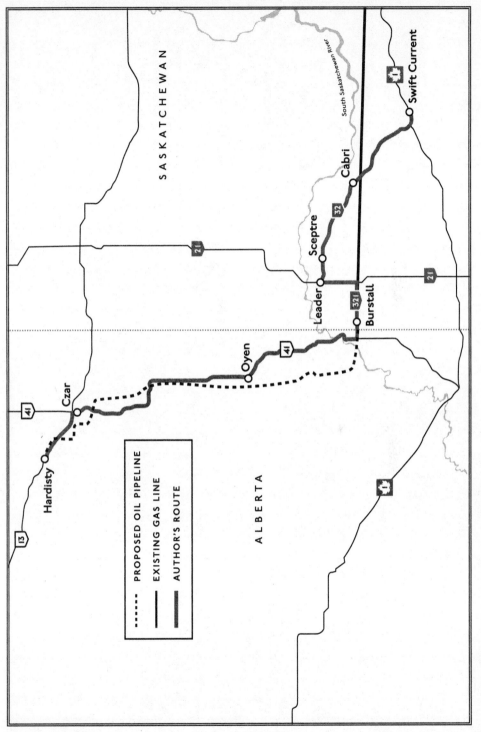

HARDISTY TO SWIFT CURRENT

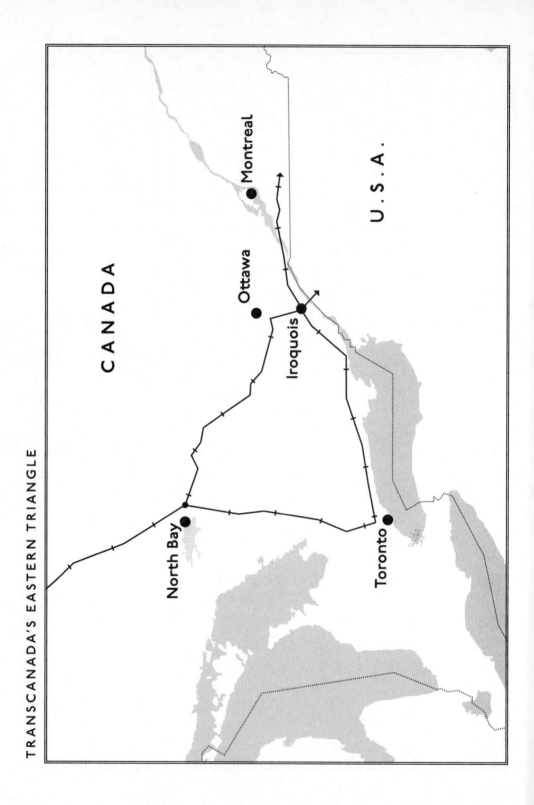

TRANSCANADA'S EASTERN TRIANGLE

CANADA

U.S.A.

Montreal

Ottawa

Iroquois

North Bay

Toronto

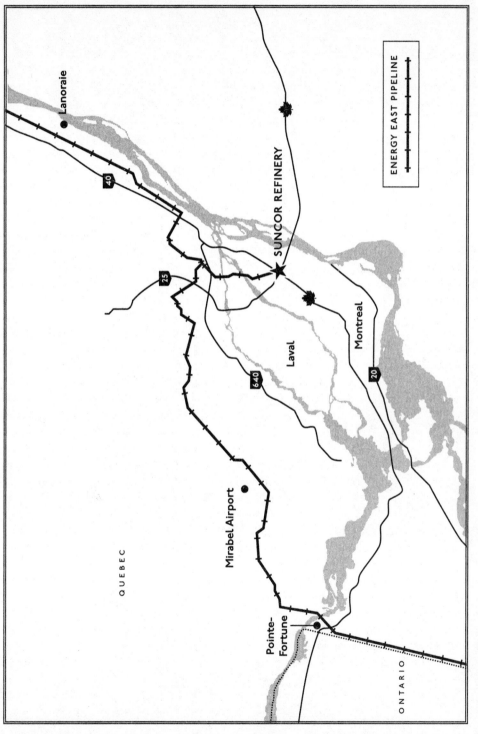

ENERGY EAST PIPELINE

Lanoraie

SUNCOR REFINERY

40

25

640

Laval

Montreal

20

QUEBEC

Mirabel Airport

Pointe-
Fortune

ONTARIO

MONTREAL:ENERGY EAST

TIMELINE OF KEY EVENTS

Nov. 10, 2011   U.S. president Barack Obama calls Canadian Prime minister Stephen Harper to tell him that the Keystone XL approval process is on hold.

Nov. 28, 2011   Former New Brunswick premier Frank McKenna floats the idea of a west–east pipeline in an opinion article in the *Financial Post*.

April 26, 2012   The Harper government introduces the omnibus Bill C-38, which streamlines the pipeline approval process, imposes a two-year deadline for a decision, incorporates environmental assessment considerations into the National Energy Board process, and gives cabinet the power to overrule an NEB rejection.

July 29, 2012   British Columbia premier Christy Clark issues demands that Alberta must meet in order to win her approval of the Northern Gateway pipeline to the Pacific coast.

Nov. 22, 2012   Alberta premier Alison Redford and Quebec premier Pauline Marois discuss the west–east pipeline concept in Halifax.

Dec. 19, 2012   New Brunswick's legislature unanimously passes a motion supporting the west–east pipeline.

Feb. 3, 2013	New Brunswick premier David Alward travels to Alberta to promote the pipeline.
June 6–7, 2013	Alison Redford visits Fredericton and Saint John to promote the pipeline.
June 18, 2013	Arthur Irving visits Frank McKenna in Toronto to discuss his frustrations with the TransCanada negotiations.
June 19, 2013	Irving Oil CEO Paul Browning and TransCanada vice-president Alex Pourbaix make key compromises to reach a deal.
July 6, 2013	An oil train derails and explodes at Lac-Mégantic, Quebec, killing forty-seven people.
Aug. 1, 2013	TransCanada officially announces that it will apply to the National Energy Board for approval of Energy East.
March 23, 2014	Alison Redford resigns as premier of Alberta.
April 7, 2014	Philippe Couillard and the Quebec Liberal Party win a majority government.
Sept. 22, 2014	Brian Gallant's Liberals win the New Brunswick election.
Oct. 30, 2014	TransCanada submits its Energy East application to the National Energy Board.
Nov. 21, 2014	Ontario premier Kathleen Wynne and Philippe Couillard announce that they agree on seven conditions for Energy East.
Nov. 23, 2014	Gabriel Nadeau-Dubois donates the money from his Governor General's Award for French-language non-fiction to Coule Pas Chez Nous.
April 2, 2015	TransCanada announces that it will not build an export terminal at the port of Gros-Cacouna.
May 5, 2015	Rachel Notley's NDP is elected in Alberta.
Aug. 13, 2015	The Ontario Energy Board concludes that there is an "imbalance" between the risks and rewards of the Energy East project.
Oct. 19, 2015	Justin Trudeau's Liberals win the federal election.
Nov. 5, 2015	TransCanada says that it will not build an export terminal anywhere in Quebec.

Nov. 6, 2015	President Barack Obama announces that he will not issue a permit for the Keystone XL pipeline.
Nov. 30– Dec. 12, 2015	The Paris summit on climate change agrees on a framework for global emissions.
Dec. 17, 2015	TransCanada files an amended Energy East application to the National Energy Board.
Jan. 21, 2016	Montreal mayor Denis Coderre and other mayors in the metropolitan area declare that they are opposed to the Energy East pipeline.
Jan. 27, 2016	The Trudeau government announces additional interim review processes for the Trans Mountain and Energy East pipelines.
Feb. 26, 2016	TransCanada signs its agreement with Carry the Kettle First Nation.
March 1, 2016	Quebec environment minister David Heurtel seeks a court injunction to force TransCanada to submit to a provincial BAPE review.
April 4, 2016	Brad Wall is re-elected premier of Saskatchewan.
April 10, 2016	In Edmonton, federal NDP delegates vote to discuss the Leap Manifesto.
April 22, 2016	TransCanada agrees to go through Quebec's environmental assessment process.
July 20–21, 2016	A Husky oil pipeline leaks into the North Saskatchewan River.
Aug. 4, 2016	Mike DeSouza's story in the *National Observer* reveals that Jean Charest discussed Energy East with NEB members during their "engagement" session.
Aug. 8, 2016	The National Energy Board hearings on Energy East begin in Saint John.
Aug. 29, 2016	Protesters halt the first day of NEB hearings in Montreal.
Sept. 9, 2016	NEB panel members and chairperson Peter Watson recuse themselves from the Energy East review.

Sept. 9, 2016	The Saskatchewan government announces a new pipeline inspection program.
Oct. 3, 2016	Prime Minister Justin Trudeau announces the federal carbon-pricing plan.
Nov. 29, 2016	Trudeau announces the approval of the Trans Mountain pipeline and the Enbridge Line 3 upgrade and the rejection of Northern Gateway. Saskatchewan announces new pipeline rules.
Jan. 9, 2017	A new Energy East panel is selected by the National Energy Board.
Jan. 10, 2017	Transition Initiative Kenora files a legal challenge calling for a restart of the project review.
Jan. 24, 2017	Donald Trump signs an executive memo inviting a new Keystone XL application.
Jan. 26, 2017	TransCanada submits a new Keystone XL application to the U.S. State Department.
Jan. 27, 2017	The NEB's new Energy East panel announces that the process will restart, and that once it deems TransCanada's application to be complete, the twenty-one-month timeline will begin anew.
Feb. 1, 2017	TransCanada reaffirms its commitment to Energy East.
March 24, 2017	Trump grants a permit to Keystone XL.
May 10, 2017	The NEB seeks comments on proposed new criteria for the Energy East review, including upstream and downstream emissions impacts.
Aug. 10, 2017	Brad Wall announces that he will retire from politics.
Aug. 23, 2017	The NEB confirms that it will apply the new criteria it proposed in May.
Sept. 7, 2017	TransCanada announces a thirty-day suspension of the Energy East application.
Oct. 5, 2017	TransCanada cancels Energy East.
May 29, 2018	The Trudeau government announces the nationalization of the Trans Mountain pipeline.

PROLOGUE

SUSPENDED

BRIAN GALLANT WAS IN the dark when the blow fell. It was the evening of September 7, 2017, not long after the thirty-five-year-old premier of New Brunswick had left a Liberal Party event in the city of Miramichi. Word arrived of a press release he had to see. An assistant was driving while Gallant, seated in the back, flicked at the glowing screen of his phone. The release was from TransCanada Pipelines. The company was suspending its application to the National Energy Board for Energy East, a 4600-kilometre oil pipeline made of steel and extending from Alberta to New Brunswick. Citing "significant changes to the regulatory process," the company said it would take thirty days to assess how the new criteria would affect the project's "costs, schedules and viability." It added that the project might be cancelled altogether.

"It wasn't a surprise," Gallant acknowledged a few days later. The NEB, the country's energy regulator, had announced two weeks earlier that "given increasing public interest" in greenhouse gas emissions, "together with increasing governmental actions and commitments," its regulatory review of the project would include an assessment of likely emissions created by Energy East—both upstream, at the point of extraction in the oil sands of Alberta, and downstream, in the combustion engines of the cars driven by buyers of gasoline. The board, long criticized as too accommodating of the oil sector, would also look at "supply and demand scenarios" under new government climate change policies in order to assess whether those measures would affect the business viability of the pipeline.

This heavy burden had never before been applied to a Canadian pipeline project. In the past, an NEB review had simply assessed the emissions from the construction and operation of the pipeline itself, not its broader impact on production and consumption. The new federal Liberal government of Justin Trudeau wanted more rigorous environmental reviews, but Energy East had filed its initial application long before he took power, and was subject, ostensibly, to the older, more industry-friendly rules. Now the NEB review panel was exercising its independent authority to add the new criteria. Would a pipeline cause more extraction, more fuel consumption, more greenhouse gases? The board would attempt to answer those questions.

From the back of his van speeding down a darkened two-lane provincial highway, Gallant took a call from Russ Girling, TransCanada's CEO. The premier had hoped that recent positive signals from the federal government, like its approval of Kinder Morgan's Trans Mountain line to the Pacific coast, would reassure TransCanada that national policy still supported pipelines. But Girling said that the new criteria introduced uncertainty. Gallant agreed. Assessing emissions was "something I can certainly live with," he would say, "but the fact that we're changing course and adding yet another twist and turn is the worrisome part. . . . It really will destabilize the market, and makes it hard for proponents to invest." He asked Girling what he could do to help; the CEO responded that TransCanada needed "clarity" on how the NEB planned to conduct the new assessments. Gallant said he'd do what he could, and they ended the call.

TransCanada's decision, though preliminary, was an economic blow to New Brunswick. Skeptics disputed Gallant's math, but the premier claimed that Energy East would create three thousand jobs in New Brunswick over nine years—no small impact in a province of 750,000 people long beset by high unemployment. Gallant hadn't included those enticing job-creation estimates in his Liberal government's economic growth forecasts, but he now seemed likely to share the fate of many of his predecessors, who had promoted big, "game-changing" energy megaprojects—a new nuclear reactor, a second oil refinery, shale gas development—only to see them fall victim to market conditions and environmental objections.

And TransCanada's decision was a political blow, too: though Gallant had inherited Energy East from David Alward, the Progressive Conservative premier he'd defeated, the young Liberal politician had worked hard to sell the project. He'd been featured in a TransCanada promotional video and had appeared on Quebec television to debate the mayor of Montreal, a pipeline opponent. Many of the Energy East jobs would have been created in Saint John, the one-time industrial heart of the province and the planned site of the pipeline's storage tanks and export terminal. Gallant's Liberals held only one seat in Saint John; just three days before the news broke about Energy East, the premier had assigned himself ministerial responsibility for the city, hoping to make gains there in the election a year away. Now he was confronting a hard reality: the project was collapsing, and his critics would link him to his Liberal ally Justin Trudeau's environmental policies. After all, Gallant's government had passed on the opportunity to file arguments against the new NEB criteria when the board was considering them. "The pipeline is now the victim of first-degree murder," a provincial newspaper editorialized. "Yet the weapon was not Macbeth's dagger or Brutus's sword, but a soft, warm, fuzzy pillow, with which the pipeline was slowly smothered."

The suspension of Energy East was also a blow to Canada's economy. In 2012, TD Bank had declared pipeline expansion "a national priority." Oil and gas accounted for 20 percent of Canada's economic growth in 2010 and 2011, the bank said, but the sector's full potential had been stifled. The shale boom in the United States had created a glut of oil at the storage and trading hub in Cushing, Oklahoma. Bitumen from the Canadian oil sands—heavier and thus costlier to process—had to be sold there at a discount. In late 2012, the discount was 30 percent, which translated into $6 billion in lost royalty revenues for Alberta in 2013, and $4 billion less for the federal treasury. A pipeline to the coast would get the oil to ocean-going super-tankers and would let producers fetch the higher global benchmark price. And Energy East, Alberta's route to the Bay of Fundy, was the key to unlocking that wealth.

So TransCanada's announcement was also a blow to Alberta's oil sector—and supporters of that sector reacted with fury. Terry Etam, a writer for an online oil industry newsletter, referred to the new NEB criteria as the "Soviet-style strangulation" of Energy East and said that if the rules were really designed to address climate change, there should be "a universal standard" for all energy projects. An "energy citizens" group, backed by an oil industry association, launched a letter-writing campaign to MPs, asking them to "tell the National Energy Board that enough is enough—that their job is done and it's time to get out of the way of nation-building infrastructure projects." Alberta Conservative MP Michelle Rempel blamed the additional criteria not on the NEB but on "extreme incompetence by an ideological Liberal government that is opposed to development of the energy sector, writ large." Even Justin Trudeau's allies distanced themselves from him: Alberta's NDP energy minister, Margaret McCuaig-Boyd, accused the NEB of "historic overreach" and said that her province's climate plan was sufficient to deal with emissions. Trudeau, she pointed out, had cited the Alberta plan when his cabinet approved another pipeline in 2016.

But if pipeline projects were suddenly endangered, it was also because of other factors—factors far more damaging than anything a prime minister could create and far beyond the control of a panel of NEB members. The impediments began in 2014, before Justin Trudeau was in power, when oil prices plunged. By 2016, the world barrel price was half what it had been when Energy East was conceived. The extraction of bitumen from Alberta was expensive, but it was prohibitively so now. "In a world of triple-digit oil prices, those costs can be absorbed; in a world of $40-per-barrel oil, they can't," the high-profile economist Jeff Rubin warned in 2015. "In that world, it's not worth having a debate over environmentally contentious pipeline projects."

A report by an internal government think tank, Policy Horizons Canada, echoed Rubin's caution: renewable energy was becoming cheaper more quickly than expected, "significantly disrupting fossil-fuel markets," it said; Alberta's most lucrative export "could lose its commodity status." ExxonMobil, the world's largest oil company, wrote down more than three billion barrels of crude from the oil sands in 2017, essentially declaring them unrecoverable.

So many blows to the oil sector—and for Energy East, another had come from the White House. President Donald Trump issued a permit in 2017 to allow TransCanada to build its long-delayed Keystone XL pipeline to the Gulf of Mexico. Given the slowing pace of production in the oil sands, Trevor Tombe, an economist at the University of Calgary, suggested that even Keystone might not be at full capacity until 2030. "In our view, Trans Mountain plus the Keystone pipeline would make the Energy East pipeline less needed," said industry analyst Divya Reddy. "It doesn't seem like that extra capacity is needed." Another economist, Andrew Leach of the University of Alberta, tweeted that TransCanada was using the new NEB criteria as a scapegoat for a decision on Energy East based more on economic fundamentals. "It might have just a little more to do with a lack of a million barrels per day of new production looking to pay ten-dollar-plus-per-barrel tolls to New Brunswick," he said.

Or maybe TransCanada's warning wasn't a blow but a feint—an attempt to pressure the Trudeau government into backing off. If so, Ottawa was calling the company's bluff: a spokesperson for the natural resources minister, Jim Carr, told reporters that Energy East was "ultimately a private-sector decision." Trudeau himself said he wouldn't interfere: "It's up to companies and proponents to figure out the best path forward." It was a stunning turn of events: for five years, political and business leaders had laboured to build support for the $15 billion pipeline. They'd infused it with symbolism, describing it as a project that would bring the country together. And now it was slipping away.

Energy East had become the canary in the coalmine of Canada's energy future. Keystone XL and Trans Mountain still faced challenges, but they had successfully navigated the arduous regulatory process. Some believed they might become the last major pipelines capable of winning approval in North America. In that way, TransCanada's halting of its application was a reflection of an entire industry wondering what the future held. Was a new fossil fuel infrastructure possible in the rough-and-tumble collision of opinions inherent in a democracy, and was it even viable in a world grappling with climate change and a possible peak in oil demand?

How different the mood had been on a bright, sunny morning in June 2013 when the premier of Alberta, Alison Redford, arrived at the New Brunswick Legislative Assembly. The sandstone building had officially opened in 1882, when the nascent Canadian Pacific Railway hadn't yet been built as far as the tiny settlement of Fort Calgary, which would grow into Canada's oil capital and the locus of Redford's political career.

The two provinces could not have been more different. New Brunswick, one of the four founding provinces of Confederation, had seen its economic strength and political clout diminish since 1882. It was, in the shorthand of the federal equalization program, a "have not" province that received funding from wealthy provinces via Ottawa. Its indicators—employment, gross domestic product, literacy, health—lagged behind the national average. Several forestry mills had closed, shrinking the province's biggest industry. The global crash of 2008 and desperate government stimulus spending had created record-high deficits. Alberta, meanwhile, was an oil giant, the linchpin of Canada's drive to become an "energy superpower," in the words of Stephen Harper. Its oil sands, with lucrative jobs and seemingly endless growth, drew thousands of workers from New Brunswick and the rest of Atlantic Canada. So many Maritimers commuted, usually on two-weeks-on, two-weeks-off rotations, that Air Canada drew up new flight schedules to cater to the migration.

And now Alberta was throwing New Brunswick a lifeline, a potential physical connection to that wealth. "There's a new friendship between our two provinces," Redford told the elected members, "one that points to how powerful we are when we come together as Canadians in the national interest."

This was an unusual message from an Alberta premier. Redford's predecessors had focused inward, treating the province's oil wealth as a resource to be guarded from rapacious non-Albertan outsiders, especially the national government in Ottawa. "Let the Eastern Bastards Freeze in the Dark," declared a bumper sticker popular when Pierre Trudeau's government tried to grab an extra share of Alberta's oil revenue. Stephen Harper and several of his fellow Alberta policy wonks once called for a "firewall" around the province.

Redford was different. Born in British Columbia, she'd lived in Nova Scotia as a child and had studied in Saskatchewan. Her peripatetic biography, and her work as an international human rights lawyer and a political staffer in Ottawa, gave her a more moderate, worldly conservatism and a more expansive view of Alberta's position. "When I was first elected premier and talked about Alberta's role in Canada, that had not been the political tradition in Alberta for many years," she said in an interview. "It had been very much a situation where political success in Alberta for premiers had always been about fighting Ottawa, which in my mind was fighting the national interest."

Now, as Redford saw it, Alberta's interest aligned with the national interest: she had a problem, and have-not New Brunswick and its premier, David Alward, a one-time cow farmer and son of a Baptist minister, offered a solution. An increasingly noisy campaign by environmentalists was pushing President Barack Obama to reject Keystone XL, blocking more oil exports to the province's traditional market in the United States. Oil companies had also proposed a pipeline called Northern Gateway to the Pacific coast, but had run up against Christy Clark, the British Columbia premier, who insisted that Alberta meet a list of conditions before she would allow it. That stymied Redford's deeper objective to broaden Canada's energy focus away from the United States, where Alberta producers were paid a discounted price for their crude. If the oil could get to China and India, where a growing middle class was buying cars, the province's royalties would soar. "When you started to look at those differentials, getting it into Asia, whether through the west or the east, was much more profitable than going to the States," Redford said. "We made a decision proactively to try to market to Asia as opposed to the United States."

The west or the east: the Pacific was so close that the latter option seemed far-fetched at first, but it made more and more sense as Christy Clark dug in and B.C. Indigenous leaders girded for a fight. Alberta's production was growing fast enough that all three pipelines would be needed, but Saint John, New Brunswick's largest city, offered two unique advantages. There was its natural deepwater port, which could accommodate the world's largest supertankers, giving them economies of scale in shipping to Asia. And there was Canada's largest oil refinery, owned by the reclusive and controversial Irving family. "A west–east pipeline will allow us to take advantage of some amazing synergies between Alberta and New Brunswick and use them for the benefit of all Canadians," Redford told the New Brunswick legislators. Eastern refineries, including Irving's, were importing millions of barrels of foreign oil, she said, sending money out of the country. "We can do better than this."

There was a third advantage: New Brunswick wanted the project. Redford's sales pitch was part of an elaborately choreographed political dance. Alward had been to Alberta to promote New Brunswick to the province's oil producers. As he and his energy minister, Craig Leonard, boarded their flight at Fredericton's airport on a cold February morning in 2013, they had met New Brunswickers travelling to work in the Alberta oil patch. "Go get 'em, Dave," they told the premier. "Bring that pipeline home." In Calgary and Edmonton, Alward was received as a hero. "This was what was going to save Alberta," Leonard recalled. "They needed us. It felt like we were really building something important." The marketing plan wrote itself: "Alberta had a definite need to find a home for their oil that could get them the market price," Leonard said, "and here was New Brunswick, desperate for jobs, with the infrastructure already in place—the port and the Irving refinery. It just made perfect sense for the two provinces to work together and try to build that support across the nation."

At a scrum with reporters after Redford's Fredericton speech, she and Alward were ebullient. Even Quebec's separatist government, normally wary of the symbolism of pan-Canadian projects, was buying in, they said. Redford had met with Premier Pauline Marois, and they'd set up a working group of Alberta and Quebec bureaucrats to exchange information. Dallas McCready, one of Alward's advisers, found Marois surprisingly agreeable on the topic. "What one would have expected from a Parti Québécois premier, we got the exact opposite. She wanted to make sure it was good for Quebec— that was first and foremost—but she had no objection to the fact it was important to the rest of the country." Alward had also met with premiers of Ontario and Manitoba. "Collectively across the country, leaders get it," he said, "how this project makes sense for Canada, individually as provinces, but very much for Canadians."

Later that day the two premiers travelled to Saint John, where Redford gave a business-luncheon speech and toured the Irving Oil refinery, the proposed destination for some of her province's crude oil after its journey across six provinces. The refinery was already receiving oil from across the continent by rail, but a pipeline would be cheaper and safer.

The sprawling facility and its owner, eighty-two-year-old billionaire Arthur Irving, were the last pieces in the west–east puzzle. They offered something TransCanada lacked: marine experience. Redford's most vivid memory was not of her meeting with the Maritime tycoon, but of her glimpse of an object floating in the bay a few kilometres from land, a buoy that anchored a pipe running back to storage tanks on the shore. "People sometimes laughed when I talked about this," Redford recalled, "but when you're standing on that point and you see those storage tanks, and you see those railway tracks that have shipped product from Alberta, and you see that one buoy in the middle of the harbour, where all of the resources that are produced and refined in Canada can be shipped out and make their way across the world—that is very powerful, it is impactful and it's important for our country." The Irvings had built it, she said, "because it was a wise investment, and they did it because it was good for Canada."

The buoy that inspired Redford's ode to nationhood didn't move Canadian oil to world markets, however. It was an *intake* tube for Saudi oil, and Venezuelan oil, and Nigerian oil, and whatever other foreign crude Irving could acquire at the best price at a given moment. Supertankers plugged into the pipe to feed imported crude *into* the refinery.

But technical precision wasn't a consideration when a new national metaphor was taking shape. After a quarter century of national unity crises and hand-wringing over firewalls and eastern bastards, after decades of rhetoric that Canada was destined to surrender to the north–south reality of continentalism and globalization, the country seemed to be getting its east–west act together, returning to its origin story to tie itself together once more with a great feat of engineering. To listen to Redford and Alward, it was a journey both new and familiar, akin to John A. Macdonald's national dream of a cross-country railway. The optimism was infectious.

It didn't—perhaps it couldn't—last.

The woman one row back on Air Canada flight 1159 was explaining environmental activism to the passenger next to her. "They would much rather the oil stay in the ground," she said, describing the militant voices opposing Alberta's oil sands and the pipelines that would carry their product to market.

"They would much rather we use Iraqi oil." It was September 6, 2016, and we were descending into Calgary, the heart of Canada's oil industry.

My fellow passenger's agitation was widely shared. The consensus championed by Premier Alison Redford three years earlier in Fredericton had shattered. She was gone, and so was David Alward; their successors continued to champion Energy East, but faced growing opposition and interprovincial discord. "We're acting like a bunch of villages as opposed to a nation," Alberta's new premier, Rachel Notley, told journalists in frustration. In Quebec, the Parti Québécois, out of power, was now firmly against the pipeline, but so was the federalist mayor of Montreal, Denis Coderre. Quebec's Liberal premier, Philippe Couillard, though initially supportive, was wavering. So was Ontario. Clean-water activists in Winnipeg were protesting, and Indigenous leaders were restive. New climate change policies were polarizing the debate further. Justin Trudeau faced "an interprovincial war of words" over the pipeline that, to *Toronto Star* columnist Chantal Hébert, evoked not Sir John A.'s Canadian Pacific Railway but the failed Meech Lake constitutional agreement of 1987. Redford's "bright new spirit of cooperation" was nowhere to be seen. Instead, Energy East had turned into "a unity minefield," Hébert wrote, exposing Canada's longstanding regional and economic divisions.

In the midst of this, I took that flight to Alberta to begin a journey along the Energy East route. I wanted to grasp the scale of the project by seeing the landscape it would span—and I wanted to understand how it was being transformed from a piece of infrastructure, an engineering challenge, and a symbol of unity into the latest front in the climate wars. I also wanted to see whether a consensus was still possible on the broader questions it raised about oil, energy, and climate change.

By the time the journey ended, however, the story had become a whodunit. I would witness the slow-motion killing of the $15 billion energy project— a series of blows dealt not just to a single pipeline proposal, but to Canada's carbon economy—a death that also signalled, perhaps, the birth of something new.

PART ONE

ALBERTA

I

KILOMETRE ZERO

IN HARDISTY, ALBERTA, PEOPLE get things done.

People like Lori Goodrich—who in the fall of 2009 "got wind," as she put it, that Canadian Pacific Railway would demolish its derelict train station at the edge of town. Word gets around fast in a town of seven hundred people. Goodrich, an amateur historian, was more alarmed than most. The CPR had made Hardisty: in 1904, the railway chose a location near the Battle River as the site of a freight depot where equipment and horses could be loaded onto cars on the new Edmonton–Saskatchewan branch line. People poured in, and in 1911 the town, named for Richard Hardisty, a Hudson's Bay fur trader who negotiated with Louis Riel and became Alberta's first senator, was incorporated. "The population then was probably bigger than it is now," Goodrich told me. Hardisty became a rail–farm hub and a commercial connection to the wider world; the station was a monument to that history. "It was the last one of this design left in Alberta," she said. "It was the oldest building in Hardisty, and it was rundown. Terrible. We took it upon ourselves to save it."

Goodrich recruited several family members and they went to work. They bought the station for a dollar, had it lifted and trucked a half kilometre to a new location near the town's main intersection, and then spent most weekends over the next couple of years sprucing it up. "We left the original walls, but we gutted it." They made one room available for a local wellness program and rented another for conferences. Oil companies used it for meetings. Tea, coffee, and smoothies were served, and the station became a going concern. But in 2012 the labour of love became a burden when Goodrich's brother-in-law was diagnosed with terminal cancer, and they sold the station to a local entrepreneur. Clayton Hinkey agreed to maintain the building "as close to the original as possible" as he transformed it into a sports bar called the Leaf, which catered mainly to workers in Hardisty's oil and gas industry.

Lori Goodrich had the open, outgoing demeanour typical of the local do-gooder. Her gold jewellery reflected her sunny disposition as the cool light of the early afternoon seeped through the windows of the Leaf. The place was buzzing, even in the post-lunch lull. A sign outside advertised for servers, cooks, and kitchen staff. Despite the recent drop in oil prices—we met in September 2016, when oil was just over forty dollars a barrel—the town was busy. "Overall, Hardisty never really gets dead or slow," Goodrich's nephew, Jeff Golka, told me. "It just keeps humming along. There's enough industry here now." New motels had opened, as had a new restaurant on Main Street, and the hardware store had a new owner who was expanding the place. "There are so many major companies here," Golka said, "there's always something going on." Golka's optimism was an occupational necessity: he was the local real estate agent, with a big sign out by the provincial highway. But Hardisty did tend to ride out short-term busts in the oil sector. The big oil sands projects were long-term ventures, built to recoup their investment over decades. "When prices decline to unprofitable levels on a short-term basis, they still produce with an expectation that profitability will return on a long-term basis," said Ben Brunnen, an economist with the Canadian Association of Petroleum Producers. The product had to keep moving, and when it moved, it moved through Hardisty.

"Calgary has had the highest hit in staffing and downturns, because that's where they start, at the corporate level," Anita Miller, the mayor, told me. "Here, luckily, most of these companies have hardly had any layoffs." Companies like Gibson Energy were still building new storage tanks. "There definitely isn't as much construction," Miller said. "Our town isn't as busy. But the hotels and restaurants are still getting good business. That's how they make their living, from all the transient workers who are here building a tank or connecting a tank."

The real danger was long-term decline. Boom-bust cycles were a fact of life in Alberta's oil sector, but if prices never rebounded, then the construction of new oil sands projects would slow down, and eventually, so would Hardisty. Jeff Rubin, the former chief economist with the Canadian Imperial Bank of Commerce, warned in 2015 that the price crash signalled "there was no longer an economic context for the huge expansion planned for oil sands production." Goodrich was seeing indicators: car dealers, used to customers trading for new trucks every couple of years, were calling their regulars to come in and make a deal. Her husband, Ed, an oil field consultant, had steady work for fifteen years, but for nine months in 2015 he found himself at home with nothing to do. After a few weeks' work, he was off again for another long stretch. "This is going to go on for a long time before we ever see the industry turn around to where it's boom times again," Goodrich said.

There was one thing that would have helped, one bit of potential good news that Goodrich had been convinced would give Hardisty, and Alberta, a boost. She'd wanted federal and provincial leaders to adopt some of the town's can-do spirit, the same spirit that had saved the train station, and get a new oil pipeline approved. Construction would boost the local economy and get Alberta's oil to lucrative foreign markets. "People started gearing up for that, as you can see—all the motels and everything that started up here a couple of years ago," Goodrich said. But the new line, Keystone XL, never arrived. Existential shivers went down the town's spine. Some experts said that if oil was facing a long-term decline, it was all the more urgent that Alberta get its oil out of the ground quickly and shipped to the coast for the higher world price—before demand dropped off for good.

Enbridge's Alberta Clipper, a 1600-kilometre pipeline from Hardisty to the port of Superior, Wisconsin, had been approved with little controversy in 2009. But now, pipelines—just a conduit for the product, in the view of the people of Hardisty—had become an easy target for environmental activists, and weren't being authorized as readily as they had been. "It's all politics," Goodrich said with a rueful little shake of her head. "Unfortunately, the provincial and federal leaders right now don't get it." Even people in the industry didn't understand at first, she said. "They're getting it now."

Hardisty is a two-hour drive southeast of Edmonton, mostly along a straight two-lane highway cutting diagonally through the fields of central Alberta. Tiny towns dot the road, each community just a couple of dusty streets wedged into the corner of a square farm site, part of the grid of 640-acre, one-square-mile sections that surveyors marked for the first settlers. The pattern still defines much of the rural west today. But Hardisty is different from the moment it comes into view: shimmering metallic forms spread across the horizon, hazy outlines of giant drums and tubes and power transmission lines sprawling over the grid lines.

The town was clean, prosperous, and bustling. Trucks, tankers, and equipment were on the move up and down 49th Street, which led into town from the provincial road. The R&R Inn at the corner was a spiffier-than-average roadside motel; signs in each room asked oil workers to use specially designated red towels "for washing excess grease/grime." A Gibson Energy lot was full of fuel trucks. Nearby low-rise buildings housed companies catering to the oil business. All of it sprang from the agglomeration of steel on the hill, the heart of the Hardisty economy. "It's actually quite a huge facility out there," Jeff Golka said, and he was right: the entire town would fit inside the complex of storage tanks, compressor stations, and pipes.

Hardisty's status as a hub, created by rail, had endured thanks to oil. Mayor Anita Miller's family once owned a farm on land where the tank farm now sits. "I literally grew up out there," she said. The first big pipeline came through in 1950, just three years after the oil strike at Leduc, which launched the modern industry in Alberta. Interprovincial Pipe Line, later renamed Enbridge, built 1816 kilometres of line from Edmonton to the port of Superior, Wisconsin, to transport oil as far as the shipping lanes of the Great Lakes. Goodrich's father-in-law was one of the consultants on the project. The line was extended from Superior through the United States and back into Canada to reach refineries at Sarnia, Ontario, in 1953.

When the oil sands shifted into high gear around the turn of the twenty-first century, Hardisty was a natural receiving point for the Athabasca pipeline running from Suncor's site near Fort McMurray. Known as "dilbit"—thick bitumen diluted with chemicals to move through the network—the oil is stored and blended in those dozens of massive drums until it's shipped out in pipelines running east and south to a hungry North American energy market. The price for Western Canada Select, the benchmark for heavy oil sands bitumen, is set there.

Golka watched the tanks spread out over the landscape as a young man. "My dad had a couple of the first trucks hauling oil out there," he told me. The complex grew and grew: more pipelines, more tanks, more shipping companies. Goodrich told me that North America was so reliant on the large volumes of crude passing through Hardisty, and the potential economic consequences of disrupting it were so high, that the town was once listed as the fourth most important potential terrorist target in Canada.

Pipelines were a normal part of the landscape, so when TransCanada first proposed the Keystone XL line in 2008, no one in Hardisty doubted that the project would get quick approval and the town would become Kilometre Zero yet again. TransCanada already had one Keystone line, from Hardisty to the Alberta–Saskatchewan border, where it fed into a converted gas line to carry the oil to near Winnipeg, and then south into the American Midwest. Keystone XL would create a shortcut, a larger pipe cutting across Montana, South Dakota, and Nebraska in a diagonal line that would move more oil more quickly to a junction in Steele City, Nebraska. An extension would reach Cushing, Oklahoma, home of the world's largest oil storage tank farm, and a final section would continue to the refineries in Texas on the Gulf of Mexico.

The National Energy Board quickly approved the Canadian section. A green light from Barack Obama was considered inevitable; George W. Bush had granted the permits for the initial Keystone system, and Obama had approved the Alberta Clipper in 2009. Moreover, TransCanada had a sterling reputation for safety and reliability. Not only did it use the strongest steel, the best welding technology, and the best coating, but it was also a world leader in monitoring. "There is no better pipeline in the world than the ones built by TransCanada and Enbridge," Hal Kvisle, a former CEO of TransCanada, told me in an interview. "We crossed the Andes not once but three times. No other company in the world has done that."

Nebraska would be a snap.

In Nebraska, the Calgary pipeline executives were seen as presumptuous big-shot businessmen. When a few cattlemen refused offers of money, declaring that they didn't want the pipeline on their land, TransCanada threatened to invoke eminent domain, a legal process used to force an owner to allow private development. This offended the cattlemen's libertarian ethos. Ranchers in the Sand Hills, a vast, ecologically fragile area of grass-covered sand dunes in the central part of the state, wondered what an accident might mean for their land and for the large freshwater aquifer beneath it. The BP Deepwater Horizon explosion in the Gulf of Mexico and the Enbridge pipeline spill in the Kalamazoo River in Michigan had occurred months apart in 2010, and the dilbit that spilled into the Kalamazoo—similar to what Keystone XL would carry—had sunk and wouldn't biodegrade, making it difficult to clean up.

Environmentalists and other progressive activists allied themselves with the ranchers, using petitions, email lists, databases, and social media to demand that the State Department reject the permit application for Keystone XL. Washington commissioned additional studies; landowners asked the Nebraska state government to demand a different route. TransCanada resisted, fearing that any change would require a restart of the federal review from scratch. And it had federal reports showing that environmental objections were overblown. Secretary of State Hillary Clinton said she was "inclined" to allow Keystone XL.

Her boss, President Barack Obama, was preparing to run for re-election, however, and he was looking for a win on climate change. Obama's push for cap-and-trade legislation had failed narrowly in 2009, and after the Republicans won both houses of Congress a year later, legislative action was out of the question. Nebraska's demand for a new Keystone XL route set off a chain reaction of new reviews and state legislation, which gave opponents, including a growing list of celebrity activists, more time to lobby the president.

Prime Minister Stephen Harper had proudly called the development of Alberta's oil sands "an enterprise of epic proportions," and predicted that they'd make Canada "an energy superpower." But the oil sands had a reputation for dirty extraction methods, making them a tempting target for activists, who put pressure on the president. In November 2011, Obama told Harper that a new State Department review would delay the decision past the 2012 presidential election. "We'd always been told that there were legally defined criteria by which their decision had to be made, and they had nothing to do with politics," a former adviser to Harper told me in an interview. But "the intelligence we picked up was [that the delay] was really a case of a political football being kicked down the field."

The Alberta government launched a U.S. marketing campaign to improve the image of the oil sands while Harper and his ministers used speeches and visits south of the border to pressure Obama. The prime minister "wanted to signal that this would continue to be an issue in Canada–U.S. relationships," his former adviser said. "We would seek to signal to the United States that this would continue to be an open issue that would irritate them, and we were going to try to undo some of the benefit that [Obama] was seeking by not deciding at that time."

After Obama was re-elected, the environmentalists gained the upper hand. "It got way, way worse," the Harper adviser recalled. An early conversation between the new secretary of state, John Kerry, and John Baird, Canada's foreign minister, "was pretty negative." Every step forward was followed by a step back. Nebraska's governor approved a new route that avoided the Sand Hills, and the State Department reported that halting Keystone XL would not reduce emissions: the project was unlikely to spur a net increase in oil sands production because, without the pipeline, the same oil would just move by rail. But the U.S. Environmental Protection Agency disputed some of the findings and suggested that the oil sands should be compared to alternative supplies, such as conventional drilling, which was less dirty. The oil sands were projected to contribute to a 23 percent increase in emissions between 2005 and 2020, so the comparison was a losing proposition for TransCanada. "The net effects of the pipeline's impact on our climate will be absolutely critical to determining whether this project is allowed to go forward," Obama said in a Georgetown University speech in June 2013. A month later, he dismissed one of the strongest arguments for the project, telling *The New York Times* that jobs created by Keystone XL would be just a "blip."

Dennis McConaghy, a former TransCanada executive, recounted how the company urged both Harper and the Canadian Association of Petroleum Producers to consider a bold gambit: the adoption of a carbon tax. Especially after Obama's Georgetown speech, McConaghy said, a price on emissions "should have been pursued more publicly and with greater conviction as the last card Canada had to play, to see if an approval could have been salvaged." A carbon tax would have "tested" Obama's goodwill, he said. "Had Canada actually done that, it might have actually allowed Obama to say within his own country, 'Here's the rationalization I have for this approval. They are doing what we ideally would have liked to have done.'"

Alberta's premier, Alison Redford, supported the approach but feared it was too late. "It was very difficult for Canadians to be taken seriously as partners on issues involving the environment and climate change because our federal government was so resistant to the issues and resistant to getting involved in the issues," Redford said in an interview. "It made it very difficult for other interested parties, whether it was a provincial government or private companies, to get done what they needed to get done."

The suggestion was a non-starter. Harper had been re-elected in 2008 by campaigning against a proposed Liberal carbon tax. And the prime minister's advisers were convinced that no climate policy would satisfy American activists, whom they considered extremists. "It wasn't being against this pipeline or that pipeline," the senior adviser said. "They didn't want production to grow, and they wanted production to cease." Harper was convinced that Obama had caved in to radicals. "Look," he told Bloomberg News, "I'm not telling any tales out of school that the reason for the holdup is politics, and it is politics of a fairly narrow nature."

The prime minister became increasingly frank about his frustration over Keystone XL, signalling that he'd wait out Obama. "My view is you don't take no for an answer," he told a business audience in New York in September 2013. "If we were to get that, that won't be final. This won't be final until it's approved and we will keep pushing forward." At another business conference, he said that Keystone's approval "under the right circumstances" was inevitable—a clear reference to the end of the president's term in January 2017. But Harper's time in office ran out first: he was defeated in the 2015 federal election. Days later, Obama officially rejected Keystone XL, declaring he wouldn't issue a permit for a project that "would not serve the national interest of the United States."

In Hardisty, the news was received with resignation. The town had seen a remarkable 483 percent increase in construction permits in 2012, some of it based on Keystone XL's being a sure thing. But many people in town could read the signals from Obama as well as any prime ministerial adviser. "I don't think any of us were one hundred percent surprised, from the statements he'd been making," Mayor Miller said. That didn't make it any easier to swallow. Jeff Golka couldn't fathom Obama's reasoning. "It doesn't really seem to be anything substantial," he said. "We're used to living with pipelines and we're used to living with decent environmental regulations—or strict, I call them." Before he got into real estate, Golka ran a company doing oil spill cleanups and reclamation. "I think our standards are very high," he told me. Hardest to accept was that it was the United States, an ally, a like-minded nation, rejecting Canadian oil. "I really don't understand why we can't make a relationship with a neighbour like that," he said. "It baffles me."

The decision was a downer, but Hardisty kept chugging along, Mayor Miller said, "because we have so many companies out there and they're doing other things. . . . It's hard to tell if it's quieter because of TransCanada, or is it because Enbridge is quiet, or is it because Husky's quiet? You can't say just because of 'this,' Hardisty's quieter."

And the oil, after all, was still moving.

The day I was in Hardisty I drove around the tank farm, spinning through the roads criss-crossing the vast complex, my tires kicking up dust along alleys of giant drums bearing names like Gibson and Enbridge. Some were painted white, some light green; some had flat tops and others shining silver domes. Fencing and electrical lines and piping filled the spaces between the tanks. Most of this elaborate metal web sat on the south side of Route 13, while on the north side sat the three white tanks that made up TransCanada's Hardisty A Terminal. Farther up the hill seven more tanks, rust-coloured and unpainted, squatted forlornly at the planned Hardisty C Terminal, designed for Keystone XL. "I'm sure they're still hoping and planning," Golka said.

Any smart business has more than one option, however, and five kilometres down the road from Hardisty was the industry's backup plan: a vast rail yard, an oval of concentric train tracks. A kilometre and a half long, tucked behind some hills off Route 13, it was too large to see as a whole unless you could get some elevation—and there was none here.

A single train of black oil tanker cars sat on the outermost track. Around the other side was a long rail shed connected by pipeline to Gibson Energy's storage tanks back near Hardisty. "The terminal's strategic location and direct pipeline connection to substantial storage capacity provides efficient access to the major producers in the region," the yard's builder, USD Group, said on its website. The terminal, which opened in 2014, could load two 120-railcar trains per day. The track connected to Canadian Pacific's main line, and thus to the rest of the continent.

The oil-by-rail boom began in 2008, around the same time that the U.S. oil glut opened a gap between the American benchmark price, known as West Texas Intermediate, and Western Canadian Select, the Alberta benchmark. Alberta oil became cheap enough that refineries in eastern North America were willing to bring it in on trains. Although shipping by rail was more expensive than by pipeline, the gap made it profitable. "When the differentials to [West Texas Intermediate] blew out, that's when we started to look at rail," Ryan Gritzfeldt, a vice-president at Crescent Point Energy, said in an interview. "There's a tipping point when rail economics become better, and they can be substantially better."

From 2009 to 2013, the number of tanker cars carrying crude east leapt from eight thousand to four hundred thousand, a fiftyfold increase. Regulations and inspections couldn't keep up. Even after the July 2013 rail explosion in Lac-Mégantic, Quebec, killed forty-seven residents—exposing the safety risk in dramatic and tragic fashion—oil by rail continued to grow, with an 83 percent increase in the barrels shipped per day from 2013 to 2014. TransCanada CEO Russ Girling told Reuters that his company, stymied on Keystone XL, might enter the rail market. "Our customers have needed to wait for several years, so we're in discussions with them now over the rail option," he said in May 2014.

Only the stunning crash in prices later that year reversed the trend, when rail's relatively higher cost made it unprofitable. But Gritzfeldt predicted it would make a comeback if prices rebounded and new pipelines weren't built. "If everybody had their choice, pipelines would be the safest, most environmentally friendly way to go," he acknowledged. But if companies followed the rules, they could reduce the danger of rail. It was striking that even after the Lac-Mégantic disaster, an industry that acknowledged the risk was willing to gamble on railways—if the return was high enough and pipelines weren't available. The yard outside Hardisty was a loaded gun pointed at the temple of public opinion: *stop us before we use this again.*

But industry and political leaders had also turned their thoughts to another option, labelled "improbable" and a "moon shot" by Bloomberg News. It was fanciful, but it would refashion the fight for pipelines into a national crusade: a line to run Alberta bitumen all the way from the big storage tanks in Hardisty across the prairies, through the Canadian Shield, down to the St. Lawrence River and into New Brunswick, where, after more than four thousand kilometres, it would reach the tides of the Bay of Fundy. From there, tankers could ship it to Europe or Asia to earn the even higher world price—about double the Western Canadian Select benchmark in early 2013—or even around the tip of Florida to the Gulf of Mexico, Keystone XL's erstwhile destination. There was enough oil to warrant three pipelines, but given Obama's stubbornness, a cross-Canada route to the east coast seemed tantalizingly easy in the short term. "Once you get on tidewater, you can get anywhere, and you don't need a presidential permit to bring oil into the Gulf Coast," Girling said in February 2013. "It's not a Plan B, it's a Plan A, and it will go if the market supports it, along with Keystone."

In Hardisty, the west–east concept was instantly popular. "To have two options is a good thing," Golka said. "In the business world, if you have something that's ready to go at the right time, you'll be successful. That's what we need to look at. Don't wait."

Hardisty was still waiting in September 2016.

More than three years after TransCanada gave the project a name, Energy East, and announced it would proceed, the same fears that had doomed Keystone XL—spills, explosions, climate impact, "big oil"—were being raised about the new project. Mayor Miller pointed out that there had never been a major leak around Hardisty, the most pipeline-laden town in Canada. "The requirements today compared to the requirements of seventy years ago have increased tenfold," she said. "There's governing bodies that check those things and make sure everybody's following the regulations."

Jeff Golka was discouraged by Obama's rejection of Keystone, but found opposition to Energy East particularly galling. Every region of Canada, every *Canadian*, should support a west–east pipeline. "Oil companies are willing to do it, and each provincial government should be willing to do the same in a tough economy," he said. "So now we're sitting here and waiting for something to happen, within our own country, to get the oil moving. Why are we sitting here? . . . Let's do something and get it going, and look at it as a country-building thing."

Golka's aunt, Lori Goodrich, was frustrated too. "It's unfortunate our leaders don't get their acts together," she said. "And all the other provinces still have their hands out, waiting for the transfer payments. How do you give transfer payments when you've got a hundred thousand people out of work?" Canadian politicians weren't responsible for the global drop in oil prices, but Goodrich thought they could show a little of Hardisty's spunky determination and get the project moving. "I believe in human energy, and when you've got leaders who are putting out a negative attitude," she said, "that's negative energy."

Mere hours after my conversations with Golka and Goodrich, while I was still puttering around Hardisty, word came of a major setback to Energy East.

Three members of the National Energy Board panel, which had finally launched regulatory hearings into the proposal, recused themselves. They were accused of bias for secretly meeting with a pipeline lobbyist. The review would have to start over, with new panellists, and there was no word on how long that might take. But it wouldn't be quick, and time was short. Warning signs were adding up that Alberta's economy itself was in doubt, and that delays to the pipeline could prove fatal.

Back in the nineties, Jeff Golka's father, Johnny, took the lead on a local community project that Golka still spoke of with pride. "We had a drought for many years—ten or fifteen years in a row," Golka said. "We were losing our lake." The lake—a big pond, really—was part of the municipal park wedged between the Lakeview Golf Course and 49th Street, Hardisty's main artery. "There were people who were saying we didn't need to spend any money to keep water in our lake," Golka recounted, "but we were watching little islands show up in the water, and water people were saying, 'It'll turn,' and once it's upside down, you can't bring it back." Johnny had a possible solution: run a pipeline two kilometres from the Battle River on the other side of town into the lake to replenish it with a new source of freshwater.

This would be complicated. There were regulations galore, environmental assessments to conduct, inspections, paperwork. "We had everybody, Fisheries and Oceans, and Alberta Wildlife, and everything," Jeff said. But Johnny was unrelenting, "and we did it. We got approvals." To pay for the line, Johnny Golka and his committee organized fundraising auctions and dances. They also convinced the big oil and pipeline companies in Hardisty, like Enbridge and TransCanada, to kick in. "When there's something that needs to get done, people get behind it," Goodrich said. Hardisty is a town of transients—she estimated that only half of the seven hundred residents had grown up there—"but when something comes up, the community gets behind it."

More importantly, Johnny built a consensus among disparate interests. The golf club, for example, was worried what the impact would be on its water service, so he put someone from its executive on his committee. "Now they were part of it," Golka said. "We were hearing all the issues and everybody's perspectives." They found common ground, the pipe was installed in 2000, and the lake was saved. Its beach and campground continue to provide a respite from Alberta's arid climate. Water skiers and Sea-Doos ply the waters.

I suggested to Jeff Golka that some of Johnny's can-do attitude and consensus-building might come in handy in the larger pipeline debate consuming Canada. He nodded. "The little struggles we had here as a community are very similar to a large pipeline," he said: the balancing of interests, the need to consult, the importance of common ground. "It brings communities together, stuff like that, projects. Even projects like Energy East—there are differences at the start, but when the economies get going and things start to happen, it's a win for the community."

But unity on a 4600-kilometre pipeline, and the bitumen oil that would flow through it, was proving more elusive, and certainly couldn't be achieved in Hardisty alone—if at all.

2

"I WILL MAKE IT FEASIBLE"

THE LAND OUTSIDE HARDISTY was just hilly enough not to be called "flat." Patches of scrub and trees dotted the terrain. The road to the rail yard, stands of birch trees, the Hughenden Golf Club, a couple of tiny towns, a sign advertising liquor and cold beer at the general store—all rushed up and fell away. The CP rail line ran along the provincial road heading southeast.

My plan was to follow the proposed Energy East route as closely as I could manage by car, from the tank farm on the edge of Hardisty to the site of the planned export terminal on the Bay of Fundy in New Brunswick. In Alberta, this meant following the ghost of Keystone XL: although the bulk of Energy East would consist of one of TransCanada's gas lines, converted for oil, the section from Hardisty to the Saskatchewan border would be new construction. To avoid having to repeat its previous engineering and environmental work, however, the company planned to use the route it had mapped out for Keystone XL, with a couple of exceptions.

Shorncliffe Lake, about thirty minutes outside Hardisty off Route 13, was one of them. A small subdivision of twenty well-maintained houses had been built on a single main road that looped back around on itself; beyond it was the shimmering lake. A private driveway became a little dirt path that ran down to the water. It was 9:00 a.m. and the calm surface reflected the clear sky. A pickup truck was parked on the grass, and in the distance a lone kayaker was moving silently across the water, followed by two dogs on the shore. I waved, and the kayak turned around and headed toward me.

Shorncliffe Lake was where TransCanada had made its first route adjustment. The Keystone XL route was to follow the southern shore, along the CPR branch line, then pass south of the little town of Czar at the far end of the lake. But the company decided to move Energy East north of the lake then turn it toward Czar, a detour of six kilometres. "This route avoids issues associated with construction space requirements, high groundwater, gravel extraction, and a sharp-tailed grouse lek," the company explained in one of its regulatory filings.

I scanned the shore for the sharp-tailed grouse, but it was the wrong season. The Alberta Conservation Association says that the bird is "quiet, well camouflaged" for most of the year, but that its spring "shenanigans"—an elaborate mating ritual that sees the males flutter their wings, stomp their feet, and spin in a tight circle—are "undoubtedly one of the most impressive spectacles in Alberta's natural history calendar." The "lek" is where this spring dance takes place. High grass increases the chance of nesting success, the association says, but loss of habitat meant the grouse's numbers were dwindling in the province. The species was listed as "sensitive." The province regulated grouse hunting by keeping the season short and setting bag limits.

"I've seen them," Diane Vincent said after she paddled her kayak up to the shore and disembarked. "They'll be in and around the foliage all around the lake." Vincent didn't know that TransCanada had shifted the pipeline route to avoid the grouse: there had been no local agitation for the change, she said, and the company hadn't held public meetings in the area where it might have been suggested. "I think it's good that they did," she offered. TransCanada's media spokesperson for Energy East, Tim Duboyce, said only that the company always tried to avoid areas with "known occurrences" of wildlife and plant species on federal or provincial at-risk, endangered, or "of concern" lists. He couldn't say how it learned of the grouse lek. "The decision was made following environmental assessments we carried out, and best practices," he said. "That is what we always try to do."

Diane Vincent and her husband moved to the lake in 2009 from outside Edmonton. Her husband worked in the oil industry, as did most of the people in their little subdivision. "It was absolutely gorgeous," she said of the moment they first spotted Shorncliffe. "We just found the area and they were selling lots." Vincent kayaked three or four times a week, usually first thing in the morning, "whenever the lake is calm," watching the birds and the muskrats.

The dogs sniffed around while she spoke. She was sixtyish, with thick, curly blond hair. Energy East didn't have her terribly concerned. "I would say that as long as the pipeline is going to do things that are environmentally responsible, and have it in writing that they're going to be able to take care of the different environmental ideas, I think it's a good idea," she said. "I don't see any problem with it." Like Lori Goodrich, she saw troubling signs for the oil economy, even in this corner of Alberta. "A lot of the businesses, they're down to 10 percent staff right now," she said. A new pipeline might help. "It would be good for everybody. It would be good for the economy. It would be good for Canada."

Calgary was cold when I was there two days before heading to Hardisty, a brisk and windy four degrees Celsius the day after Labour Day. And the chill air gave the city's office-tower downtown a metallic hollowness. The tall glass buildings were the most visible symbols of Alberta's wealth, but now they told a different story: oil patch tenants in spires such as the fifty-eight-storey Bow Tower were laying off staff and subleasing office space they no longer needed. After slashing sixteen hundred jobs since the end of 2014, Cenovus Energy required only half the square footage it had agreed to rent in Brookfield Place, a skyscraper still under construction.

Boom-and-bust was an old story in a city built on commodity prices, but this bust was two years old and counting. Oil sands projects were being cancelled and investment was declining. "It's all the way through the city economy," Ben Brunnen, the economist with the Canadian Association of Petroleum Producers, said in an interview. Retail sales were down; employment insurance claims and mortgage defaults were up. "The restaurants aren't as busy," he said. There had been forty-four thousand layoffs in the oil business. Including indirect employment, the job losses had soared past six figures. "These people aren't finding jobs elsewhere, either, and if they are, they're finding lower-paying jobs," said Chelsie Klassen, the association's director of communications. The oil and gas industry had contributed 42 percent of the provincial economy in 2014; the following year, that figure dropped to 28 percent. The day I arrived, a newspaper reported that the property value of condominiums in the city had fallen. The same day, Enbridge announced it was buying Houston's Spectra Energy; analysts said that the company saw better prospects for growth in the United States. "They just don't see it happening in Canada," wrote columnist Gary Lamphier.

Corporate Calgary was on edge about something else: a Liberal government in Ottawa that was planning new climate policies, including a price on carbon—a measure already adopted by the NDP government in Edmonton—and new requirements for the approval of oil pipelines like Energy East. The big oil sands producers based in Calgary rebuffed my interview requests, but executives at a smaller company, Crescent Point Energy, were willing to talk, so I rode an elevator to the twentieth floor of Eighth Avenue Place's west tower to meet Ryan Gritzfeldt, one of the company's vice-presidents. The reception area offered a sweeping view of the Rocky Mountains to the west, but the company's orientation was east: most of its oil production was from conventional drilling in Saskatchewan and from the Bakken shale deposits, on the border between Saskatchewan and North Dakota.

Crescent Point had been cutting costs to keep up with the drop in the market. When prices were high, expenses tended to rise, Gritzfeldt said, in part because there wasn't as much time to scrutinize them. Now, "everybody needs to sharpen their pencils and look at doing things differently." If the barrel price rose back to fifty or sixty dollars, Crescent Point would survive, he said, but if it remained stuck at forty, "that's a whole lot of hurt."

Gritzfeldt liked the idea of Energy East, though Crescent Point hadn't committed to shipping its lighter, non-bitumen oil on the pipeline. "We couldn't quite get the terms that we wanted," he said. The existing Enbridge pipeline went "right past our doorstep" in Saskatchewan, he added, but the company was talking to TransCanada and might eventually put some of its oil on a planned Energy East lateral line running from southwest Manitoba. "That could make sense for us." Either way, he said, the pipeline would reduce bottlenecks that sometimes forced Enbridge to limit how much oil Crescent Point and other producers could ship.

An earnest and boyish engineer, Gritzfeldt had grown up in Strasburg, Saskatchewan, a town of seven hundred people, many of whom became instant oil experts whenever he was home to visit. "My dad always says, 'Why aren't you drilling here?'" Gritzfeldt chuckled. "That's the funny thing. Some of the farmers hearing about farmers in southern Saskatchewan getting wells and pipelines in their fields and collecting rent—they want it. 'When are you going to drill on my land?' 'When you are going to put a pipeline on my land?' 'Just drill over here.'"

That opportunity was threatened by new government climate plans, Gritzfeldt said. Crescent Point, he insisted, was perfectly able to explore shifting to non–fossil fuel sources without being coerced by laws and regulations. "We're starting to look at 'green energy' initiatives more seriously," he said, using air quotes. "It can be looking at strictly new, renewable energy alternatives, but it could also be reducing emissions with technology—capturing stranded flared gas." A carbon price wasn't necessary to encourage this, he noted. "Instead of monies going to a government—and who knows where that money goes—can we somehow create initiatives to spend that money to reduce emissions right away, to see some baby-step improvements right away?"

That was preferable, he said, to "having something forced down on you, because who knows how that will affect the economy?"

Other industry leaders were resigned to a price on carbon. Hal Kvisle, the retired CEO of TransCanada Corporation, said that a tax was the least-bad option—even though he wasn't persuaded that the problem it was intended to address even existed. "I'm not going to argue that there's climate change and we need to do something about it," he said in an interview. "I don't know that. . . . But if policymakers and scientists decide we need to do it, let's do it." Kvisle favoured a carbon tax because 85 percent of fossil fuel emissions come from end-use consumers: forcing everyone to pay was the best way to reduce consumer demand, he said. It was also the lowest-cost alternative for oil producers.

Gritzfeldt agreed—to a point. "If you really want to reduce emissions, tackle the demand. Get more cars off the roads, or get cleaner-burning cars moving. That's ultimately where the issue is. If the demand is there, the oil will find its way to those markets." But he also said that a carbon tax would put Canada at a disadvantage relative to other oil-producing nations. "Where do you get your best bang for your buck?" he asked. "If Canada does its one hundred percent, what does that mean for the rest of the world? Not much, right? It's kind of an uphill battle."

Gritzfeldt echoed the industry view that demand for oil would continue to rise, and that Canada couldn't afford to let others step in and supply it. "The internal combustion engine is still the cheapest form of power, and India, China, all these countries aspire to drive cars, and they can't afford Teslas," he said. It was a central tenet of the Alberta industry that the basic trajectory of oil—ever greater demand—would continue unchecked, and that Ottawa shouldn't interfere. The case for maintaining the status quo, and for building more pipelines, rested on this faith.

Ryan Gritzfeldt's frustration—his resentment of government, particularly of the federal government and its meddling in resource industries—had deep roots in the west. In 1870, the new Dominion of Canada had acquired the North-West Territories, the future prairie provinces, from the Hudson's Bay Company, and Ottawa had retained control over the land and its resources so that they could be offered to settlers and railroad investors. This domineering attitude created a cycle of perpetual grievance. "In essence," wrote Mary Janigan in her book *Let the Eastern Bastards Freeze in the Dark,* "Manitoba and the North-West Territories were colonies." Resentment grew when Ottawa began giving oil companies exploration leases during the First World War. Mackenzie King finally gave the western provinces power over natural resources in 1930, but the image of an arrogant, grasping federal government remained etched in the political culture of Alberta.

Oil became the crucible for the Ottawa–Alberta relationship. Recorded mentions of the stuff date back to the eighteenth century, and in 1914 there was a strike in the Turner Valley southwest of Calgary. But the discovery that changed the province was at Leduc, near Edmonton, in 1947. Alberta was soon awash in cash, selling exploration rights and charging royalties. A modern industry sprang virtually from nowhere, with U.S. companies setting up subsidiaries and advising Premier Ernest Manning on how to create a production chain. Three refineries were built in Edmonton by 1951, and Interprovincial Pipe Line ran its line from the capital via Hardisty to Superior, Wisconsin. Pierre Trudeau's National Energy Program, which attempted to divert the province's oil wealth from foreign markets to eastern Canada, was viewed as an effort to confiscate a resource Albertans saw as their own.

The oil sands, a thick, gooey tar in the vast northern reaches of the province, became a contentious battleground more recently. Back in the early twentieth century, federal researchers had found that the oil, attached to grains of sand by a thin layer of water, could be separated and processed. But extracting it was difficult and prohibitively expensive, and diluting the thick bitumen so that it could move through pipelines was also costly, so there was no incentive to commercialize the sands while conventional wells offered cheaper, lighter crude. Production began slowly, in 1967, while research into more efficient extraction continued. By 1996 there had been enough progress—and there was enough potential money to be made—that the Alberta government was persuaded to overhaul its royalty rates, allowing companies to pay just 1 percent of revenues until they'd earned back their capital costs. Meanwhile the Chrétien government in Ottawa changed tax policy so that firms could write off their investments immediately instead of over the lifetimes of the projects.

The oil sands were thus poised for lift-off when prices soared in the early years of the twenty-first century. In 2004, Washington-based lobbyists for oil companies and the Alberta government persuaded George W. Bush's Department of Energy to officially recognize that the province had recoverable reserves from "unconventional sources," meaning oil sands bitumen. The Securities Exchange Commission, run by Bush appointees, followed suit in 2008. This allowed oil companies to list the estimated 176 billion barrels in the oil sands as assets, which in turn attracted investors to fund more exploration and extraction. "That was really the pivotal moment that got those people into the game," said Hal Kvisle. Geopolitics also drove growth: China's hunger for oil and Russia's use of pipeline diplomacy to reassert itself on the world stage made bitumen from stable, democratic Canada all the more attractive to the U.S. Bush called for *North American* energy self-sufficiency. "America has turned its hungry eyes towards Alberta," author William Marsden wrote in 2007.

Between 1996 and 2015 the oil sands brought $38 billion in new royalty revenue into Alberta's provincial treasury, but they also deepened the province's dependence on oil and gas. When Conservative Alison Redford became premier of Alberta in 2011, the industry had recovered from a global crash—all the jobs lost had returned, unemployment was back down to 3.8 percent, and royalty revenues from oil leases had more than doubled. But she and her government faced a dilemma: how to cash in on oil while making Alberta less dependent on it. In her government's first budget, in February 2012, Redford's finance minister, Ron Liepert, acknowledged that the province was spending all its resource revenues on day-to-day operations. That had to stop. Oil was a "depleting public asset," he said, that would inevitably enter "a period of irreversible decline. This may be far in the future, but that day will eventually arrive."

Liepert also described a more immediate challenge: his budget documents included a half-page box explaining how the world price benchmark for oil, known as Brent, had soared much higher than the West Texas Intermediate price paid at Cushing, Oklahoma. And because of the shale glut in the U.S., Alberta producers were being forced to accept an even deeper discount on their benchmark price, Western Canadian Select—a punishing 30 percent reduction by early 2013. "Our biggest customer has now become our biggest competitor," said Ben Brunnen, the industry economist in Calgary.

Redford may have aspired to turn Alberta away from oil dependence in the long term, but her immediate goal became getting the province's oil to coastal waters, where it could be shipped to foreign markets on tankers for the higher Brent price. "We were going to start to have systemic structural issues in the budget if we didn't deal with it," Redford said. "And that was one of the reasons we were such strong advocates of pipelines."

Pipelines began as an efficient way to deliver product to customers, a simple cost–benefit equation. John G. Rockefeller, the creator of Standard Oil and the original oil baron, started building them in the 1860s, when the Teamsters tried to charge him high rates to haul his barrels by wagon in Pennsylvania. Rockefeller's competitors later built the first long-distance line to get around his growing monopoly. Three pipelines were already carrying crude oil at the time of the 1947 Leduc strike in Alberta: from Turner Valley to Calgary; from ships docking in Portland, Maine, to Montreal; and from other regions of the United States to Ontario. They were not constrained by borders, and they were not instruments of politics.

But in Canada, a country established on the very notion of resisting the north–south gravity of the United States, it was perhaps inevitable that pipelines—like railroads and highways—would become national symbols.

In 1954, a consortium that included Clint Murchison, a political ally of Dwight Eisenhower's; Lehman Brothers, the merchant bankers; and a law partner of the brother-in-law of the late prime minister R.B. Bennett proposed building a natural gas pipeline from Alberta clear across the prairies and through the Canadian Shield to the lucrative population centres of Ontario and Quebec. Although the consortium was dominated by American ownership, the partners, wise to political realities and to the Canadian psyche, called the venture TransCanada Pipe Line.

Piping gas across the country, particularly through the rocky landscape of the Canadian Shield, was seen as far-fetched. "The breadth of this barren wilderness has always defied Canadians to make a single country of east and west," William Kilbourn wrote in *Pipeline*, his account of the TransCanada saga. A rival proposal pitched a more practical continental approach: pipe Alberta gas into the United States south of Winnipeg, and bring American gas to Ontario and Quebec in a pipeline crossing at Niagara Falls. But this did not suit the Liberal government's economic nationalism. Murchison, Kilbourn wrote, understood this: "He was conscious that as an American his best chance to win the licence for building the line would be to outdo his Canadian rivals, who had been first in the field, in the national and patriotic character of their enterprise." It worked. "The all-Canada line is national policy," declared the powerful federal cabinet minister C.D. Howe. "I will make it feasible."

Howe used his political power to tip the scales. First, he pressured the rival suitor, Western Pipe Line Ltd., to merge with TransCanada. Then Louis St. Laurent's government deployed regulatory rulings to block an American gas company, Tennessee Gas Transmission, from selling to distributors in Ontario, who had their own doubts about the cross-country route from Alberta. When the Ontario companies hesitated to sign contracts with TransCanada, putting private financing at risk, Ottawa took an ownership stake in the project through a Crown corporation. Howe was determined, Kilbourn wrote, to complete "the greatest engineering feat of his lifetime and the crowning point of his career."

It was also his downfall. The opposition Progressive Conservatives, led by prairie populist John Diefenbaker, punched holes in the Liberals' nationalist appeal, objecting to the lack of Canadian control over the pipeline. Supported by the CCF, which wanted a government-owned line, the Tories stalled parliamentary approval of necessary legislation, forcing the Liberals to ram it through—a heavy-handed manoeuvre that led to their defeat in the next election. But by 1958, thanks to a sell-off by U.S. shareholders, three-quarters of the TransCanada stock was owned by Canadians, and the country, improbably, had its west–east natural gas pipeline. "The miracle of dynamiting a pipeline through northern Ontario . . . is one of the most incredible engineering achievements in Canadian history," Kvisle, TransCanada's former CEO, told me. "It's comparable to the CPR blasting its way through the Rockies from Calgary to Vancouver." The vast distances forced the company to develop such innovations as computerized monitoring, a cleaning process to improve flow, a jet aircraft–type turbine to power the gas compressors, and mobile units to replace broken equipment quickly.

TransCanada went on to use that expertise to build pipelines in Mexico and South America, but "none of those are as difficult and burdensome as dynamiting your way through the granite of the Canadian Shield," Kvisle said. A magazine would compare the final weld of the last section in northern Ontario to the driving of the CPR's last spike at Craigellachie, B.C. Kilbourn called it "one of the great physical accomplishments in Canadian history." And one of the great business accomplishments, too: TransCanada was in the black by 1961, and two years later, it bought out the Crown corporation Ottawa had created to save the project. In northern Ontario, TransCanada became the largest payer of property taxes in more than half of the communities through which the pipeline passed.

The gas line battle left another legacy. The same day TransCanada's line was completed, a Royal Commission on Energy released its report. The new Diefenbaker government, astute enough not to halt the project mid-construction, instead appointed the commission to examine how to avoid future polarizing pipeline debates. The answer, the report concluded, was for Ottawa to create a legal, arm's-length approval process for future pipelines—a regulator called the National Energy Board, which would take politics out of the oil transportation business.

Politics returned to the pipeline world just as Alison Redford went looking for a path to the ocean for Alberta's bitumen. She and her colleagues saw great wealth in the oil sands, but environmentalists saw an extraction process that consumed half a barrel of oil and two-fifths of a barrel of water for each barrel produced, accelerating pollution, ecological destruction, and climate change. If Canadian activists couldn't stop oil sands production itself, they would mount, like their U.S. counterparts in the fight against Keystone XL, a "collateral attack"—a term adopted by the industry and used by Ryan Gritzfeldt— to stop the sinews of steel that carried the product to its customers.

Alberta politicians were accustomed to having the National Energy Board approve projects with little fuss. "There was sort of an assumption that whatever was going to go on in terms of pipeline development was really a private-sector issue," Alison Redford recalled. "There was a regulatory process, and they would do the work that they needed to do to get pipeline approvals." When she was a minister in the cabinet of her predecessor, Ed Stelmach, other ministers would tell the premier "that it was not the role of government to be involved in pipeline discussions around [Northern] Gateway out west," she recalled. Now she saw that this was changing.

Stephen Harper was learning the same lesson, thanks to Keystone XL. It threatened his vision of Canada as an "energy superpower." Not long after Obama announced that he was putting off a decision on Keystone, Harper headed to China. "We must diversify our energy export markets," he would say. One possible route was Northern Gateway, a line Enbridge was proposing to build from near Edmonton to Kitimat, British Columbia, on the Pacific coast. But the proposal faced opposition from Indigenous communities and environmentalists. A joint review by the NEB and the Canadian Environmental Assessment Agency was soon bogged down by activists; the same delays were likely to plague a plan by Houston-based Kinder Morgan to twin its Trans Mountain pipeline from Edmonton to Burnaby, B.C., a project that would lay new pipe along the existing line to triple its capacity.

Before Kinder Morgan filed its application, Harper's Conservatives passed two pieces of legislation, Bill C-38 and Bill C-45, to eliminate many regulatory barriers to pipelines and streamline the NEB process. It provoked environmentalists even more and sparked a new Indigenous movement called Idle No More. But Harper was showing that although he couldn't control the U.S. regulatory process for Keystone XL, he'd do whatever else he could to get Canadian oil to world markets—to "make it feasible," as C.D. Howe had put it.

Redford adopted a different strategy, using her image as a new kind of Alberta Conservative—a moderate, pan-Canadian woman—in a personal campaign to rebrand the oil sands, salvage Keystone XL, and blunt opposition to the other pipelines. Her predecessor, Ed Stelmach, had introduced a levy on large-scale emissions in 2007, with big emitters like oil sands companies and power producers paying fifteen dollars for every tonne of carbon over their individual limits. The money went into developing energy-efficiency technologies. Though the levy didn't apply to consumers or small energy producers, Redford claimed in speeches across Canada and in the United States that Alberta had "put a price on carbon. . . . We're the first in North America to do it." But the politics remained difficult: Keystone XL was beyond rescue, and in B.C., Premier Christy Clark listed five conditions for her support of Northern Gateway—including an extraordinary demand for a share of Alberta's royalties, for which there was no legal basis or precedent.

It was a pipeline stalemate. But, Redford recalled, "slowly people were starting to see an alternative." TransCanada executives told her that "there might be another viable economic option."

———

At TransCanada's head office in Calgary, Hal Kvisle had a working group—
"half a dozen guys," he recalled—looking at ways to get oil out of Alberta.
They examined converting existing lines to Chicago and California, buying
out Trans Mountain, or racing Enbridge to Kitimat, Kvisle said. But the U.S.
was clearly becoming a problem, and Kvisle had spent eight frustrating years
trying to win approval for a second attempt at the Mackenzie Valley pipeline,
which had first stalled in the seventies. By the time the new bid was approved,
the U.S. shale boom had wrecked its business case. "I said to our team, 'I'm
not going to do another one of those.'"

Then, he said, "one of the guys who looked at it was asking, 'Well, how
about converting the Canadian mainline all the way to Montreal?'"

In that moment, Energy East was born.

There was a business case. The TransCanada mainline pushed through by
C.D. Howe had grown to six parallel pipes carrying Alberta natural gas across
the prairies to Winnipeg. From there, two turned south to supply the United
States and one fed customers in the Manitoba capital, then continued with
three others toward northern Ontario and the lucrative market in the
Toronto–Montreal corridor. Built over four decades, the lines could move
seven billion cubic feet of natural gas per day. But the National Energy Board
had made what Kvisle called "a fatal mistake," approving a pipeline called
Vector to bring gas from Chicago into southern Ontario. Beginning in 2000,
gas retailers in Ontario and Quebec had access to American product—undoing one of the barriers C.D. Howe had erected to make the original gas line
feasible. "That started what was nothing less than the death spiral of the
Canadian mainline," Kvisle said. "The need for the Canadian mainline has
shrunk and shrunk." By 2013, the mainline was operating at less than half its
capacity. Converting one line to oil would make up some of the lost revenue.

TransCanada's engineers got to work. "Technically we knew the steel was
in perfect condition and there was no external or internal corrosion," Kvisle
said. Gas pipelines operate at higher pressure than oil, so that wasn't a concern. Disconnecting the line from compressor stations that pushed the gas

east and building new pump stations to move the oil would be costly, but the expense would be offset in part by a key calculation: the National Energy Board bases the tolls oil producers pay to ship on pipelines in part on what pipeline builders need to pay down the line's capital cost. Tolls on a line that was newly built across most of the country would be prohibitively high, but the excess capacity on the gas mainline had devalued it to the point that it was "approaching zero," Kvisle said. So TransCanada had almost no costs to recover, allowing it to charge lower tolls for oil and thus make the line attractive to producers and financially viable for TransCanada. "If it weren't for the fact that the pipeline exists all the way to Montreal," Kvisle said, "Energy East would be a ridiculous idea."

In TransCanada's early discussions, the idea was to run the line to the Suncor refinery in Montreal, or possibly Valero's facility near Quebec City. But farther east, the billionaire Irving family was already buying discounted western oil and shipping it by rail to its Saint John refinery. Irving's facility sat on the Bay of Fundy, another outlet to world markets. The Irvings were enigmas to many of the big players in Calgary, but TransCanada knew them: Alex Pourbaix, a young executive at the company, had secured a contract in 2003 to build a cogeneration plant within the Saint John refinery, using the refinery's own byproducts to generate and supply it with electricity. "I know they have their reputation in New Brunswick of trying to own the whole province, and I know that there have been a lot of senior management changes," Kvisle said. "But they're very credible, ethical, straight-up business people and I don't have any complaints about the deals I've done with them."

As Kvisle retired in 2010, the west–east pipeline concept was still taking shape. "The relationship with the Irvings was there," he said, "but the pieces had not yet been put together." It would be up to his successors to complete what was looking like TransCanada's next great epic adventure.

3

THE BUFFALO TRAIL

AT THE OPPOSITE END of Shorncliffe Lake was Route 41, a north–south, two-lane provincial highway nicknamed the Buffalo Trail. Robert Dewald and Gary Sayer sat chatting on a bench outside the Race Trac Gas Bar and Convenience store in the little town of Czar. Dewald's ball cap bore the logo of AGSI, an agricultural services company. He worked for the municipal district of Provost. Sayer, retired from the "MD," as the districts were known, had grey, slicked-back hair. Like Diane Vincent, the two men were unaware that the pipeline route had been moved for a grouse lek. "They're not endangered when *we* hunt," Sayer said, cracking himself up. TransCanada's decision, though, indicated that it was serious. "They want it in if they're willing to do that," Sayer said.

A maintenance crew was working on the CPR line across the road from the gas station. From their perch, Sayer and Dewald had seen hundreds of tanker cars roll down that track, carrying crude oil loaded at Hardisty. "It's a lot better putting it in that pipeline than it is putting it on this railroad track," Dewald said. "I would think 99 percent of the people would rather see it in the pipeline." There were fewer oil cars passing through Czar these days—"Things have slowed right down now," Sayer noted—but in his view, that didn't change the fundamental issue of getting the product to market. "You got to get it to a place where it can be put to good use," Dewald said. "What the big holdup really is, is our politicians. We need to do something with them. Change the politicians. Change the government."

But the government *had* changed, I reminded them. Pipeline-friendly administrations had been in power both federally and provincially—and had been sent packing by voters.

"Isn't that the truth," Sayer said ruefully.

In the marble rotunda of Alberta's massive Beaux-Arts legislature building, there was a new flash of colour, orange-auburn, coming from a second-floor balcony. A row of portraits of former premiers hung there. Alison Redford's red hair made it easy to pick out her likeness from below. I learned later that the painting had been quietly mounted just a couple of hours before I arrived, while the city's attention was focused on Wayne Gretzky's arrival for the official opening of a new downtown hockey arena. There was no announcement and none of the usual ceremony for the unveiling—no speeches, no VIP guests, certainly no Redford. Instead, a couple of employees hung the work under the watch of an official from the Speaker's office. Alberta seemed determined to forget Alison Redford.

Redford won the 2012 election she was supposed to lose to Wildrose. The upstart right-wing party had been fuelled and funded by an oil sector angry over an increase in royalty rates—eventually reversed—imposed by her predecessor, Ed Stelmach. But Redford's triumph was short-lived: her trip to South Africa for the funeral of Nelson Mandela, whom she'd worked with as an international human rights lawyer, cost taxpayers $45,000. The revelation outraged Albertans and led to more scrutiny of her office expenses, including her personal use of the government airplane. In March 2014, facing a PC caucus revolt, Redford resigned.

That shock was followed by a broader crisis: between June and December of 2014, the price of a barrel of oil dropped by half. Facing a glut of cheap oil and shale gas in the United States, OPEC members, led by Saudi Arabia, refused to cut production. It was seen as a bid to keep prices low and push higher-cost oil—like that in the Alberta oil sands—out of the market. If demand for oil was poised for a permanent decline, some analysts said, the Saudis wanted to sell the very last barrel. The result was a stark reminder of Alberta's overreliance on oil revenues: one out of every seven dollars projected to flow into the provincial treasury evaporated, close to the annual budget of the education department. Royalties from oil sands bitumen plunged 73 percent. The new finance minister, Robin Campbell, repeated the same refrain as his predecessors: spending could no longer outpace "stable"—non-fluctuating, non-oil—revenue. "We need to get off the rollercoaster of energy prices," he said.

Campbell and his boss, PC Premier Jim Prentice, raised fuel taxes and income taxes for higher earners to replace the lost revenue—a necessary decision, but one Albertans didn't like. Still angry about Redford, they tossed Prentice and his party from office in May 2015, ending more than four decades of Progressive Conservative rule.

Down one of the corridors off the legislature's rotunda, in a large, cluttered office, Alberta's first NDP environment minister, Shannon Phillips, was darting from desk to table to shelf, gathering briefing books for a race to the airport to catch a flight. She stopped long enough for a short interview about the new NDP government's climate plan and its support for Energy East. "We are moving at lightning speed for a way a government [typically] moves forward," she said, as if to explain her own frenzied movements. "The pace that we have worked at during the past fifteen months has essentially, for government, been overnight."

This was no exaggeration. The climate plan had been put together in six months, barely enough time for Phillips to absorb the magnitude of the task. "It became clear to me in August or September, before we made the announcement, that, like, my God—I'm going to be the face of a carbon tax in Alberta," she said. "Top ten jobs you don't want, right?"

The NDP's historic win in Alberta made Rachel Notley, a lawyer and one-time union staffer, the first non-PC premier of the province since 1971. One of the most pressing questions after she was sworn in was how she would honour her vague campaign commitment—made before she had any expectation of taking power—"to take leadership on the issue of climate change and make sure Alberta is part of crafting solutions with stakeholders, other provinces and the federal government." One early signal was her choice of environment minister: dubbed "Alberta's minister of hard hits" for her sport of choice, roller derby, Phillips had worked for the Alberta Federation of Labour. The NDP's union supporters saw the construction of energy infrastructure as a way to create well-paying jobs. Another indicator was the hiring of Marcella Munro, a veteran NDP organizer, to staff Notley's satellite office in Calgary. "There is no planet on which I could try to argue against the oil sands," Munro told a newspaper columnist, describing herself as "a labour-side New Democrat, a jobs-first New Democrat."

Notley implemented such standard NDP initiatives as a minimum wage increase, an apology to Indigenous people for Alberta's residential schools, and an extension of workplace safety rules to farms. But she also quickly signalled her support for pipelines. The federal review had approved Northern Gateway, as had the Harper cabinet, but it was being challenged in court, and Ottawa had seemingly abandoned any political effort to overcome opposition in British Columbia. So Notley put her weight behind the Energy East and Trans Mountain proposals. Alberta would need to move its oil for a long time, Phillips told me in her rapid-fire speaking style. Even if everyone eventually drove electric cars, we'd still need oil "to make our plastics and our leisure suits," she said, using a well-rehearsed line. She sounded a lot like Alison Redford as she blamed anti-pipeline activism on the lack of Conservative climate action in Ottawa. "The pipelines themselves became about what was in them, and what they represented. They did not become about the fact that they're a piece of infrastructure that delivers energy and, quite frankly, they're the safest way to do so."

Critics said the NDP's embrace of pipelines underscored that the oil industry had "captured" the political process in Alberta: top bureaucrats and academics drawn from, or funded by, the fossil fuel sector formed a fossil fuel "deep state" that kept government policy from veering off course. Alberta New Democrats argued that they were trying to strike a balance: if Notley's government could get a couple of pipelines built, Albertans could conceivably swallow a carbon tax and an emissions cap that would eventually wean the province from its carbon dependence and allow it to adjust to a world that needed less oil.

And from another perspective, if the NDP could show Canadians that Alberta was acting—moderately, but concretely—on climate change, public opinion might allow for the construction of new pipelines that would create jobs and generate higher royalties. That, in turn, might pull the province out of its slump, smooth the transition to a lower-carbon world—and show that the NDP deserved more than a four-year fluke opportunity to govern.

It was, in short, a rare opening to reshape both the province's politics and its role in the debate over energy and the environment.

Across the river from the minister's office at the legislature, a short ride away on Edmonton's light-rail transit system, sat the main campus of the University of Alberta. Andrew Leach's office at the business school was a typically cluttered professorial habitat filled with books, posters, his bicycle, and a toy replica of the iconic Caterpillar 797 heavy-hauler truck used in the oil sands. Leach was red-haired and impish-looking, an appearance that belied his training as an economist, his serious personality, and his importance to Shannon Phillips: she chose him to chair a panel of experts to draft the provincial climate plan. "I didn't know exactly what I wanted," Phillips told me, but after she met Leach, "it immediately became clear to me, first of all, how smart Andrew is, and second of all, that he had been cooking this up in his mind for a long time, what the path forward is."

Leach had grown up in Miramichi, New Brunswick, not far from where the Energy East pipeline would begin its final approach to the Bay of Fundy. He studied environmental science at the University of Guelph and stumbled into a course on environmental economics. Arriving at U of A in 2006, he was asked to teach a class in energy markets, the financial side of the oil and gas business. "That just grabbed my interest," he said. He spent a sabbatical in Ottawa as an in-house economist working on the Harper government's proposed oil and gas regulations, which gave him a firsthand look at how government policy is crafted.

At the time, Barack Obama was expected to pass a cap-and-trade system and lead the world to a stringent climate treaty at the United Nations conference in Copenhagen in 2009. The Conservatives proposed a faster coal phase-out, a requirement for carbon capture at new oil sands facilities, and other measures— not a bad package overall, Leach said. But the proposals were panned as too weak by environmentalists and too severe by industry. Most were never implemented. "Watching that happen has been as influential on this file for me as anything else," he told me. "You ask Canadians, 'Do you want action on climate change?' and they'll say yes. You ask them, 'Do you want any of the following seven things that add a reasonable level of stringency that'll accomplish a particular goal?' and they will say no. 'Do you think this goal is stringent enough?' They will also say no." The message, Leach said, appeared to be "'We want you to go further, without doing any of the things that would get you there.'"

Despite that experience, he didn't hesitate when Phillips asked for his help. "As far as I'm concerned, if the clerk—or the premier, or the prime minister, or the head of executive council—calls, you take the call." The new NDP government wanted Leach to do what seemed the impossible: find a consensus among oil executives and environmentalists.

As it turned out, the two sides were already talking. "Industry was ready for the war to be over," Phillips said, "and environmental groups were looking for a way forward for Canada." A decade earlier, Greenpeace had led the crusade to brand Alberta oil as the dirtiest on the planet, hoping to make it unmarketable, but in 2014, Tzeporah Berman, a former director of the organization's climate change program, began meeting with Steve Williams, the CEO of the oil sands giant Suncor, and other industry executives. "We were viewed to be one of the bad guys in the world around what was called the tar sands," Williams recounted. "We want to be at the leading edge of this debate so we can challenge people to come with us." Pat Carlson, the CEO of the natural gas producer Seven Generations Energy, agreed: "What jurisdiction in the world has the technology and the hydrocarbon resources to take this leadership role? Who should we look to, if not ourselves?"

Phillips and Leach discovered that the big producers operating in the oil sands—companies that planned in decades-long increments—were ahead of the politicians on fossil fuels. "These folks who have a little bit of a longer view, they're looking at a post-combustion future, right?" Phillips said. Oil would always be needed for some products, but "carbon pricing will reach a point where it will become too expensive to do something silly like combust it, because it will be too valuable." The corporate executives knew how costly it was to get a barrel of oil out of the oil sands; the seemingly radical chant of the environmental left, "Leave it in the ground," made good business sense in a world where extraction of the hardest-to-reach oil was no longer profitable. "The last barrel that we take out is very environmentally inefficient and very economically inefficient, and I'd like to leave it in the ground," Williams said. "But we're regulated to take it out." Alberta's policies created incentives for companies to extract every last barrel, no matter how costly, he explained—a dubious proposition for shareholders. A shift away from that "helps me going forward."

That made it easier than expected to find a consensus between CEOs and environmentalists. On the day Phillips and Notley announced the NDP government's climate plan—a cap on emissions, a carbon tax that funnelled rebates to low-income Albertans, a phase-out of coal—they were flanked not only by climate activists but also by Williams and three other oil sands executives: Brian Ferguson, the CEO of Cenovus; Murray Edwards, the CEO of Canadian Natural Resources Ltd.; and Lorraine Mitchelmore, the head of Shell's Canadian operations. "This plan will position Alberta, one of the world's largest oil and gas producing jurisdictions, as a climate leader," Edwards said, "and will allow for ongoing innovation and technology in the oil and gas sector." (Cynics noted that it was easy for the big producers to support a carbon tax: "It's not about reducing emissions on upstream production. It's about making grandma pay more to heat her home," Conservative politician Jason Kenney told *Maclean's* magazine. "It doesn't add significantly to their bottom line. It imposes the cost downstream.")

The NDP's emissions cap would be one hundred megatonnes, enforceable with financial penalties. Oil sands emissions were only 24.5 megatonnes in 2000, but had more than doubled a decade later. They reached seventy megatonnes in 2017 and were forecast to hit the cap around 2030. It was far enough away for some planned projects to go ahead, but it would eventually force producers to rein in emissions. Alberta, Williams would say, was thinking about the long term. "The political cycle is not the capital-cycle world I have to live through," he said. "My cycle is ten, twenty, fifty years of future for my shareholders. Often politicians are in a five-year world. And if you're in a four- or five-year world, this problem can't be easily solved."

Williams did not speak for everyone. In the summer of 2016, the *Financial Post* reported a "growing fissure" in the oil patch: many smaller companies were angry that the four big CEOs were endorsing policies they considered "suicidal." The oil sands producers had decades to adjust, but smaller conventional drillers needed short-term returns on their investments and were more vulnerable to Notley's policies. Some of the most vehement disagreements on his panel, Leach said, were between different fossil fuel companies. The split prevented the industry's main lobby group, the Canadian Association of Petroleum Producers, from joining Notley at her announcement—though it didn't oppose the plan, either. "CAPP represents a broad membership base," the organization's Chelsie Klassen told me. "We have juniors, we have smaller producers, we have oil sands. . . . It's not because we didn't support it, but because we have such a difference of opinion that we couldn't stand up there and represent everybody."

Crescent Point Energy was one of the dissenters. Ryan Gritzfeldt from Crescent Point had told me that companies could start reducing emissions "right away" if they were allowed to keep the money they were instead paying to the carbon tax the NDP "forced down" on them. Leach dismissed that: the industry would never make the necessary turn to green energy without a nudge from government, he said. "Why would they do it? These companies have fiduciary responsibilities to their shareholders. They're going to invest in things that provide a return on investment. The whole point of pricing greenhouse gases is it creates a return on investment for those new technologies." In 2017, Crescent Point and several other smaller conventional producers quit CAPP over its perceived acquiescence to the NDP's carbon tax and its focus on the big oil sands producers.

Notley had scored an early victory by winning the support of the major CEOs for her effort to balance climate action and oil development. But, clearly, there were more battles to come.

On a downtown Edmonton side street, along a block of red-brick buildings housing tony shops and cool wine stores, sat an office that had once seemed out of place in oil-mad Alberta: Greenpeace, the world's best-known environmental group. It still didn't advertise its name on the door. It, too, was sorting out how to deal with Notley's government.

Mike Hudema, the organization's first paid staffer in the province, had set up the office a decade earlier to make the oil sands a climate *bête noire*, and he succeeded largely by bringing celebrities and prominent activists to see the unsightly tailing ponds. It was confrontational, but "at that point, you had a government that was never going to do climate policy unless it was forced to," said Bronwyn Tucker, a Greenpeace organizer in Edmonton. "Being as loud and blunt as possible was one of the only ways." Now, with the NDP in office, the organization was trying to be "a lot more solutions-based . . . a bit less controversial," Tucker said, issuing reports on green jobs and community-owned renewable energy projects. Tzeporah Berman, the Greenpeace activist who had opened the dialogue with Suncor, was named along with a former CAPP president to the committee designing the details of the NDP emissions cap penalties. Even so, Hudema, after applauding the cap, denounced it as insufficient: it would still allow emissions to grow enough to wipe out reductions in other provinces and to miss Canada's Paris targets.

Notley's government presented the environmental left with a dilemma: support her initiatives—inadequate but real—or agitate for tougher action. In April 2016, a federal NDP convention in Edmonton, intended to showcase the Alberta party's historic victory, instead became a public display of this tension. A group of activists led by broadcaster and author Avi Lewis wanted federal delegates to vote to study the Leap Manifesto, which advocated a rapid transition to renewable energy and a ban on all new oil pipelines—a notion that threatened Notley's effort to establish the Alberta NDP's moderate bona fides. Phillips, who lobbied delegates to vote no, was incensed that activists like Lewis and Hudema wouldn't acknowledge the realities of governing. "No lunatic is going to phone up Mike or Avi's office and threaten to kill them over their climate plan. They phone me all the time," she said. "And also, no one elected Avi or Mike in the time of the worst recession in essentially a generation with tens of thousands of job losses." Notley used a keynote speech to plead for pragmatism, pointing to her climate plan. "That is what you get to do when you move up from manifestos to the detailed, principled, practical plans you can really implement by winning an election," she said. Despite that plea, the Leap motion narrowly passed.

Tucker, from the Greenpeace office, said the NDP was being too pragmatic. "I think the strategy there is to get re-elected." She saw this as wrong-headed; the party's win was a one-time fluke that it should use to go for broke: Notley should delay all pipelines to buy time for the world to shift further away from fossil fuels, despite the electoral cost. "Four years from now, regardless of what government is in power in Alberta, pipelines are not going to get through,"

Tucker said. "The rate at which that social licence for fossil fuel projects is changing is really fast. International pressure will also be mounting."

But it wasn't in a political party's nature to concede power after having won it. Phillips wanted to move faster on climate, she told me, but she had to recognize "the actual meat and potatoes of what the economy is in this province. It has been highly dependent on one product, one market, one price." The two right-wing parties whose vote-splitting helped the NDP win in 2015, the Progressive Conservatives and Wildrose, voted to merge two years later and were vowing to undo Notley's policies when they returned to power.

Those policies were designed to make repeal difficult. Incentives for renewable energy would create not just a market for it but a constituency for it, too—companies and customers—and therefore a political cost for eliminating incentives. "That's always part of the thinking," Leach said. Repeal would also go against an increasingly clear global trend. "By 2019 you're going to be going straight into the headwinds of every industrialized economy and a number of industrializing economies as we see China moving into a carbon market, Mexico, and so on," Phillips said. "So I invite any opposition party to design their election offer to Albertans around repealing the price on carbon and all the other investments that we are and will be making in the economy to ensure that we're competitive for the future."

This wasn't far from what Tucker argued, but Phillips didn't see changes happening quite as fast, so the NDP also needed to ensure "that the folks who elected us are seeing the benefit of how we're starting to move the ship of the economy," she said. "I'm not talking about forty years from now, when we might be talking about a post-combustion future. I'm talking about four months." That meant bringing back oil jobs, including with pipelines.

It was the classic incrementalist argument of Canadian politics, one mastered by Liberal politicians but also adopted by Conservatives like Stephen Harper: to achieve its goals, a political party must be moderate enough to win the trust of voters in the first place and gain power. Notley was often described as philosophically closer to the new Liberal prime minister, Justin Trudeau, than to her own federal party. Trudeau, too, walked a fine line on pipelines, promising to reform a National Energy Board that he claimed favoured industry while telling Albertans that more credible regulatory reviews would make it easier to "get those resources to market." Trudeau invited Notley to brief his cabinet on her climate plan—she received a standing ovation—and she, in turn, supported his NEB reforms. *Maclean's* proclaimed the prime minister "Rachel Notley's new BFF." The NDP, once derided as "Liberals in a hurry," was learning to take its time.

In November 2016 Trudeau handed Notley her reward: he approved the expansion of Kinder Morgan's Trans Mountain pipeline from Edmonton to Burnaby, B.C. "We could not have approved this project without the leadership of Premier Notley and Alberta's climate leadership plan," Trudeau said. "It has been rightly celebrated as a major step forward, both by industry and the environmental community."

The same day, the Trudeau cabinet officially rejected Northern Gateway. The Federal Court of Appeal had struck down the Harper cabinet's approval because of its lack of Indigenous consultations. Rather than reopen those consultations, Trudeau let the project die; he said that the Great Bear Rainforest on B.C.'s Pacific coast "was no place for a crude oil pipeline." But Trudeau also approved the replacement of Enbridge's Line 3 from Alberta to the U.S., giving the industry, and Notley, two wins out of three. She declared victory: her emissions cap, she said, was aimed at "Canadians who are concerned about the relationship between pipeline construction and greenhouse gas emission increases." They could be reassured that "approval of this pipeline does not mean an increase in production at all," and that Alberta's emissions would not grow past a hundred megatonnes—"so that those conversations are de-linked." Trudeau's announcement suggested that her calculation was working.

But what about the other calculation, the one where more pipelines would increase so-called upstream emissions—those generated at the source of the oil—by encouraging more production? It was a question that would follow me the length of my journey from Hardisty to Saint John, and in a world threatened by climate change, it was the most fundamental equation of all. I asked Andrew Leach about it. His answer: *it would depend.*

It would depend, Leach said, on the intricate workings of the global oil market, and the cost—relative to the rest of that market—of extracting a barrel from the oil sands. Let's say a barrel of Alberta bitumen cost $30 to extract, and the next most expensive barrel, somewhere else in the world, was $30.10. Shut down Alberta, and customers could easily switch to that other source, because the cost wasn't much higher. There would be no significant change in the amount of oil burned worldwide; emissions would be roughly the same.

But imagine if that next most expensive barrel cost $40, or $50, or $60 to extract: it would be prohibitively expensive to substitute that barrel for a barrel from the oil sands. Block a Canadian pipeline, strand some bitumen in Alberta, and the demand *could not* be met elsewhere. In that scenario, "you're materially changing the effective global supply curve for oil," Leach said, "so you're going to ensure less total oil is burned globally." Emissions would go down.

Which scenario was more realistic? That was a source of debate among economists, who posited a range of dizzying models and scenarios. Rail, for example, would be a viable alternative to pipelines only if the price of oil reached a level where it would cover the higher cost of train transportation. Some of the calculations were brimming with internal contradictions, Leach said. But none of these considerations had any bearing on governmental action on climate, he added. Building Energy East did not preclude a government's capping emissions or taxing carbon. "Yes, you build a pipeline, and it's more likely that the oil sands will be part of the global supply mix than without it. But that doesn't mean it's more or less likely there'll be global action on climate change."

That, too, would depend.

The Energy East path crossed Route 41, the Buffalo Trail, just south of the town of Czar, and then turned south, beginning a long, generally straight trajectory toward the bottom of the province. The highway headed south, too, into a landscape of undulating hills, large cattle herds, and scattered oil derricks pecking at the ground like giant steel birds. At the town of Consort, Route 41 turned left and ran east for a few minutes. Near a cow pasture along the shoulder of this stretch of road was an array of pipeline warning signs. "TransCanada Keystone," it said. "Warning—High Pressure Oil Pipeline."

Beneath the ground was the original Keystone, the first section of the oil pipeline that TransCanada began operating in 2010. This right-of-way would have become part of Keystone XL, and it was where the company also planned to build the first section of Energy East, parallel to Keystone, from Hardisty to the Saskatchewan border. It was a reminder that oil wasn't just the Fort McMurray boom, and the Hardisty tank farm, and the executives on the twentieth floor in Calgary: pipelines were part of the landscape all over Alberta—part of daily life, as natural and unremarkable as a lobster boat in the Maritimes, a paper mill in Quebec, a manufacturing plant in Ontario.

Farther south, the Buffalo Trail led into the Neutral Hills. Small oil wells pumped away, and occasionally a hawk perched on a field post, looking for prey forced out of their holes by farm equipment starting the fall harvest. At Oyen I left the highway, cut through the centre of town, and headed into the grid of dusty township roads, looking for N51°19'32" W110° 31'22"—coordinates listed in TransCanada's regulatory documents, filed publicly with the National Energy Board. The spot was at the top of a gentle hill along the same Keystone right-of-way, the future site of one of the seventy-one Energy East pump stations TransCanada would need to push diluted bitumen, or dilbit, from Hardisty to Saint John. That would require up to six 6500-horsepower motors, access roads, "field services buildings," and electrical substations connecting to the local power utilities. All that marked the spot now were a few TransCanada signs indicating the existing gas lines below the ground, some barbed-wire ranch fencing, and another hawk watching me from a cattle fence.

The landscape south of Oyen stayed flat for a long time. In the fields stretching out to my left and right, trucks and combines kicked up great clouds of dust. Route 41 carried me over the Red Deer River. To the west, TransCanada's right-of-way passed beneath it. The Energy East route split from the existing path there: a company assessment team had decided that the Keystone corridor didn't provide enough space to build new pipeline "through critical habitat of [Species at Risk Act]-listed plant species," one of its filings said. It also cited "the presence of other species of management concern, and archaeological sites near these existing pipeline routes."

South of the river, the road wound through a range of low, small hills. Traffic was sparse. A sign pointed to Medicine Hat, little more than an hour away, but my time in Alberta was coming to an end. The road plunged into another river valley, a steeper drop this time, and the hills became smaller but sharper, like a forest of earth cones. This was the valley of the South Saskatchewan River. The river was to the left, and in the hills lining the opposite bank, horizontal shades of sediment were visible—layers of time revealed by the erosion of the river. They spoke to the age of the earth itself— a world that was seemingly immutable but was constantly changing.

In 2002, a Dutch chemist coined the term "anthropocene" for the earth's current geological epoch. After five mass extinctions in which life on earth was brutally culled by a random, natural event—the meteor that killed the dinosaurs was the best-known example—civilization was now bringing the sixth such event upon itself, transforming the physical world through fossil fuel combustion and deforestation. A few months earlier, Rachel Notley had been confronted by wildfires that swept through Fort McMurray, covering a million and a half acres and destroying more than two thousand homes in the city most identified with Alberta's economy and its contentious reliance on the oil sands. Canadians were transfixed by dashboard-camera videos posted to YouTube of residents fleeing through a hellish landscape of red-glowing cinders and blinding ash. Scientists said that intense fires were becoming more common because of drier soil and vegetation, more frequent lightning strikes, and longer fire seasons. The Fort McMurray fire was another example of how the human need for energy was altering nature itself.

What was it those two men had said, back in Czar, about TransCanada redrawing the Energy East route around Shorncliffe Lake to avoid the nesting area of the sharp-tailed grouse? "It would be a lot cheaper to move the grouse, wouldn't it?" Gary Sayer had remarked, and both men had roared with laughter.

How easily we think of the world as permanent. How casually we are willing to alter it.

A road bridge spanned the South Saskatchewan River. On the other side were more layers of rock and a small riverside park. Then the road rose up out of the valley to another flat landscape. On the horizon, the imprint of our modernity picked at the sky: tanks and chimneys and flare towers, metal silhouettes glistening in the sun, their giant, belching beacons beckoning me to the next leg of my journey.

The Keystone XL path crossed the river near here and turned away, heading southeast to the United States. The Energy East route came east, though, back toward Route 41. A sign marked "Empress Area Gas Plants" pointed east as well, down a side road labelled Route 545. I turned off the Buffalo Trail and followed the road into Saskatchewan.

PART TWO

SASKATCHEWAN

4

THE GREAT SAND HILLS

CUTTING THROUGH RECENTLY HARVESTED fields, Route 545 in Alberta became Route 321 in Saskatchewan, marked only by a subtle change in the texture of the asphalt, a different pattern of cracks and patches, and a lonely "Saskatchewan, Naturally" billboard. But the provincial border mattered here. Across fields to the left, on the Alberta side, were the towers, flares, and pipes of the four gas plants I had glimpsed, belonging to Spectra Energy, Plains Midstream Canada, Pembina Pipeline, and Atco Energy Solutions. They drew gaseous components out of the natural gas piped in from the carbon-rich Western Canadian Sedimentary Basin, processed them into products such as propane and ethane, and sent the remaining "lean gas" across to Saskatchewan. The configuration, developed with the blessing of Alberta governments and regulators, was deliberate: by keeping all but the final step within the province, the local gas network mostly avoided the regulatory clutches of distant Ottawa.

A kilometre and a half inside Saskatchewan, the gas reached TransCanada's first compressor station in its Canadian Mainline network—the starting point for six underground pipelines, built over four decades, that carried

Alberta gas thousands of kilometres east to Quebec and the United States. The station, built in 1957, was a short drive up Range Road 3295, and it was literally humming when I pulled up. Low metallic buildings were interspersed with pipes and valves emerging from the ground.

Across the dirt road was new construction: a small crane dangled over several large white pipes, each with one end suspended in the air and the other buried in the soil. A couple of workers were on the site. This was where the newly built Energy East pipeline originating in Hardisty would connect to one of the existing gas lines, which would be converted to feed dilbit toward New Brunswick. A major pressure-control station would transfer the oil from the higher-pressure new line to the existing pipe, but TransCanada told me that this wasn't the new construction I saw. "I don't really know what kind of activity you spotted," spokesperson Tim Duboyce said in an email. "There is nothing happening . . . related to the development of Energy East, as the project still needs to go through the regulatory approval process." The TransCanada foreman came over when I started taking photographs, and when I explained my book project, he asked aggressively, "Are you for it or against it?" I demurred. "Well," he shot back, "I can tell you I'm one hundred percent for it." He was one of many pipeline supporters who demanded to know my views, a defensive reaction to the industry's being questioned as it had never been questioned before—including by a lot of eastern journalists who knew little about it.

Burstall, Saskatchewan, the first community up ahead, was tucked on an angle into the corner of one of the township sections created by the nineteenth-century survey grid. It called itself the Turbo Expander Capital of the World for the turbine-like devices used in the gas plants, the town's economic lifeblood. "We are just minutes away from five huge natural gas facilities that provide unlimited employment and contract opportunities," the town's website crowed.

Railway Avenue ran diagonally from the provincial road into Burstall. Customers shuffled into and out of Shevy's restaurant; a giant community yard sale was around the corner, and local children were enjoying horse and wagon rides. Across the street, residents were streaming into the community hall to take their chances at Chase the Ace. "I was born and raised here," Daryl Thomas said as he stood on the sidewalk watching the activity. "I like it." Thomas worked at the Atco gas plant across the line in Alberta. Don Bodnarchuk, another Shevy's patron, lived in Burstall but worked for Natural Gas Petroleum and Resources, a utility owned by the city of Medicine Hat, Alberta, an hour away. It supplied customers, including power companies, in both Alberta and Saskatchewan. Gas was king here, and those five plants out off Route 321 were its castles. "They do a lot of things there," Bodnarchuk told me. "There's a sheet two pages long of things they make from natural gas, like paint and plastic. It's just phenomenal."

So the shipping of fossil fuels over great distances, and across political boundaries, was entirely natural in Burstall. An oil pipeline like Energy East from Alberta to New Brunswick was a no-brainer. "I've worked in the oil fields and the gas fields since I was eighteen years old," Bodnarchuk said. "I'm kinda pro-pipeline." He'd read about a major spill from a Husky Energy pipeline in the North Saskatchewan River in July. "That was bad," he said. "But as far as ground leaks, everything's fixable." Thomas was also unfazed. "Our company and I think all the companies around here, especially in Alberta, are pretty up on pipeline integrity," he said.

But another question was gnawing at Burstall—and it applied to both Energy East and those gas plants. Gary Kondra, another Shevy's customer, wondered about the business case for shipping western bitumen to eastern refineries like Irving Oil. "Right now I know that they're buying twenty-dollar-a-barrel oil from OPEC," he said. "Why do you need a pipeline if you're buying it for twenty dollars a barrel?"

Cheap fossil fuels also threatened Burstall. Even before the price crash of 2014, the town was struggling. "It used to be a lot bigger when I was growing up here," Thomas said. When the gas companies began providing company cars to employees, many of them moved to Medicine Hat and commuted. "And then we lost our high school, and we lost our grocery store." Now the basis for what remained—the gas plants—was in doubt. Cheaper ethane from the U.S., the result of the North American gas glut, had hurt sales at the Atco plant where Thomas worked. More gas was being stored than sold, and the plant was being decommissioned. "They're going to tear it down and turn it back into farmland," he said. He wasn't sure whether he'd find another job in a sector that had promised "unlimited" employment. "Maybe, maybe not," he said. "Some of the other plants went through some cutbacks because of the price."

In the Canadian psyche, Alberta and Saskatchewan are distinct, one a free-market industry haven, the other the social-democratic cradle of medicare. But in Burstall, they were indistinguishable, linked physically by pipelines and economically by a fossil fuel sector facing an uncertain future.

Along Route 321 the fields were gold, the colour of the bundles of wheat found on Saskatchewan's flag and coat of arms. The road east was straight and virtually free of traffic. Twenty-five kilometres out of Burstall, the TransCanada mainline, running underground on a slight angle to the road, passed under it; a meter station surrounded by a barbed-wire fence marked the spot. From here, the six gas lines—including the one already carrying oil as part of the original Keystone and another to be converted to Energy East—would travel on a more or less straight line, and would be easy to spot: little "Don't Dig" warning signs would appear again and again, tracing the trajectory that Alberta's crude would eventually follow toward New Brunswick.

But it wasn't possible to follow every kilometre of the route. The mainline cut across challenging terrain or below impassable obstacles. The first such obstacle wasn't far from Burstall, at a crossroads called Liebenthal, where the six lines headed into a vast, unique, and dramatic ecosystem called the Great Sand Hills of Saskatchewan.

Spanning 190,000 hectares of sandy grasslands, the hills form an arid ecosystem distinct from the surrounding agricultural land. Famous for their striking open sand dunes, the Great Sand Hills have been debated, studied, protected, regulated, farmed, and drilled for decades. "The basic conflict remains the same and it has grown rather than gone away," Rebecca Grambo wrote in *The Great Sand Hills: A Prairie Oasis*, an environmental *cri de coeur* masquerading as a coffee-table book of photographs.

Route 321 ended at Liebenthal and became a dirt track into the sand hills. The roads through the hills were not good, so I drove north to the town of Leader, detouring along the western edge of the hills, then east on Route 32 to skirt their northern reaches. On one side of this road was the hulking Great Sand Hills Terminal, a 23,000-tonne grain terminal straddling a short-line railway that runs around the hills from Burstall to Swift Current. On the other side, golden fields stretched north to a hazy, distant horizon, a snapshot of Saskatchewan's vastness.

In the town of Sceptre was the Great Sandhills Museum and Interpretive Centre. It was closed for the season, but Mary Ann Peters, who'd stopped in for a minute to grab some paperwork, gave me an informal tour, moving through shadows, flicking on lights. "I'm not sure if I'm the chairman of the board or the president," she said. "I think the chairman." The museum, which began accepting credit cards only in 2016, was run by volunteers. "In 2009 I went to a meeting to step down from the board because I'd been on it for sixteen years or so, and I ended up chairman of the board," Peters said. "There were other people leaving and there wasn't anybody taking over. All the other previous board members are deceased. I think that's how you get off the board."

Most of the displays constituted less a linear story of the hills or the community than a repository for anything that was old, local, and worth preserving: hospital equipment, school desks, agricultural tools, an RCMP uniform from Maple Creek, CPR paraphernalia. "It pretty much deals with every aspect of early pioneer life," said Peters, who admitted little knowledge of local history. "I have tried to educate myself on a whole lot of stuff here, and it's been very fascinating." A couple of rooms included panels explaining the fragility of the hills. "It's subject to blowing out really easily," Peters said. "It's such fine soil. It can drift pretty easily."

I mentioned that I was following the route of the Energy East pipeline. "And is it meant to go through the hills, then, too?" she asked.

One of the existing gas lines would be converted to carry bitumen, I explained.

"I haven't heard anything about that," she said. She admitted that she hadn't followed the pipeline issue closely because the project had seemed "not really a go."

The sand hills were formed by glaciers fourteen thousand years ago. Indigenous people used them for millennia; the Sioux chief Sitting Bull met the Blackfoot chief Crowfoot in their southern reaches. They were seen by some nations as the afterworld: "Death gives the soul its release, which is to go to the Great Sand Hills, and continue to live and practise our traditional Blood way," the Blood Tribe elder Louise Crop Eared Wolf once said. Pat Provost, an elder of the Piikani First Nation, told the Energy East panel in 2015, "When we pass on, we go to the sand hills. That's where we meet our people." TransCanada noted in its studies that after European settlement, Indigenous people had "reduced access" to the hills to hunt and to mourn.

The hills were not easily farmed by settlers who poured in after Confederation, so the area escaped what Grambo called the "intensive alteration" of the more arable land across the prairie. Depression-era programs established by the federal and provincial governments saw wheatgrass planted. It stabilized the soil so that land could be leased to ranchers, who learned to manage the grasslands for their grazing herds. The hills were also home to two hundred plant species, a hundred and fifty types of birds, and dozens of animals, reptiles, and amphibians: a 2003 survey showed that ranches in the hills had more diverse plant life and fewer non-native species than nearby nature preserves. TransCanada catalogued many of them during its Energy East research, calling the hills a "nationally and internationally significant area." Grambo described them as "a 190,000-hectare island containing an irreplaceable combination and juxtaposition of ecosystems—an island with the waves of development slowly eating away at its shores."

The open sand that gave the hills their name makes up only about half of 1 percent of the surface area; the rest is thin vegetative cover that sustained the cattle ranches and farms. "This is thirsty land," Grambo wrote: what little water exists is in near-surface sand and gravel aquifers, some of them just a few metres down. "The same soil permeability that allows rain water to quickly disappear in the sand hills allows biological and chemical contaminants to travel rapidly through the aquifers," she noted.

A 1980 study concluded that the hills were "intolerant of greater than natural physical disturbance," but the pressure to develop natural gas reserves in the area was unrelenting. In 1991, after the Progressive Conservative government of Grant Devine began selling oil and gas rights in the sand hills, four regional municipalities formed a planning commission to draft a land-use plan banning gas development in close to 60 percent of the surface area. But one municipality broke ranks and sought rezoning to allow gas well development. The NDP government of Lorne Calvert created even more of an impetus for exploitation when it cut royalties for oil and gas and gave tax breaks to exploration companies; the party had denounced the PC sale of oil and gas rights only a decade earlier. "What has changed now besides the name of the party in power?" Grambo asked. Another report acknowledged that development was inevitable and urged that it be managed carefully, with more monitoring and more land protection. Calvert's government responded by creating the Great Sand Hills Representative Area Ecological Reserve, but it represented less than 20 percent of the hills and was broken into four separate areas.

By May 2007, when the last major study was released, the sand hills were home to fifteen hundred gas wells. Saskatchewan, like Alberta, was now fully embracing the prosperity created by fossil fuels. Forty percent of sand hills residents reported "some dependence" on income from the gas industry, and two-thirds supported an increase in development. But the study warned of "disturbance of native habitat at drilling sites, disturbance of habitat during pipeline construction, and an overall increase in human activity in the region." It called for restrictions on new roads, a reduction in existing roads, greater environmental monitoring, and the creation of thirty-five new "core bio-diversity areas" on top of the existing ecological reserve. But the right-leaning Saskatchewan Party, which took office later that year, ignored the report. "It's as if it's dead in the water," NDP MLA John Nilson, a former environment minister, complained in 2011.

Peters pointed out some large display panels in one room of the museum: several of them contained excerpts from one of the environmental reviews. Another, provided by TransCanada and bearing its logo, described the construction of its pipelines through the sand hills. The first line was built in 1956, and the five subsequent ones were installed "without compromising the integrity of this unique and natural landscape," the panel said. The land-use restrictions of the nineties came after the company's fifth line had been approved, so the company worked with the province to "minimize impacts to this sensitive environment" and to restore the landscape by spreading mulch to stabilize the soil and applying seed to restore the grass cover. "By 1994, soil erosion was almost negligible and the plant coverage was restored beyond our objectives," it declared. The company's sixth and final pipeline went in that same year, with the same reclamation methods. "Complete restoration of a sustainable native plant ecosystem can take as long as 20 years," the panel said. That period would have ended a year or two before my visit, but so far there was no panel presenting a final assessment of TransCanada's efforts.

"Someone said, 'That's really out of date,'" Peters remarked, nodding at the panel, "and I said, 'Well, it's a museum.' We're collecting history, not really what's today, right?"

With a copy of the museum's hand-drawn map in my lap, I drove south from Sceptre into the sand hills along a road the map called Dirt Road. Twenty-seven kilometres south was a single parking lot, the only facility for visitors. "It wasn't developed for tourism," Peters had told me. "You stay on the main road that goes through the hills, but being able to go where you want—basically you can't." Ecotourism would create more stress, one review panel concluded. More roads would mean more breaks in the grass cover that held the soil together. Camping, horseback riding, and fires were banned, as was the recreational use of all-terrain four-wheelers.

Saskatchewan's grid of sections and roads was mildly disorienting in the sand hills, where some roads weren't named. The flat fields soon gave way to slight hills, and what green there was yielded to a dull brown. The road began winding through ever-larger hills, and what passed for the shoulder grew visibly sandier. At an opening in a barbed-wire fence, a sign declared the land the private property of the Sand Hills Stockmen's Association. A Texas gate, a widely spaced metal grate, was built into the road to deter cattle from venturing beyond the fence. Soon the route became more sand than gravel, like the approach to a beach. Two large sand dunes came into view, three or four storeys high. The visitor parking lot was next to them.

The dunes were magnificent and otherworldly. I hiked along a narrow path through tall grass and climbed to the top. The sand, fine and white, would linger in my shoes for days. A few other visitors stood at the summit as well, equally enchanted by the desert-like formation in the middle of the country's wheat basket. Two children squealed as they slid down the side of the dune on their bottoms, toboggan-style. Their parents gazed past nearby hills of brush to other dunes visible in the distance. Grambo was right: the sand hills were unique.

One of the tourists asked me what had brought me to the hills. I told him I was writing about the heavy bitumen that would be passing under the sand.

He shrugged. "It's safer than rail," he said.

Neil Block's cattle ranch was about twenty-two kilometres east of the visitor area, on the far side of the sand hills. He met me back on Route 32 at Portreeve, not far past Sceptre—a giant man with rusty hair and beard that were going grey, sitting in his equally giant black Dodge pickup. We headed back into the hills through the dry, grassy eastern edge of dust and scrub and Texas gates, a route marked only by an abandoned farmhouse, a cornfield or two, a few incongruous ponds, and eventually, a lot of cattle. At the edge of Block's ranch, six TransCanada warning signs sat on each side of the road—the gas lines, the converted Keystone pipe, and the proposed Energy East route.

Block had appeared in an online TransCanada promotional video, part of a "Good Neighbour" series that extolled how easy the company was to deal with. "We always get along well," he told me as several dozen cows mooed in the grassy green field behind him. "If there's a problem, they fix it right now. We deal with some other gas companies, and you can't pick up the phone and expect an answer from them right away. But with TransCanada, if there's a problem and you phone them, by the end of the day you'll have something. You might not have closure, but they're on it."

Block took over the ranch from his father, Carl, who bought it from the family that had owned it since 1890. Eighty-five percent of the land in the sand hills is government-owned, but Block's ranch belongs to him. The 2007 government review said that 40 percent of the residents in the sand hills lived outside towns; the unemployment rate was lower than the provincial average. "We've got a roof over our head and food in the cupboard," Block said. The cattle mooing in the distance were destined for a feedlot that fall. Business had been better, he added, "but we're here for the long term, so we weather the ups and downs."

Rebecca Grambo concluded her book by arguing that the sand hills environment "should be kept as it is . . . not as a static, glassed-in museum exhibit but as an example of humans working and making a living as a contributing part of an intricate, interwoven, living, breathing ecosystem. Like the Great Sand Hills themselves, that is truly unique." Block was one of the humans she was referring to—someone who understood the fragility of the ecosystem but also called it "pretty darn resilient. . . . It could be blowing away, right? But it's not." He agreed with the premise, though: "We have to treat it differently." He was always aware of how many cattle were on which of the ranch's forty-five pastures and for how long. "It's essential," he said. "How quickly [the grass] can recover from grazing determines how soon you can come back. . . . They eat a certain amount of grass, and we move them somewhere else, and we have to take them away from there for a year, or a year and a half or two years, before they go back and graze it again."

For Block, this was a day's work, and pipelines were another human creation to be factored in and managed. The fifth and sixth gas lines were built after his father bought the ranch. "It's always been there for me," he said. "I'm not concerned about it at all. For the benefit that we, as Canadians, get from it, it's a small price to pay." He pointed to how close the lines came to his land. "If I was concerned about safety, we wouldn't have a yard here. If one of these gas lines goes, we're not here!" Nor did the conversion to oil bother him. "It's certainly safer than on a rail car or on a truck," he said. Heavy bitumen's tendency to sink into the ground was "a concern" because he relied on groundwater for his cattle, but one of TransCanada's pump stations would be just over the hill to the west, which Block figured would allow the company to shut off the flow quickly if there were a break.

The angst about oil in eastern Canada was "laughable sometimes," Block said. "I don't see how it's going to be a problem. The pipe leaking into the St. Lawrence would be a huge deal. The pipe leaking into our ground here is a bigger deal to me. I'm more concerned about that. And I'm not worried about it happening."

A few sections to the east of Neil Block's farm, the TransCanada mainline passed through the property of Gary Nieminen, who in early 2015 had applied to intervene at the NEB hearings into Energy East. Nieminen wasn't nearly as confident as Neil Block. "You can't just go and put a resource at risk these days," he said of the aquifers under the hills. "Whether anyone's using that water today, you don't go and put it at risk. It's a groundwater resource. You don't just put your dilbit over it and risk it." One of TransCanada's NEB filings said that it had rejected building an entirely new pipeline from Hardisty to Saint John in part because that would "necessitate crossing sensitive environmental features," including the sand hills.

Nieminen rented his farm in the sand hills and lived in Regina, where I interviewed him a few days later. But he'd grown up on the property and attended a tiny country school on the main road that ran east from Block's farm. He'd read Grambo's book and the various government studies. None of the 2007 recommendations were acted on, he said, though the province created conservation areas in the most sensitive parts of the hills. "And guess what, TransCanada goes right through the middle of it!" He acknowledged that the gas lines were there before the studies, but converting them to oil was another issue entirely, he said: gas dissipates in the air. Oil sinks.

Nieminen's father had bought the plot from another family in 1953, three years before the first gas pipeline. "Then every few years, another one would come across," he said. "I don't think any of those pipelines went through any kind of environmental assessment. Just go get your right-of-way from the farmer and go for it." Many landowners consented in return for new cars. "That's kind of the way a lot of people treated it out there. They don't worry about the environment or the hazard or anything else. They say, 'What's the compensation this time?'"

Nieminen studied environmental engineering when he left the farm, including hydrology—the movement of water—and he worked for the city of Regina for years, including on hazard planning. That landed him on a national committee that developed guidelines for pipeline setbacks within municipal limits. When he first heard about the proposed conversion of another gas line to dilbit for Energy East, he started researching the project and attended an open house organized by TransCanada near Regina. The company was reticent about providing the information it promised, he said: copies of its documents showed up in municipal libraries along the route, an NEB requirement, only after Nieminen complained. "The guy from TransCanada called me, all apologetic—'Dunno what happened, mix-up in the mailroom or something,'" he said. Even then, libraries were sent a USB thumb drive rather than hard copies. Nieminen complained again, and TransCanada said it would provide hard copies. "Was it me who gave them a little bit of a poke to move? I don't know."

Despite those frustrations, Nieminen said, he'd formed some conclusions. TransCanada had not modelled how a bitumen spill would affect the sand hills. "They haven't done any of this work," he said. When I asked the TransCanada spokesperson, Tim Duboyce, for a spill plan, he told me that because an existing gas line would be converted, "that means much less environmental disruption during construction"—not the concern Nieminen was raising. "In converting the line for Energy East we will ensure the integrity of the pipeline and place safety equipment such as valves and emergency response tools in strategically appropriate locations," Duboyce added, "so in the very, very unlikely event of an incident we can limit any potential impacts." He pointed out that the converted Keystone line had been carrying oil through the hills since 2010. "Several pipelines that currently run through that area all have site-specific emergency response plans in place."

Nieminen was following the fallout from a Husky Energy accident in Saskatchewan in July 2016. The line broke when the bank of the North Saskatchewan River shifted during a rainstorm. It contaminated the water source for the cities of North Battleford, Melford, and Prince Albert with more than two hundred thousand litres of oil. The break happened after a pipeline expansion that the province approved without an environmental impact assessment. The mayor of Prince Albert, Greg Dionne, questioned why the company couldn't stop the spill before it reached his city almost four hundred kilometres downstream. "It didn't happen on a tanker in the ocean where it can go in four directions," he told the CBC. "It happened in a river channel that's controlled. . . . I don't know why it got away from them."

The accident prompted a new round of debate about Saskatchewan's regulatory regime for pipelines. The rules came under the same department that promoted oil and gas development, and they let companies monitor themselves. This made Nieminen nervous. Regina, the provincial capital, drew its municipal water from Lake Diefenbaker, which was fed by the South Saskatchewan River, beneath which Energy East bitumen would pass. "If they ever had a failure there, it would be a humongous impact," Nieminen said. "It would be a spill ten or twenty times larger than Husky."

He wanted to intervene at the NEB hearings so that he could urge the board to order TransCanada to build forty-five kilometres of new pipeline; that way, Energy East could go around the Great Sand Hills—a detour he estimated would cost an extra $90 million. "Do I give a shit?" he said. The additional construction would boost employment, something he thought Premier Brad Wall should welcome. "TransCanada has got to learn that if you want a pipeline you should put it on an appropriate route, and you're probably going to get a pipeline."

Nieminen told me that in 2014 his tenant farmer had noticed something peculiar along the pipeline right-of-way. "He had weeds growing all over the thing, and he couldn't kill the goddamned things," he said. "The productivity along this corridor is the shits." It appeared to be a variety of herbicide-resistant weed that he figured TransCanada had tracked onto his land after not cleaning its equipment properly. So Nieminen wasn't feeling generous when company representatives made their annual visit in 2015 to check on the corridor and write a cheque for a few hundred dollars for continued use of the right-of-way. "I hounded them, like, 'Have you guys even got a proto-col?'" he said. "'Maybe I should be telling you guys when you want to come to work on my land to get the hell off.'"

A year later, Nieminen was still holding out. "I'm not signing anything," he told me. He didn't expect the company to bend, either, and legally, they probably didn't have to. At one point during their flurry of email exchanges, a TransCanada representative told Nieminen that the company was willing to test a soil sample from his land. He promptly asked what methodology she planned to use. "I haven't heard back from her," he said. "They're probably going, 'Geez, this guy's a real pain in the ass.'"

———

Neil Block and Gary Nieminen knew of each other as sand hills neighbours, but they weren't acquainted. They were linked only by the unique landscape of the hills, and by their respective instincts to be moderate and reasonable. "I'm not against pipelines," Nieminen said. "You need to know that. Sure, we've got to have a way to get product to tidewater if we're going to sell oil. That's an issue that I'm not into, like the Council of Canadians: they don't want to see this pipeline built at all. 'It doesn't fall in line with our goals to reduce greenhouse gases,' and this and that. I'm not into that. I'm just saying a route that was selected for gas lines is not necessarily a good route for liquid product."

Block, too, wanted to be reasonable. "I can understand the environmental questions that everybody has," he said. "If this was a new line going through our place, I'd be worried about it, too." Still, oil was "what makes the country go 'round, really, whether people like to admit it or not. We use it. Everybody uses it. . . . I'm not saying that people should just roll over and let it happen. People want to be very sure on how everything's installed, and where it goes, and what protections are in place." But, he said, accepting that risk, helping to get Alberta oil to lucrative markets—through safer means than rail—was the Canadian thing to do. "We have it right in our backyard and I don't mind it going by. So I think everybody's got to take a piece of it, for the country."

5

OUR NATIONAL METAPHOR

THE GRID ROAD THAT ran east from the Neil Block and Gary Nieminen farms crossed provincial Route 32 near the town of Cabri. Relieved to be back on smooth asphalt, I drove southeast through spare, flat countryside until I reached Saskatchewan Route 1, the Trans-Canada Highway, the country's primary thoroughfare. A few dozen metres to the right was the Canadian Pacific Railway. The city of Swift Current lay a few kilometres ahead.

The CPR created Swift Current in 1882, when a train crew detached a boxcar to mark the spot for a new settlement. The city's commercial life had since migrated to the highway, but its downtown was still that of a railway town: the tight grid of streets, the massive rail yard splitting the city into north and south sides, the hulking grain terminals down the tracks. From Swift Current, the CPR began to converge on the Energy East pipeline route: the existing gas line crossed many of the same farmers' fields and small towns as the steel tracks, passing through the same cities—Regina, Winnipeg, Kenora—as it left the prairie, entered the Canadian Shield, and continued to the Great Lakes, the beginning of another Canada.

And the pipeline followed the CPR another way: rhetorically.

Before TransCanada's grand Alberta-to-New Brunswick project had a name, politicians were using the CPR to brand it. Frank McKenna, the former New Brunswick premier turned oil industry cheerleader, may have been first. In an opinion piece for *The Globe and Mail* in June 2012, McKenna wrote that the railroad had pit "the indomitable will of our early railroad pioneers against the rugged Canadian terrain. In a country where gravitational forces often move north and south, this ribbon of steel has helped knit the country together both symbolically and economically." He called for "another bold project, national in scope," a pipeline from Alberta to New Brunswick that would not only deliver oil to market but also become "a powerful symbol of Canadian unity."

Others echoed McKenna's conjuring of Sir John A. Macdonald's ghost. "The pipeline is as important today . . . as the railway was in the past," New Brunswick premier David Alward said in 2013. His Saskatchewan counterpart, Brad Wall, called Energy East "the modern-day version" of Macdonald's national dream. On Canada Day 2016, Mark Scholz, president of the Canadian Association of Oilwell Drilling Contractors, pushed the analogy so hard that it almost jumped the tracks. The CPR was "bold and ambitious," he wrote in the *Calgary Herald*, a project that required "tremendous political courage and leadership" yet also "crossed party lines." Scholz noted that politics were different in Macdonald's time: there were no polling data, no tweets restricting debate to a hundred and forty characters. "In those days, debates were won by delivering sound arguments, not political rhetoric. Decisions were made based on facts and evidence." Substance trumped style, and leaders "were not afraid to make difficult decisions." That courage had linked western resources with eastern manufacturers, creating "a great nation of the north." Justin Trudeau, Scholz concluded, should show the same courage.

The message was clear. Energy East could not fall victim to too much debate or too long a deliberation: it had to be pushed through by force of will—by gutsy politicians who, if successful, might someday be described in the same reverential tones as Sir John A.

———

The CPR's presence was felt everywhere on the prairies. Hardisty's social life revolved around the Leaf, the train station turned bar. CPR museums dotted the landscape in towns like Empress, Alberta, and Herbert, Saskatchewan. Railway artifacts filled the Great Sandhills Museum and Interpretive Centre in Sceptre and the Sukanen Ship Pioneer Village and Museum outside Moose Jaw. All these places had been linked to the wider world by the CPR; on the broad vista of the prairies, it remained a powerful symbol in the west, an epic of Canada that lived deep in the national soul.

"The east-west cousinship, a nation's rise," the Canadian poet E.J. Pratt wrote in his narrative poem "Towards the Last Spike." In breathless blank verse, Pratt compared Macdonald's political struggle to that of the railway crews fighting the forces of nature. "The feel of it was in the air," Pratt wrote. "'Union required the Line.'" Gordon Lightfoot invoked the same themes in 1967, when the CBC commissioned a song for Canada's centennial. "Canadian Railroad Trilogy" acknowledged difficult working conditions but cast the CPR as an inevitable and necessary triumph: "Open 'er heart, let the life blood flow / Gotta get on our way 'cause we're movin' too slow." Three years later, Pierre Berton's two-volume history of the railway's construction, *The National Dream* and *The Last Spike*, became a publishing phenomenon. The story, the author would recall, "had everything—a huge cast of larger-than-life characters, a major political scandal, an engineering feat of immense complexity, a prairie revolution, and, most important, the stitching together of the new nation from sea to sea." At a time of rising Canadian nationalism and, paradoxically, existential anxiety about the country's future, "*The National Dream* was now the historic litmus test of national vision for all Canadians," wrote Berton's biographer, A.B. McKillop.

Other artists challenged the prevailing narrative. "Where are the coolies in your poem, Ned?" asked the poet F.R. Scott in his "All the Spikes But the Last," a response to Pratt's epic poem. "Between the first and the million other spikes they drove . . . who has sung their story?" In 1992, the Canadian roots-rock band the Cowboy Junkies released an album that included a moody song called "The Last Spike," the story of a small town in decline:

> *Mornings feel so damn sad these days*
> *without the call of the 8:15*
> *That old familiar echo*
> *has finally died away*
> *leaving nothing but a chill*
> *where there once was a mighty scream . . .*

"We had been a very American-centric band in some ways," Michael Timmins, the lead songwriter, recalled in an interview. "So I wanted to write something more Canadian, but something that made sense in global terms as well." The song wasn't explicitly Canadian, and the title didn't appear in the lyrics, but "by calling the song 'The Last Spike,' that gave the song a Canadian twist, or a wink of the eye to Canadians," Timmins said. Coming at the end of the Mulroney years, the track, quiet and haunting, reflected the anxieties of the age—free trade, American hegemony—and the CPR's renewed potency as a national metaphor. "The Canadian railway in many ways was what we think it was, a real bonding of this country, a tying together of the country from coast to coast, a protection against American expansionism. So that's why it's such a striking, defining image: it had a purpose as well as being a grand gesture."

But the song also subverted the image, because Timmins's lyrics evoked the train not as the bringer of nationhood but as a darker presence—"the sense of it destroying things and carrying things away," he said.

> *I've watched the flat cars*
> *take away our timber*
> *I've watched the coal cars steal our rock*

And now that we've got
nothing left to take we're told
that the wheels will stop turning,
the whistles will stop blowing,
these foolish dreams must stop

The railway was fraught with meaning, both good and bad; any politician who invoked it was inviting it to be applied in full, including the less savoury and more contentious elements of the story, Timmins said.

I carried a copy of Berton's *The Last Spike* on the western leg of my pipeline journey. My route tracked closely to his map of "The Prairie Line," and I, too, was struck by elements of the CPR story with which no sane politician would want to be associated: land speculation by corrupt public officials; price fixing; poor working conditions; shoddy, unsafe construction; conflicts of interest, including one that led to the selection of Regina as the capital of the North-West Territories; and cost overruns that required government bailouts. The backroom deals, favouritism, brinkmanship, and corporate welfare hardly lived up to the soaring rhetoric of twenty-first-century pipeline boosters.

Along the pipeline route, people who knew the oil business—including its ardent supporters—rolled their eyes or shook their heads at politicians comparing Energy East to the CPR. "The railway is probably a little bit different," Jeff Golka, the Hardisty real estate agent, told me. The CPR had multiple uses, he said, while a pipeline had just one function. "I'm not sure we should be comparing the railway to the pipeline." The town's mayor, Anita Miller, pointed out that there were several ways to ship oil, but "when John A. Macdonald was building the rail, that was the only way to get across Canada." Neil Block was also dismissive: the pipeline "does tie the country together, but I don't think on the same scale that the railway does." Hal Kvisle, the former TransCanada CEO, thought the better analogy to the CPR was the company's original gas pipeline in the fifties. "It is enormous, and it is the second-largest pipeline transmission system in the world," he said. "So that's the real comparison."

As resistance to Energy East grew, the CPR metaphor became a cudgel. "Thank goodness that kind of thinking wasn't around at the start of this country," Saskatchewan premier Brad Wall said of pipeline opponents. Alberta Conservative Jason Kenney tweeted, "Our national railways would not have been built if we had been governed by 'social license' rather than rule of law," a reference to the vague phrase activists on the left used to define the threshold for pipeline approval. Bronwyn Tucker, the Greenpeace activist in Edmonton, called the CPR "a weird comparison" for Energy East, but said it applied in a way that pipeline supporters hadn't anticipated: environmental groups in provinces touched by the project were working together for the first time, holding weekly conference calls to coordinate strategy. "So it's nation-building in terms of the climate movement," she said, laughing.

Even by the standards of 1885, the CPR was a questionable symbol of unity, as Berton acknowledged in *The Last Spike*. Macdonald was now governing a country larger than the one created in 1867. He struggled to reconcile increasingly diverse interests and constituencies, "tugged this way and that by a variety of conflicting environmental and historical strains, and all now stirred into a ferment by the changes wrought through the coming of steel," Berton wrote. Macdonald faced criticism from Manitobans over the company's rail monopoly, which prevented local entrepreneurs from building short lines to settlements not on the main route. Farmers in the west were angry that the railway would let their resources be exploited by the east, while easterners resented paying for a railway that would benefit a part of the country foreign to them.

"From the beginning he had seen the railway as a device to unite the nation—to tie the settled East to the new country beyond the Shield," Berton wrote. "Now in the very first year of its construction the railway had become a divisive force, antagonizing the very people it was supposed to link together."

That passage, written at the time of Canada's centennial, seemed to anticipate the pipeline debate of a half century later.

"When we talk about the great myth of the railway—at the time, there was no thought of First Nations rights, and now we're doing that again," Michael Timmins said. "Maybe if we hadn't had that attitude then, we would have dealt with the land rights issues at the time, and our relationship with those First Nations would have been a hundred and fifty years healthier."

To facilitate the settlement of the west and the construction of the railway, the federal government signed a series of numbered treaties with the Indigenous peoples of the prairie. According to the English text of Treaty Four, thirteen Cree and Saulteaux chiefs agreed to "cede, release, surrender and yield up" a vast stretch of land from western Manitoba through the southern half of Saskatchewan to southeast Alberta. In return, they were promised annual payments, farming equipment, and clothes; chiefs were granted extra incentives. There would be reserves of one square mile for every five people, selected "after conference with each band of Indians," and each reserve would have a school. The treaty also promised the Indigenous people that they could pursue their "avocations of hunting, trapping and fishing throughout the tract surrendered," subject to Canadian law, except on land needed for "settlement, mining or other purposes." Reserve land could be expropriated "for public works or building of whatsoever nature" as long as "due compensation" was paid.

This bargain, Treaty Four, was signed at Fort Qu'Appelle, a Hudson's Bay Company trading post, on September 15, 1874, by Alexander Morris, the lieutenant-governor of Manitoba and the North-West Territories; David Laird, the federal Indian commissioner; and the thirteen chiefs. Having learned that the signing was being commemorated during my pipeline journey, I drove to Fort Qu'Appelle to attend the ceremony.

When I arrived, the chiefs of the thirty-five First Nations of the treaty— additional tribes had signed between 1874 and 1877—were gathered in their large semicircle legislature at the Treaty Four Governance Centre, which itself had been the subject of a land claim: in 1874 the chiefs were promised land where they could conduct treaty business, a promise it took Ottawa until 1995 to honour. The centre, a modern office building with a giant replica of a teepee out front, dominated the edge of town.

Inside, Perry Bellegarde, the national chief of the Assembly of First Nations and a former chief of the nearby Little Black Bear First Nation, was updating the assembly on his discussions with the new Liberal government of Justin Trudeau. He introduced Joe Wild, the assistant deputy minister for treaties and Aboriginal government at the Department of Indigenous and Northern Affairs, who'd flown in from Ottawa for the commemoration. Trudeau's government, Wild said, was looking for ways to "decolonize" the relationship. There would be challenges: Canada had reorganized Indigenous nations to suit its purposes, like the building of the CPR, Wild said, but "we have to decide whether the values we espouse as Canadians—democracy, human rights—are real or not." The chiefs faced a decision, too: to cooperate with Ottawa or hold out; to believe Trudeau's rhetoric or reject it. "We're an order of government," Senator Ted Quewezance of the Keeseekoose First Nation told Wild. "We're not just bands controlled by the Indian Act. We're human beings." But Sakimay chief Lynn Acoose said she felt that a new process was beginning: "This is a good day for us."

The ceremony began after lunch, under a tent outdoors, when David Johnston, Canada's twenty-eighth governor general, arrived to the sound of ceremonial drums. Johnston represented the same Crown on whose behalf Alexander Morris had signed Treaty Four in 1874, and he said he'd come to reaffirm its terms. "In this country, we are all treaty people," he told the gathering. "Today is about much more than simply marking an anniversary. Yes, Treaty Four was signed near here 142 years ago, but that doesn't make it history." Treaties, he said, were "living, breathing documents," and the compromises of the agreements signed after Confederation represented "the first confederal bargain" of Canada's history. They remained fundamental to the country's conception of itself, he continued, but not the paternalistic and destructive narrative of the past. "It's a story that's told in the treaties, including in Treaty Four," he said. "It's a story of partnership: balanced, reciprocal, and respectful."

One of the Indigenous elders, Noel Starblanket, spoke after Johnston. His comments carried a weary tone: promises had been made before. "One hundred and forty-two years ago, your forebears and mine came together on this very ground," he said. "We are now privileged to welcome you back. One hundred and forty-two years ago, the office of the treaty commissioner and other government representatives promised that they would revisit the following year. They're late." Laughter rippled through the tent. "But we welcome you nonetheless."

Starblanket brandished a copy of Treaty Four in book form—"our Bible," he said, "a solemn agreement in the eyes of God"—and reminded Johnston of the Indigenous interpretation of the pact: the chiefs hadn't *ceded* the land, they had shared it. "We continue to agree to share this land," he said. "We have not surrendered it. Our people share it so readily as to become impoverished in material terms and poor in physical spirit—but strong yet today in our spirituality." The people of Treaty Four were "buoyed" by Johnston's reaffirmation, Starblanket said. "The future is calling us, Excellency. Your visit here is historic. It restores the relationship that was begun 142 years ago."

Johnston returned to the stage, where Starblanket and others presented him with a gift: a copy of a pictograph that had been created in 1883 by Chief Paskwa, one of the treaty signatories, and that outlined its terms in drawings. The negotiators were depicted on the left; on the right were the various tools, clothes, and money the Crown had promised to provide.

The pictograph's own journey to Fort Qu'Appelle echoed the themes of the day. Paskwa had drawn it when a British traveller passed through the valley in 1883, nine years after the signing. Already the Crown wasn't honouring the treaty's promises, and Paskwa asked the traveller, William Henry Barneby, to deliver the pictograph to Queen Victoria as a reminder. Instead, Barneby kept it. After his descendants put it up for auction in 2000, it was eventually bought by the Pasqua First Nation for $200,000, with the Royal Saskatchewan Museum, the province, and other donors helping to cover the cost. It was the only recorded account of the treaty from an Indigenous perspective. The museum held the original, but in Fort Qu'Appelle a copy was finally handed to the Crown, like an overdue bill.

One of the chiefs at the Fort Qu'Appelle ceremony—the one I came to see— was Elsie Jack of Carry the Kettle First Nation. For Jack, Johnston's reaffirmation of the treaty and Starblanket's avowal that the bands would continue sharing the land were pressing concerns.

In a May 2016 band election Jack had defeated the incumbent chief, Barry Kennedy, who had accused her of orchestrating, ahead of the vote, an agreement with TransCanada on Energy East that he said was "taking all of Carry the Kettle's rights away." The deal, negotiated by Jack and signed by five band councillors over Chief Kennedy's objections, would pay the First Nation $18 million. Part of that was compensation for the company's original building of gas pipelines, starting in the fifties, through the reserve east of Regina. In return, the company gained a new easement to convert one gas line for crude oil and "the right to pass and repass over the reserve to such extent as may from time to time be reasonably required." The band promised to "not oppose, interfere or try to set aside Energy East project approvals."

Jack had worked for TransCanada in the past and had advised the councillors who signed the deal. Kennedy told the Aboriginal Peoples Television Network that it was "sneaky and conniving" to sign with TransCanada "at the eleventh hour on the eve of an election." But his complaint that the agreement took away the band's rights was belied by a clause that said Carry the Kettle wasn't waiving any of its Aboriginal or treaty rights. (Another clause stipulated that TransCanada wasn't acknowledging those rights.) After Jack was elected chief, the company used its Energy East Twitter account to congratulate her on her election victory.

Jack had studied accounting in university, and had learned how to value land and assets for tax assessments. She became a treaty and land claim consultant, she told me, doing gas well valuations at Carry the Kettle. Her work for TransCanada in 2012 hadn't influenced her negotiations on behalf of the council or compromised the band's position, she insisted. "Maybe other people saw it that way," she said. "I had a knowledge base to help my people." The gas lines already crossed Carry the Kettle, she pointed out. "We can't say yes or no to it because we've been living with it for sixty years." Instead, the band had to get the maximum benefit.

Jack's story was entwined not just with Energy East but with its metaphorical predecessor, the CPR. She was the great-granddaughter of Chief Man Who Took the Coat, one of the Lakota chiefs who witnessed, and resisted, the expulsion of his people from their original home in the Cypress Hills to make way for the railway. "There was genocide that happened to my people, starting with John A. Macdonald and Mr. Dewdney"—the federal Indian commissioner—"who fulfilled his policies," Jack told me. "They stopped at nothing to get what they wanted." History was young here: only four generations separated the woman sitting in front of me, who negotiated with TransCanada, from the chief who endured his tribe's forced resettlement from its traditional territory four hundred kilometres away.

Confined to reserves, the Indigenous people of the prairies became dependent on government relief. The promise of the treaties, that their life could continue as it had been before, proved hollow. Canada sought to transform these hunters into farmers, pushing them onto better agricultural land north of the railway, far from their ancient grounds. "Thus," Berton wrote in *The Last Spike*, "the CPR became the visible symbol of the Indians' tragedy." Seventy years later, TransCanada built its first pipeline through the present-day reserve, where Chief Man Who Took the Coat's people had been forced to resettle.

Carry the Kettle First Nation "brings an alternative perspective which is significantly different from [that of] other First Nations," the band wrote in its application to intervene at the NEB hearings on Energy East, "because of years of on reserve experience with the pipeline." It also embodied the fraught history of Canada's colonial behaviour on the prairies, a narrative from which the CPR—the central metaphor of the Energy East debate—was inseparable. Many of the pipeline debate's themes came together at Carry the Kettle.

Elsie Jack was raised by her grandmother Katie Jack, whose husband, Joseph Jack, was the son of Man Who Took the Coat. As a girl, Elsie told me, "I would always be in the kitchen and she would have a lot of her friends over who spoke fluent Nakota. I would be mingling around in there until I got kicked out for asking too many questions." She laughed at the memory. "My grandmother would always share with us stories, oral history, of our family and where they came from." Jack spoke Nakota as a little girl, but eventually lost the language. Her aunt and her friends "always talked a lot about our removal from the Cypress Hills. They talked a lot about the massacre of our people. So I got to hear the stories that were passed on to them by some of the people who were there at the time."

Before colonization, the Cypress Hills, twenty-five hundred square kilometres of uplands straddling today's Saskatchewan–Alberta border, were frequented by the Assiniboine people who would become known as the Carry the Kettle band. Oral history described the hills as "the permanent wintering ground of the Assiniboine tribes," an abundant source of game and plant medicine. Saskatchewan author Candace Savage referred to them as "a secret kingdom in the middle of a cactus plain," a land "filled with ghosts" because of an 1873 massacre of a group of Assiniboine by American wolfers—an event still marked by an annual pilgrimage to the site by Carry the Kettle band members. The killings are recounted in Guy Vanderhaeghe's novel *The Englishman's Boy*; in the wake of the massacre, the holy man Strong Bull hands a younger Assiniboine, Fine Man, a trader's book filled with his drawings of their people's way of life—women dancing, men skinning buffalo, a feast—so that their disappearing world would be remembered by their grandchildren.

The massacre prompted the federal government to establish the North-West Mounted Police, precursor to the RCMP. The police built Fort Walsh, which became a trading hub for settlers and Indigenous people, and it was there that the Assiniboine—represented by the four chiefs Man Who Took the Coat, Long Lodge Tepee Hoska, Wich-a-wos-taka, and Poor Man—became the last Indigenous nation to sign Treaty Four on September 25, 1877. And it was at Fort Walsh that their people would collect their annuities under the terms, "this being their country and the majority of them could not be induced to go elsewhere," NWMP superintendent James Walsh wrote in a letter to Ottawa later that fall, recognizing their attachment to the Cypress Hills.

The story becomes murky in 1879, around the time the Assiniboine were to select land for their reserve in the Cypress Hills. The Macdonald government appointed Edgar Dewdney as Indian commissioner, giving him wide powers to prepare the prairies for the construction of the railway and white settlement. Dewdney, who arrived at Fort Walsh to find the Assiniboine and other nations suffering from famine, ordered that they be taught to farm. He also directed a surveyor, A.P. Patrick, to survey the reserve for the Assiniboine. However, as a land claims inquiry would conclude in 2000, back in Ottawa the Indian branch of the Department of the Interior was being turned into a stand-alone department, and "there was some confusion" about who had authority to instruct surveyors.

That confusion proved tragic for the Assiniboine. By the time Patrick's survey of a reserve in the Cypress Hills reached Ottawa in July 1881, Dewdney had decided to relocate the Assiniboine away from the hills. Better land elsewhere would allow them to be "independent of the Government, if properly assisted and instructed in agriculture," he wrote in a letter to Ottawa. One official recommended cutting their rations in half to coerce them to leave, though he was overruled. "Regardless of whether farming or ranching would have provided a feasible livelihood for the Assiniboine Band in the Cypress Hills," the 2000 inquiry report said, "larger political and economic factors were at work." The contract for the CPR had been signed three weeks earlier, and, the inquiry inferred from letters, it had been decided, apparently by Macdonald himself, "to clear the Cypress Hills of Indians."

The Assiniboine were encouraged to settle hundreds of miles away, on reserves near Indian Head, not far from Fort Qu'Appelle. By the fall of 1881 some agreed to go, though Man Who Took the Coat and others tried to persuade government officials to let them stay. "These Indians have always looked upon the Cypress Hills as their home," one NWMP colonel wrote in a report to Ottawa. Dewdney himself acknowledged their attachment, writing that the hills were, for the Assiniboine, "places associated with thoughts of freedom and plenty. . . . Leaving these hills behind them dashed to the ground the last hope to which they had so strenuously clung," a return to life before European settlement.

The forced migration began in May 1882. By late summer, many of the Assiniboine were unhappy with their new, distant reserves and longed for the Cypress Hills. Hundreds, including Chief Man Who Took the Coat, returned to Fort Walsh. Ottawa responded by creating a permit system to restrict the Assiniboine's movements, and local officials at Fort Walsh were ordered to reduce their food allowance. In the spring of 1883, they were banished again. Chiefs Man Who Took the Coat and Long Lodge concluded that they had no choice but to return to the new reserves. In a further indignity, they were sent, under armed escort, by train. The railway track had just been laid, and the CPR that had cost them their lands also became the vehicle for their final expulsion.

Chief Long Lodge died in 1884, and the two tribes merged under Man Who Took the Coat on the reserve that is the present-day Carry the Kettle First Nation. In 1992, the band filed a federal land claim for its ancestral territory in the Cypress Hills, arguing that Patrick's 1880 survey had legally created a reserve there under the terms of Treaty Four. The commission of inquiry agreed it was "incontrovertible" that the Assiniboine had told federal officials of their wishes, and that Patrick had completed the survey. But it concluded, "somewhat reluctantly," that there was an "absence of evidence" that the survey was officially accepted by the Canadian government, one of the legal requirements. Canada owed Carry the Kettle nothing.

The commission also concluded that its own findings, though technically correct, were unfair. The Carry the Kettle band's connection to the Cypress Hills had been "tragically severed," the report said. The band "repeatedly fought the government's attempt to relocate it to other reserve lands" and succumbed to pressure "reluctantly and only when faced with the spectre of starvation as an alternative." The scene of the 1873 massacre should be a historical site, the commission said, and Ottawa should secure a location in the Cypress Hills for the band's annual pilgrimages. "The Government of Canada does not have a legal obligation to do either of these things, but in our view it would be the right, just and moral thing to do," the report said: the band's claim to the Cypress Hills was "historically accurate and morally compelling."

Carry the Kettle challenged the 2000 land claim decision, a case still before the Federal Court sixteen years later when I met Elsie Jack. "Take a look at today now," she said. "We had parts of land illegally taken from us with no consideration and no consultation, then we had our lands expropriated." When TransCanada built the first gas line through the reserve in the fifties, it paid fifteen hundred dollars in compensation, a one-time sum. "That was it," Jack said. "We've never received a payment after that." And Enbridge's first oil line to Superior, Wisconsin, built around the same time, went through the former Long Lodge reserve without the band's consent.

Jack blamed the band's acquiescence to both projects on "all the detrimental things that happened to our people." The agreement she helped negotiate with TransCanada for Energy East would hardly undo the betrayal and displacement of the Assiniboine, but it was all she had at the moment. Its terms, she said, would let Carry the Kettle recoup a share of "the billions and billions of natural gas and billions of dollars that went through those lines" crossing the reserve.

It included "legacy payments" of $550,000 per year for twenty years—$11 million in total—to redress that grievance. "We should be one of the wealthiest First Nations in Saskatchewan and it's not true," Jack said. "We have deteriorating infrastructure. The last time we had new housing was eight years ago." The deal even provided for a $3 million lump-sum payment by the company to the band in the event the pipeline did not go ahead. TransCanada, said the band's consultant, James Tanner, was "making up" for decades in which it ignored the people of Carry the Kettle. The company, he added, wanted "to re-establish goodwill with the First Nation across which their pipeline runs."

But in the short time between the band's signing the agreement with TransCanada and my meeting with the chief in Fort Qu'Appelle, the terrain had shifted on pipelines. Opinion was hardening at Carry the Kettle. "One of the turning points this year was the Husky spill," Jack said. "Those issues have become a reality now. Those issues that they said were never going to happen became a reality." Another was the confrontation at the Standing Rock reservation in North Dakota, where the Sioux were fighting a pipeline called Dakota Access. Many young people from Carry the Kettle supported them, Jack told me. "Hearing all these issues in the last little while is making our people very nervous. Our elders are getting nervous."

The agreement with TransCanada had gone through the first round of approval, but Jack said that it still needed consultation with the band membership. "It's not a sure thing. We'll have to go back to our membership and get a mandate to see which way we're going with this." She had a wish list: Ottawa already provided five thousand dollars a year for the fire department, but she wanted a twenty-four-hour service that could respond to a pipeline accident. Jack wasn't optimistic. "It may be dead in the water," she said of the Energy East agreement. Band members "may say, 'We don't want any part of this.' They may say, 'Reroute your pipeline.'" On the other hand, TransCanada had been better to deal with than Enbridge, which was planning to replace its Line 3 oil pipeline through the Long Lodge reserve. "There's been no consideration whatsoever," Jack continued. "There's been no consultation."

On both projects, she said, "it's hard to say something positive. It's very hard, because of all the things that have happened to my people. It's not just about the pipelines. It goes all the way to the treaties."

In November 2015 the NEB panel reviewing Energy East hosted a session in Regina to gather oral traditional evidence from Carry the Kettle band councillors. They told the band's history, and Jack, in her role as adviser, called the lump-sum payment TransCanada paid in the fifties "disgusting." She also spoke about Ottawa's duty to consult First Nations on resource projects, a principle enshrined in court rulings. Too often, the federal government left it up to industry, "which I'm totally against," she told the panel. "It's not consultation when you call Elsie on the phone and say, 'Hey,' and you write it up and say, 'I tried to contact the chief three times.' That is not consultation, but that's how they're documenting consultation."

It wasn't easy to pin down what Elsie Jack would do next. Maybe she was exerting leverage for a better pipeline deal. Maybe, like other First Nations leaders, she was taking a stand against fossil fuels for the environment. Or maybe she was a good politician, trying to appease more militant members of her community. "I'm not pushing that agreement forward," she told me. "I am looking for a mandate from the people." Whether they would grant it was something she couldn't predict, especially with Husky, Standing Rock, and other battles over oil becoming more intense and adding more uncertainty to an increasingly complex debate. "It's a critical time right now," she noted.

"If you take a look at the CPR, the railroad lines coming through, and now the pipelines—we've been affected by those," Jack said. "If any First Nation in Saskatchewan has been affected, we have, to the point where we lost our people." She told the NEB in Regina in 2015 that "the blood of my people rests in the decisions of your governments." But history was turning: the lifeblood of the Alberta economy might well rest in part on the decisions of Elsie Jack, the great-granddaughter of Chief Man Who Took the Coat.

The CPR was the metaphor of choice for pipeline supporters, but it was also Canada's original sin. Could Carry the Kettle forgive?

6

"NEXT YEAR"

GORD ROSS KNEW THE Canadian Pacific Railway, and he knew pipelines.

Ross was raised and still farmed on the parcel of land northwest of Moose Jaw where his family settled in 1882. They arrived before the railway; after reaching their land, they had to go back to Brandon by horse to register it. "My uncle's got a Dominion of Canada map, 1883, and my great-grandfather's name is on it, so that's how long we've been here," Ross told me. The TransCanada mainline passed within fifty yards of the property, he estimated. One of the grounding grids installed to dissipate static electricity came onto the land where he grew cereal crops, canola, lentils, and oilseed. "Anytime there's anything to do with the pipelines, I get notifications," he said. "I've been getting all the letters on all this Energy East."

Ross was in the back of the small ticket office of the Sukanen Ship Pioneer Village and Museum, located at a crossroads in the prairie grid ten minutes south of Moose Jaw. He wore a cowboy hat, and his faded denim jacket was the same colour as his eyes. Hundreds of people were on the grounds for the annual end-of-season threshing bee, an all-weekend affair of pancake breakfasts, evening dances, music jams, and demonstrations of rope making, square dancing, blacksmithing, quilting, and plowing. A rally of mid-century antique cars was snaking its way through old buildings: a drugstore, barn, barber shop, blacksmith, and small railway station complete with CPR telegraph office. All had been relocated from ghost towns in the area.

Like the Sandhills Museum in Sceptre, the place was an attempt to keep the past alive. It began as a ten-acre storage site for Moose Jaw's antique car club in 1969. "There were a couple of members who were interested in other old stuff—farm machinery—and they decided they would start a museum," Ross said. "People decided they would drop stuff off here." Ross, president and senior volunteer, spent five or six days at the museum from May until September. "There are some days I get up in the morning and ask, 'What am I doing to myself?'" he laughed. He and a core group of aging volunteers have stuck it out because they believe people should understand their history. "We want to keep it alive so that this generation and future generations realize where farming has come from in this province, how hard it was for our forefathers to settle this country, and how hard they worked," he said. "A certain segment" of the volunteers would favour "'the good old days,' as opposed to the way things are now," he added.

There was a new Saskatchewan now, a rising economic power in Confederation, embodied by Brad Wall, the province's premier. Ross disdained elected officials—"They're all self-serving people"—but he allowed that Wall was "probably one of the best politicians we've ever had." Still, this man devoted to preserving the past cast a wary eye at Energy East, a project that, for Wall, exemplified the new Saskatchewan. Those mailings Ross received about the pipeline? They came from TransCanada, he said. "It's always going to make it look in their favour, when we know that *shit happens.*"

Ross wasn't convinced the gas lines were properly maintained. He often saw crews north of his property, digging up a section. Repairs like that, TransCanada would argue, proved that its safeguards worked, that whenever the slightest risk was detected, it was fixed before disaster struck. But Ross reserved the right to worry. "I'm realistic, put it that way. Do I think it could happen? Yes, I think it could happen." Others who supported the project didn't have to live as close as he did. "It's like anything else. 'As long as it doesn't involve me, I don't care.' That's how society is, isn't it? 'It's not in my backyard, so I don't care.'"

And with that, Gord Ross ambled his way back to the festival grounds to continue celebrating the old Saskatchewan.

"You can see things here," Rebecca Grambo wrote of the prairie in her book on the Great Sand Hills. "Land and sky are open to your questioning senses." The downtown office towers of Regina, the capital city—official motto: "Infinite Horizons"—were visible far before its outskirts came into view. The CPR had crossed Route 1 and was now well north of the highway. The TransCanada gas lines were just a few hundred metres from the road, running parallel beneath the ground. They continued east into a surprising milieu: a neighbourhood of brand-new townhouses, streets, and parks on the edge of Regina, a landlocked subdivision that someone had named Harbour Landing.

The development was five years old, the product of the city's rapid growth fuelled by Saskatchewan's own oil boom. Regina's population grew by 20 percent from 2005 to 2015, and it needed subdivisions like Harbour Landing. The maze of homes, box stores, and casual restaurants was tucked into the southwest corner of the city, between the airport and the highway. Many lots were still being landscaped, and there were contractor trucks everywhere. The townhouses were pressed together, their facades dominated by giant garages close to the street that left little room for the huge pickups hogging many of the driveways. "They're fairly squeezed in," said Rob Preston, whose house was the second one built on his street. "But then you have these massive parks all over." Harbour Landing was so well known for its parks that families from other parts of the city brought their children there for an afternoon of play.

One park in particular was striking, though it wasn't so much a park as a green belt, a long alley of grass and trails 750 metres long and 75 metres wide, running west–east between residential streets. It then turned ninety degrees and continued south for another 350 metres to the highway. Along its route were those telltale no-dig warning signs from TransCanada, revealing this green belt as the right-of-way for the gas mainline—running beneath the most densely populated urban setting I'd seen so far.

And residents seemed fine with that. Mitch Sochoski, out for a walk with his wife and their baby, told me that they knew the gas lines were there when they bought their house. "No hesitation," he said. "They couldn't put houses here if it wasn't safe."

Rob Preston wasn't bothered either, though his realtor hadn't flagged the right-of-way. "The only reason we knew was because of the pipeline markers," he said. "Once we bought, we got a package from TransCanada in the mail outlining what the pipeline was for, where they were, and why there were markers there." Preston liked that the line had forced the creation of those open green spaces. "If not, they'd try to pack these homes in as tightly as they could," he said. Gary Nieminen, whose land in the Great Sand Hills was crossed by the mainline, had worked at Regina city hall when Harbour Landing was approved, and was one of the officials who told the property developer to honour the setbacks in the guidelines he'd helped develop.

TransCanada had held an open house in Harbour Landing about the planned conversion of one line for Energy East, a spokesperson told me, "so residents of the neighbourhood could come and speak with engineers, safety specialists, and other subject experts from the project to have their questions answered and so we could properly assess any concerns people had and try to address them." Preston wasn't worried about oil replacing gas in one line. "I'm in the pipeline integrity business, so I know how regimented they are at testing their pipelines. Especially knowing TransCanada and doing some work for them, I know exactly what kind of company they are, so it wouldn't change our opinion at all. They're fantastic, one of the better ones."

Preston, thirty-five years old, was walking a dog he'd named Gordon Downie Jr. He'd grown up in Regina and moved to Calgary for school and work, but the rapid expansion of the oil and gas sector in Saskatchewan had let him come home and still work in his field. Nervous easterners didn't understand how normal pipelines were here, he told me. "I just don't think they're that familiar with them. They're everywhere and you're used to them, and they're a giant percentage of the population's income as well. A lot of people rely on the pipelines."

Preston's view fit neatly into the Saskatchewan mainstream. No wonder Brad Wall—an eloquent evangelist for the new Saskatchewan who spoke proudly of the oil and gas sector and who relentlessly promoted pipelines— had become, by the measure of most public opinion polling in Canada, the most popular provincial leader in the federation.

Wall came to power in 2007 after sixteen years of New Democratic government in the province and only a decade after the creation of his centre-right Saskatchewan Party. His move into the premier's office was exquisitely timed: his NDP predecessor, Lorne Calvert, had cut taxes and lowered oil and gas royalties to stimulate the economy, and it was starting to pay off. Oil royalties surpassed $1 billion annually for the first time in 2006–07; they would exceed $1.5 billion three times in the next seven years. And the province's population, which had declined between 2001 and 2006, would balloon by 19 percent over the next decade. Budget surpluses and low unemployment made Saskatchewan a "have" province under the federal equalization program. "For as long as I can remember, Saskatchewan has been 'next year' country," Wall said in a speech to Toronto's Empire Club in 2008. "Next year has arrived."

Wall was expansive and ebullient in that speech. With his wavy fair hair and stylish glasses, he looked the part of a political golden boy. He'd already mastered his trademark speaking style, a mix of CFL jokes, self-effacement, and rootsy anecdotes combined with a digestible serving of statistics and policy wonkery. He mentioned his decision, in his first year as premier, to not raise oil royalties, "the first and probably the only time that I have ever received an ovation for our government doing precisely nothing at all." Wall could afford to keep rates low: oil prices were soaring and the province was poised to break revenue records. He could also afford to sound a generous note about the equalization program and Canadian cooperation. "Because of fiscal federalism, we have had the support and the help and the assistance of other parts of the country when we were not a have province," he said. "You need to know that part of our vision—part of our exhilaration about our new status as a have province and our determination to stay that way—is so that we can pay back a little bit, so that we can contribute more to the country and in the future of this country than we ever need to get in return."

Energy was central to Wall's ambition. He rejected the idea of a carbon tax, or of a cap-and-trade system, to address carbon dioxide emissions, but he did so soaringly, speaking of other solutions: "Who knows what can come of a concerted and continental effort with respect to innovation, especially in the area of environment and energy?" he asked. "What is possible with respect to renewables—solar and wind and biomass? What is possible with respect to cleaning up fossil fuels?" Energy, he said, represented "the next great moment of fate" for Canada, "and I want Saskatchewan to be right in the middle of it." Wall's government had inherited a pilot project near Weyburn to bury carbon emissions from oil production. "We are not shifting it around, not putting a price on it, but putting it in the ground," he said. And, he added, his government was preparing to spend more than $1 billion on an even more ambitious "clean coal" project in southeast Saskatchewan. It was an early hint of an initiative that Wall would one day tout as one of his signature accomplishments—and one that he would use, when the debate about climate and carbon began to turn against him, as a cudgel for those who challenged him and the industry that made his province wealthy.

———

On the way into Weyburn on Route 39, a series of large billboards announced the town's attractions; one heralded it as "Home of the Greatest Canadian—Tommy Douglas." The former premier, who pioneered medicare in the province, is commemorated with a statue in the centre of the city he represented in the legislature, befitting his place in the traditional Saskatchewan brand.

The new Saskatchewan—Brad Wall's Saskatchewan—was also on display along Route 39. Oil wells lined the highway past Weyburn toward Estevan, a corridor at the heart of the province's fossil fuel boom. Here oil was drawn from the shale rock of the Bakken formation, a vast deposit straddling Saskatchewan's border with North Dakota. Wall used the revenue to build roads and schools for the growing population while cutting taxes and, in most years, paying down public debt.

And Wall reaped the credit. "He's not a normal politician," said Nick Tsougrianis, a restaurant owner in the premier's hometown of Swift Current. "You know where Brad stands." Wall reminded Tsougrianis of Ralph Klein, another folksy premier whose success was funded by oil. "He's Ralph, but he's calmed-down Ralph." After Rachel Notley's NDP took power in Alberta and Stephen Harper was defeated in Ottawa, Wall—dubbed "Alberta's other premier" by *Maclean's* for his unequivocal support of the oil industry and pipelines—was often mentioned as an ideal potential federal Conservative leader.[*] By then, anyone interested in energy politics in Canada identified Brad Wall with the towering plant on the horizon ahead: SaskPower's Boundary Dam coal-fired generating station outside Estevan.

One part of the massive structure looked fresh, clean, and new, with the orange SaskPower logo and the words "Carbon Capture and Storage" emblazoned in white letters several feet high. Inside the entrance to the main office, a framed *New York Times* front page from 2014 hung on the wall. The story,

---

[*]   I requested an interview with Brad Wall during my trip, but despite several promises at the time and later, I was never given a chance to speak to him.

headlined "Corralling Carbon Before It Belches from Stack," was the kind a premier touting a megaproject can usually only dream about—especially when trying to burnish his environmental credentials. "This fall," the story recounted, "a gleaming new maze of pipes and tanks—topped with what looks like the Tin Man's hat—will suck up 90 percent of the carbon dioxide from one of the boilers so it can be shipped out for burial, deep underground." It was the equivalent of taking a quarter of a million cars off the road. "If there is any hope of staving off the worst effects of climate change, many scientists say, this must be part of it—capturing the carbon that spews from power plants and locking it away, permanently."

There was, however, no framed copy of a subsequent *New York Times* story from 2016, which reported that clean-coal efforts, including Boundary Dam, were "stumbling." The plant's carbon-capture system was operating at only 45 percent of capacity, had been forced to shut down several times, had missed emissions targets, and was requiring tens of millions of dollars in repairs and replacement equipment, the *Times* revealed. It was bleak news for SaskPower, which hoped to market the system to other countries. The utility's chief executive officer had promised that as more companies and countries bought the technology, the price for new units in Estevan would go down. But the bad publicity piled up: the British government cancelled plans for a carbon-capture plant in 2015; a project in Mississippi went billions of dollars over budget; and Joe Manchin, a U.S. senator from the coal state of West Virginia, called Boundary Dam "a failed operation" on Fox News. *Power* magazine, a U.S. publication covering electricity generation, had labelled Boundary Dam its "Plant of the Year" in 2015 but later said that its flaws were "more substantial" than anyone outside SaskPower had known.

"I'm not going to sit here and tell you we didn't start it up without any problems whatsoever," said Howard Matthews, SaskPower's vice-president of power production. Its second-year numbers were better than the first—"it's actually running pretty well now," he said—though the plant was still falling short of capturing 90 percent of emissions.

The process involves a liquid chemical, made with a proprietary formula, that's sprayed onto combustion gases; the chemical then attaches itself to carbon dioxide molecules, and when the mixture is pumped into a tall cylindrical "stripper" and heated, the carbon dioxide peels away. This all takes place in a giant building of valves, tubes, and vats attached to the plant housing the six coal-fired turbines. Matthews and Mike Zeleny, a retired plant manager who now gave tours to official visitors, asked me not to photograph some areas: the technology and its configuration were trade secrets licensed to SaskPower and owned by Shell, which hoped to sell them to other utilities.

The system, and the tour, ended at a single pipe coming out of the side of the plant and running into the ground. It carried some carbon dioxide via pipeline to Cenovus Energy for its oil operations around Weyburn. Cenovus injected the CO_2 into old wells, making it easier for oil to flow and the company to pump it out, a process called "enhanced oil recovery." These sales were part of the carbon-capture business case, but the first-year problems at Boundary Dam caused SaskPower to miss some deliveries and pay a penalty to Cenovus, wiping out most of the expected revenue in the first year. To avoid more penalties SaskPower renegotiated the contract, but that meant forgoing some sales and accepting lower revenues.

"I don't think I'd be talking out of turn to say the jury's still out on whether that's going to be their long-term solution, whether from a technical or economic perspective," said Leah Nelson Gay, the CEO of the First Nations Power Authority, which helps Indigenous bands develop small renewable energy projects to sell electricity to SaskPower. The organization stays away from coal projects and looks at natural gas only reluctantly. Carbon capture and storage (CCS) is "one part" of the climate solution, Nelson Gay said, "but there are other pieces to it." Renewables "honour Mother Earth in a way that you're not creating potentially irrevocable damage. We're able to offer a business solution that doesn't carry many of the same impacts that a gas pipeline would."

Brad Wall touted carbon capture as a glimpse of the future, but it was also about preserving part of the past: coal. Although the economic boom in the province was driving up electricity consumption, Boundary Dam's Unit Three had to be retired or refurbished by 2019—and if it was refurbished, new federal coal regulations would kick in, requiring it to emit less carbon dioxide. "The conventional coal fleet was no longer going to be able to exist," Matthews said. A natural gas plant might have replaced it, but gas prices were unpredictable and coal was reliably cheap.

There was also plenty of it around Estevan. And as Mike Zeleny pointed out, there were "the people," the coal miners who lived in the area and would lose work if the utility bought less coal. The final decision belonged to Wall, who knew that of the thirteen thousand people who lived in Estevan, a full thousand worked at Boundary Dam. "Politically, if there's no more coal plants, it's a given there'd be pushback," Zeleny said.

Wall gambled that carbon capture would let him save part of old Saskatchewan—its coal jobs—while living within the new federal rules. It was a costly bet: two-thirds of the $1.5 billion capital cost was for the carbon-stripping equipment. The other big expense, the new coal boiler, would earn back its purchase price during its thirty-year lifespan, according to a report by wind energy advocates, but the carbon-capture unit's estimated $713 million in revenue wouldn't recoup the cost of construction or of the electricity required to run it. It would, however, provide Cenovus with cheap carbon dioxide that rendered its enhanced oil recovery project in Weyburn viable—but this meant Wall was subsidizing the oil industry through SaskPower utility rates. "It's effectively a very high carbon tax, charged only to SaskPower's captive customers, with the revenue used to produce more fossil fuels," the report said.

Wall's own 2016 climate plan came close to acknowledging this when it said, "Saskatchewan taxpayers have . . . contributed to the development of many industries and technologies that contribute to climate change mitigations," including CCS. When SaskPower applied to the province's utility regulator for two 5 percent rate increases within six months—made necessary by Boundary Dam's cost overruns—the energy minister, Bill Boyd, said that taxpayers "know very well that the cost of mitigation in these areas is expensive. The cost of any kind of other alternative sources of energy are going to be expensive as well." Boyd's successor, Dustin Duncan, would later acknowledge that ratepayers were "implicitly" paying a carbon tax on their bills to cover Boundary Dam's costs.

SaskPower wasn't just conducting a pricey experiment in Estevan; it had to decide whether it was financially feasible to build two more expensive CCS plants to reduce emissions at two other Boundary Dam coal units, which otherwise would also soon be forced to close under the same federal rules. "Now we know what it takes to get one running," Zeleny said optimistically, and it's generally true in such industrial-scale projects that the second unit is less expensive than the first. At the Paris climate summit in December 2015, Wall led a presentation on the technology. "SaskPower is engaged with interests around the world who are taking a look at it," he told reporters, noting that twenty-four hundred coal plants were under construction globally at the time and suggesting that any sales of SaskPower's CCS model abroad should count toward Canada's meeting its Paris commitments.

But buyers would need to know if an individual CCS plant could break even, and SaskPower was tight-lipped on whether the first unit would. "I can't answer your question in terms of dollars and cents, whether it's net revenue positive or negative," Matthews told me. The argument he made for carbon capture was that it lowered the cost of an expensive waste product by generating revenue from it; losses were offset by the utility's other revenues. Boundary Dam's own balance sheet, however, was confidential, even during provincial regulatory reviews. "You'd have to disclose what the price per tonne of CO_2 is, and that's a confidential thing in the contract," Matthews said. "You'd never be able to disclose that particular price component."

At the end of the Boundary Dam tour, Mike Zeleny paused by the big orange pipe that carried carbon to the Cenovus oil fields near Weyburn. The day the plant started up "I hugged that pipe," he said, laughing. Walking back to the main entrance, he described how SaskPower's plant managers and its unions—who shared an interest in its survival—had "pulled together" to forge agreements that made the project possible. Zeleny gazed proudly at the massive building. "This is the future, right here," he said, seeing not cost overruns and controversy, but hope—hope that the plant would meet its high expectations "next year," as they used to say in Saskatchewan.

In June 2016 Brad Wall returned to Toronto's Empire Club, almost eight years after his first upbeat speech there, in which he'd announced that "next year" had finally come to Saskatchewan. His Saskatchewan Party had just won a third consecutive majority government, but Wall seemed cranky this time. After a couple of his trademark football jokes, he declared sombrely that "I have some good news about a pipeline that's been approved." He waited a beat. "In Uganda."

Wall was on a cross-country tour to defend the Energy East pipeline from a growing number of opponents. He made his now-familiar and compellingly positive case—pipelines were safer than rail cars, and this one would mean less foreign oil in eastern refineries—but his opening argument appeared to be that Uganda, a country with a spotty record on poverty, human rights abuses, and child labour, should be envied for its fast approval of oil projects. Canada, he said, had "this entangled and protracted and interminable process. . . . We have yet to approve a major pipeline in the last decade or so."

Wall had joined other premiers who travelled to the Paris climate summit with Prime Minister Justin Trudeau the previous December. While most of them happily attached themselves to the new Liberal government's climate change goals, the Saskatchewan premier loudly dissented. Trudeau and Rachel Notley were working together to win support for pipelines by approving them in tandem with the creation of stronger environmental rules, including a price on carbon. But Wall refused to entertain the trade-off, saying that Boundary Dam was reducing emissions. "Carbon-capture technology works," he declared in October 2016. "Carbon taxes don't."

Trudeau was vowing to impose a federal carbon price on provinces that did not introduce their own. Wall said he would refuse, and pointed instead to Boundary Dam and Saskatchewan's goal of 50 percent renewable electricity generation by 2030. "We'll be a participant in the battle against climate change," he said. "But if it's a carbon tax imposed federally, we're not signing on." Even if a carbon price reduced Canadian emissions—which Wall didn't believe—those reductions would have little impact globally. Meanwhile, Saskatchewan's agriculture crops, potash, and oil would become uncompetitive in the world market. "You think the Russians or the Belarussians will ever have a fifty-dollar carbon tax?" he told the *Financial Post*. "They won't."

Trudeau's edict offered Wall some plausible options. By one calculation, a Saskatchewan carbon tax would bring in enough revenue for Wall to virtually eliminate provincial income taxes. Or he could give generous tax breaks to the industries he said would be at risk. At Boundary Dam, Matthews told me that a made-in-Saskatchewan carbon tax could be crafted to boost the plant's business case. "Based on CO_2 emissions, it's the most efficient fossil plant in Canada," he said—better than a state-of-the-art natural gas plant. Once Boundary Dam was capturing 90 percent of its carbon dioxide, a carbon tax applied not to the plant's input (its fuel source) but to its output (its emissions) would make Boundary Dam competitive with natural gas because it would raise the cost of the gas plant's emissions to the same level.

In other words, Wall could design a provincial tax that would favour his showpiece project—but he refused to do so. An expert had told *The New York Times* that carbon capture could also be made competitive by imposing a cap on CO_2 emissions, forcing other emitters to find equally costly reduction measures. But Wall opposed caps, too. Instead he threatened to challenge the constitutionality of Trudeau's carbon-pricing edict in court. "I'm not sure how much company we'll have, but I don't care," he said.

Eight years after his Empire Club ode to pan-Canadianism, Wall had become the bad boy of Confederation. Back then, he thanked Canada for years of equalization payments and declared Saskatchewan ready to give back.

Now, when Montreal-area mayors came out against Energy East, Wall asked in a snarky tweet if they would "politely return their share of $10B in equalization supported by [the] west." He questioned the motives of premiers who didn't embrace the project, accusing them of trying to "leverage domestic politics to their advantage," and warned that Trudeau's climate initiatives represented a threat to national unity akin to his father's infamous National Energy Program. "We are heading toward an unhealthy debate, just as we did when another Trudeau introduced his energy policy," he said.

Wall was at his most apocalyptic a few days before his 2016 Empire Club speech, when he addressed the Explorers and Producers Association of Canada at Calgary's Petroleum Club. There was "an existential threat" to the oil and gas sector, the premier said. "We are in the middle of a battle and, frankly, we haven't been winning very many battles." As if realizing that his use of the first person plural might imply that he and the industry were one, he quickly added: "When I say 'we,' I mean this sector and the resource importance of western Canada." He lashed out at environmentalists, including supporters of the Leap Manifesto, who showed "profound snobbery" by wanting Canada to use only renewable energy by 2050.

Much of what Wall said was true: a rapid and complete shift away from fossil fuels was unrealistic, and pipelines were safer than rail. But his tone was notably far from the sunny, hopeful notes he once struck. Murray Mandryk, a veteran columnist with the *Regina Leader-Post*, called the Calgary speech "divisive, hyperbolic and highly partisan . . . a bizarre rant that will likely only widen divisions between the oil industry and environmentalists."

At the heart of Wall's message was an exhortation for pipeline supporters to stake their claim to the political centre and appeal to the common sense of ordinary citizens. "Let's engage in debate," he said. The facts were on the industry's side, he added: Canadians, reasonable people, would accept them. "We're pragmatic, and we're strangers to dogma."

But Wall also told his Calgary audience, "Let's not make the mistakes of the past where we ceded some ground." He was, in effect, asking environmentalists to meet him halfway on Energy East while he resisted a national compromise on climate change.

Brad Wall's isolation on energy and climate wasn't the only political challenge that followed his historic third majority victory. After the Husky spill on the North Saskatchewan River highlighted gaps in the province's inspection system, his government introduced legislation to give officials more investigation and audit powers, a significant concession. There were considerable cost overruns on a major highway project around Regina, and a scandal over inflated land prices for a government-backed trade facility. And after Wall offered subsidies to Calgary-based energy companies if they moved their head offices from Rachel Notley's Alberta to Saskatchewan, it was revealed that he and his wife owned shares in three of the companies he'd wooed.

But Wall's fortunes depended mainly on the price of oil. A political genius when it was high, the premier suddenly had a less magical touch when it fell. In 2016–17, Saskatchewan collected the lowest revenues from the sector since 2001, driving up the deficit to $1.2 billion, three times what had been projected. The premier raised the provincial sales tax and pushed to cut public sector wages—necessary moves that nonetheless hurt his once-invincible popularity. For the first time since he became premier, the NDP led his Saskatchewan Party in a public opinion poll. On August 10, 2017, Wall announced he would resign as party leader and retire from politics.

Boundary Dam's carbon-capture unit was offline at the time. It had been shut down in the spring for regular maintenance, but engineers ran into unexpected problems replacing the carbon unit's compressor coolers, and the plant remained idle all summer. The unit would not resume selling carbon until September—adding more red ink to its balance sheet. Two months later, SaskPower CEO Mike Marsh said that it was "highly unlikely" the utility would seek to retrofit the plant's other two aging coal turbines with carbon-capture technology. And the newest iteration of Saskatchewan's climate plan, released late in 2017, again rejected a carbon tax on oil and gas—a measure that might have made Boundary Dam competitive.

It was a fitting bookend to Wall's time in office. He had placed two enormous bets: he'd gambled that carbon capture, with its veneer of the future, would let him preserve the high-carbon coal jobs of Saskatchewan's past. It was working, though barely and at tremendous cost.

He'd also gambled that the high price of oil, which made popular decisions affordable, would last forever. But those prices had fallen, and there were grim predictions that they'd never fully come back. Oil, once the fuel of the new Saskatchewan, was increasingly seen as belonging to the past.

PART THREE

MANITOBA

7

PUSHBACK CITY

MOOSOMIN, SASKATCHEWAN, WAS SOMETHING of a border town before provincial borders even existed on the prairie. Back when the CPR was being built, the North-West Territories were officially dry, with Brandon marking the westernmost point in Canada where liquor could be legally sold. Eighty miles west of there, at the little station in Moosomin, police officers would board westbound trains to search for contraband. For eastbound travellers on today's Trans-Canada Highway, Moosomin is the last Saskatchewan town of significant size. It was also the location of one of Energy East's lesser-known cross-jurisdictional manifestations.

I exited the highway and drove north, zigzagging along grid roads out into the brown, arid scrub toward a set of coordinates. A handmade sign with stencilled red letters read "Pipeline X-ing Ahead. 200 m. Slow 50 km." Plastic mesh fencing surrounded a freshly filled ditch. Nearby was a small marker made of rough stones commemorating a school opened in 1898 by the Little Bluff School District No. 387. The school closed in 1960, the plaque said, and the land was sold in 1962. Below, it noted, "Trans Canada Pipeline Station No. 25-1958." A Canadian flag flapped overhead.

The compressor station was back from the road, behind some trees, moving natural gas east on the Canadian mainline. The company proposed to build an Energy East tank terminal on the site. Three storage tanks and a pump station would occupy about twice the footprint of the existing compressor station. The tanks would receive and store oil carried here through two other pipelines known as laterals—smaller lines that feed into or branch off from a main line. One, the Upland pipeline, would bring oil from the Williston Basin in North Dakota four hundred kilometres north, across the Canada–U.S. border into the southeast corner of Saskatchewan, and then across the provincial boundary into Manitoba. There it would connect to the Cromer lateral, named for the hamlet of Cromer, Manitoba. It would cross back into Saskatchewan to carry the oil to the tanks near Moosomin, from which it would be fed into the main Energy East line.

The specifics of the two projects were unclear. In 2015 TransCanada claimed that Upland could carry 300,000 barrels of North Dakota crude a day, a figure the company later revised to 220,000. But CEO Russ Girling said there were contracts for only 70,000 barrels—about 6 percent of Energy East's capacity—and that those barrels could come from "either Canada or the United States." And since there were also conventional oil wells along the Saskatchewan section of the Upland line and around Cromer in Manitoba, perhaps Canadian oil would be part of the Upland-Cromer mix. One thing was clear: the pipeline from North Dakota to Moosomin—allowing U.S. oil to reach world markets, or even U.S. Gulf Coast refineries, via tankers berthed in New Brunswick—meant that Energy East's business case rested, at least to a small degree, on American production. "U.S. Bakken producers who haven't been able get a 'yes' from their own government on Keystone XL," wrote *Financial Post* columnist Claudia Cattaneo, "are now signing up to move their oil in a pipeline through Canada." And that pointed to an irony: Moosomin was where American oil would enter a pipeline promoted on explicitly nationalist grounds as an all-Canadian enterprise.

———

Along the highway in Manitoba, a CP train chugged down the tracks and oil derricks pecked the soil near Virden. The landscape began to change. The topography, though still flat, became greener. There were more trees and rivers. A dank feeling signalled that the arid west was mostly behind me. Route I rolled past Brandon and Portage la Prairie and down Portage Avenue into the heart of Winnipeg. Once the great metropolis of the west, it was still the prairie capital of protest politics—the first city on the Energy East route where the pipeline faced real resistance.

Louis Riel first rebelled here, and the Winnipeg General Strike of 1919 was a milestone in the history of organized labour. The city's universities fostered a progressive constituency willing to charge into the latest struggle. "Winnipeggers aren't actually looking for a fight," said Mary Robinson, an anti-pipeline activist with the local chapter of the Council of Canadians, "but when they finally get pushed, they will fight back pretty strongly." Now the fight was about oil: the TransCanada line that was converted to Keystone sent its oil to the U.S. from a pump station south of Winnipeg; Energy East would carry bitumen east of the city, crossing paths with the municipal aqueduct. "Manitoba has a very agricultural identity, so people really get arguments based on protecting water and soil," said Alex Paterson, another activist. "Everyone has someone in their family who farms and knows the food system would be messed up by a big pipeline spill."

In January 2014, Phil Fontaine, an Ojibway from Manitoba and a former national chief of the Assembly of First Nations, was confronted by the latest iteration of that activism when he was scheduled to deliver a lecture at the University of Winnipeg. Fontaine was widely respected in mainstream politics for his career as an Indigenous leader. He helped put the issue of residential schools on the agenda in 1990 when he revealed that he and other former students were abused at the Fort Alexander Residential School north of Winnipeg. In 2013 Fontaine took a job with TransCanada as a liaison with

First Nations communities. Younger Indigenous people, radicalized by the Harper government's pro-pipeline stance, saw it as a betrayal. "We call it co-optation, being co-opted," one of them, Kevin Settee, told me.

The lecture never happened. A small number of activists opposed to Energy East unfurled banners as Fontaine began. One banner, held in front of the podium, showed a bloody arrow piercing a snake labelled "TransCanada." Other protesters began drumming. When Fontaine pressed on, he was shouted down. "How dare you, Phil!" one woman yelled. "On your own people? Anishinaabe people? How dare you sell us out to work for the enemy that's destroying this earth?" The scene turned chaotic as supporters of Fontaine shouted back, and the lecture was cancelled. Derek Nepinak, the grand chief of the Assembly of Manitoba Chiefs—though he opposed Energy East—tweeted that Fontaine had been "drowned out by anger and misunderstanding," and asked, "Which wolf did we feed today?"

Fontaine argued that his TransCanada job was to be an advocate for First Nations. "Have I been satisfied with everything that I've learned? Absolutely not," he said later. "Have I expressed those views with industry? Absolutely." But, he told *The Globe and Mail*, Indigenous communities "live in resource-rich parts of the country that offer very little alternate opportunity." That meant working with oil companies to share in their wealth. "We cannot make decisions that doom First Nations to a life of perpetual poverty," he said.

For many Indigenous people, including Settee, there was no compromising on pipelines like Energy East. Sitting at Stella's, a café packed with students near the University of Winnipeg's main downtown campus, Settee told me he'd grown up associating pipelines with snakes. "That's what really caught my attention, this idea of the snakes, the prophecies of snakes coming to our territories," he said matter-of-factly. "They're not myths; they're not fantasies."

Settee had dark eyes and a wispy goatee, and wore his hair in a ponytail. His mother was Anishinaabe, like Fontaine. In 2016 he was elected the first Indigenous president of the University of Winnipeg's student association. He was enrolled in the school's urban and inner-city studies program, which is based at the satellite campus in Winnipeg's north end, an area known for its poverty and symbolically cut off from the rest of the city by the CPR tracks. "Student unions and student politics have always been very white," Settee noted. "A lot of the issues Indigenous students are working on have to do with survival." As president, he travelled six hours to the Standing Rock reservation in North Dakota in 2016 to join protests against the Dakota Access pipeline. "The idea of having all these pipelines through our territory is unhealthy for our water," he said. In Winnipeg, the city's water supply is fed by the aqueduct that crosses TransCanada's lines east of the city. "If that becomes contaminated, our water is affected for quite a long time."

Pipeline politics in Winnipeg were more acute because of the large Indigenous population. The student body Settee represented was 13 percent Indigenous; Aboriginal people made up 11 percent of the metropolitan population. It was a constituency that couldn't be ignored and was becoming increasingly vocal. But Indigenous opinion wasn't monolithic: in 2016 the Fort McKay First Nation, near Fort McMurray, bought a one-third stake in a nearby Suncor oil tank farm and looked at launching its own extraction project. At a conference the same year organized by the Indian Resource Council, a pro-oil Aboriginal group, some chiefs complained that anti-pipeline activism was endangering the economies of their reserves. And Perry Bellegarde, the national chief of the Assembly of First Nations, observed that "there's a stigma that somehow you're not a First Nations person if you support a pipeline. . . . Some of those chiefs are quiet and yet I know they support [them]. It's about who's the loudest sometimes."

Settee argued that, given the poverty and desperation created by a colonial system, the chiefs who signed deals with oil companies had no other choice. "The government has a chokehold on us," he said. Chiefs were being "forced to exploit their own land." He pointed out that Indigenous people are taught at a young age not to criticize someone in their own territory. "How do I know what's best for them?" he said. "They should have the right to say and do whatever they want. On the other hand, it's different today with climate change. . . . The stakes are higher with agriculture, with jobs, with protecting the water."

In Winnipeg, there were other potential targets for climate activism. A few blocks away was the headquarters of Tundra Oil. Why go after pipelines instead of a company that drilled for oil? I asked Settee. Why not protest in front of Tundra's office, or at a local gas station in a Winnipeg neighbourhood? "You've got to make systemic change," he answered. "What's the use of being ugly with one person?" The oil sector had grown thanks to government support, he said: arguing with a random Winnipegger while he or she filled up was pointless. "Systemic change is more important than individual arguments." But shutting down a speech by Phil Fontaine didn't change the system, and neither would stopping one pipeline.

Ken Neufeld, the CEO of Tundra Oil, figured it was easier to be a climate activist in Winnipeg than in Calgary or Edmonton. "People tend to see the world from their own self-interest perspective, and Manitobans wouldn't even be aware that we have an oil industry," he said. "The fact that there's that level of investment, a billion dollars—nobody knows that. And it is a significant investment." But Manitobans "think of themselves as a hydroelectricity-producing province, which is greener. Obviously in Alberta and Saskatchewan people connect [oil] very closely to their standard of living, unemployment rates, government revenues, so they're going to speak from that perspective. Sometimes it's easier to hold certain principles if there's no personal cost involved."

Neufeld ran Tundra Oil from his corner office on the seventeenth floor of the Richardson Building, overlooking the corner of Portage and Main. Activism didn't preoccupy him: he had other concerns during the Energy East debate, like the dark clouds gathering over the oil industry. Tundra operated mainly in southwest Manitoba, in the area where TransCanada planned to build its Cromer lateral. In 2015 Tundra bought hundreds of new wells from a Houston company, a gamble that assumed an imminent rebound in prices. It hadn't happened a year later, and the company had to cut 10 percent of its workforce. "It was the first time in our history and it wasn't fun," Neufeld told me. Tundra had been contracting seven drilling rigs before the price crashed; now it had one. "A lot of the wells we could drill today are not economic by our standards," he said. As a private, family-owned company, "we need a rate of return to take that risk." Things could be worse, however: Tundra was selling at hedge prices locked in two years earlier, before the worst of the crash. "I won't give you specifics, but we would have had a good percentage of 2016 production sold at over ninety dollars Canadian," Neufeld said. "That's a game changer right now." But those hedge prices wouldn't last forever.

Neufeld oozed regular guy. His craggy but affable face gave him the look of a man who'd been around and had aged into a straight shooter. He was dressed in a checked shirt and jeans for a casual-Friday fundraiser in support of the United Way; the outfit and his manner distinguished him from the crisp-shirted executives in the glass towers in Calgary. The Richardson Building was the tallest building in western Canada when it was finished in 1969. It had less shine than the office towers of the Alberta oil giants, but it was solid and utilitarian, like Neufeld himself.

Tundra Oil and Gas was owned by the billionaire Richardsons, ranked by *Canadian Business* in 2017 as the ninth-richest family in Canada. They got into the grain business in 1858, adding oil more than a century later, in 1980. Neufeld joined the company in 1988, when Tundra bought Manitoba Oil and Gas, a provincial Crown corporation privatized by the new Progressive Conservative government. He'd been its chief financial officer. "I came along with that deal and I just survived," he said. Tundra became the biggest oil producer in Manitoba in 2004, when it struck large reserves that are part of the Bakken field.

Another Richardson company, Tundra Energy Marketing Ltd., had a network of pipelines in the area that it had created through acquisitions, but Energy East was on Neufeld's radar. The Cromer lateral would be "close enough that it would be a strong connection" to get Tundra's lighter, non-bitumen oil to market, he said. "We have had no direct conversations with TransCanada in terms of tying into their line. But I think that will happen. I think they will approach us, and I think we'll be very receptive." From the Cromer lateral, Tundra's oil would enter the main pipe at Moosomin. "If we can get to refineries in Montreal, Irving's refinery in New Brunswick, and tidewater, which is then European markets, it gives us more opportunities," he told me. Tundra shipped its oil south to the U.S. on an Enbridge line and, like Alberta producers, was forced to sell at discounted, American-glut prices. Energy East could break that stranglehold. "The overarching positive is it gives Canadian crude producers, including Tundra, optionality—access to different markets."

Neufeld recognized that the tide was turning, though. Tundra wouldn't fight government climate measures that he considered inevitable. "There's a political reality that we're going to live with that isn't always supported by science," he said, "but it doesn't matter. If that's the political will and the public discourse and so forth, that becomes our reality."

Not always supported by science? "Climate change has always gone on," he explained when I asked what he meant. "I don't know if the cause and effect is as direct." He mentioned "some of the scientific studies and lectures I've listened to, sort of webinars and something like that"—it sounded like denialist material—but then decided not to elaborate. "I don't really want go there, because then people dismiss me as an oil guy talking," he said. "So let's accept that."

Tundra was looking at building a carbon-capture plant like Saskatchewan's, expecting Ottawa to craft incentives for companies that embraced greener energy and disincentives for those that didn't. If that included a carbon tax, "we'll live with it," Neufeld said. Still, he was frustrated that anti-pipeline activists weren't more realistic. "It would be nice to have a perfect world, but we don't have one." Electric-powered cars were a fine idea, but not all provinces generated electricity the way Manitoba did, with hydro dams. Some used coal. "I don't think coal's a good substitute for oil, and oil's probably not a good substitute for natural gas in terms of its overall GHG [greenhouse gas] impact. I think people don't understand that particularly well."

Before the bottom fell out of the market, Tundra had been working on a project with Suncor to move oil by rail to its refinery in Montreal. "But it's not a good Canadian solution," Neufeld said. "Those rail cars derail, they run along riverbeds." He called it "a terrible alternative"—but one Tundra would be forced to consider, he said, if prices rose to make it viable and if additional pipeline capacity such as Energy East was blocked by activists.

"I'm disappointed there's so much opposition to it, but it is ideologically driven right now," he said. "I think a lot of people feel if we can stop the pipelines, we can stop the industry, and I don't think it's going to be like that."

But at least one of the sixth-generation Richardson cousins who stood to inherit Tundra admitted that there was a discomfort, "certainly a dissonance," in profiting from carbon-emitting fossil fuels. "I think it's time for a change," said Colby Richardson, who worked for a non-family company that made electric buses, "and I think that change has to happen sooner than most people may be ready for."

Ken Neufeld had been generalizing about the anti-pipeline left in Winnipeg, and yet—like Indigenous opinion—it wasn't monolithic. The Manitoba Energy Justice Coalition was the main umbrella group fighting Energy East, but in the summer of 2016 the Winnipeg chapter of the Council of Canadians left the coalition. In my interview with chapter member Mary Robinson, she underscored that she spoke "solely" for the council, which, she said, "rarely, rarely" agreed with the coalition on tactics. Alex Paterson, one of the coalition's leaders, agreed that there was a divide. "We charge through, we're bombastic, we're edgy," he said. "People either agree with us or they don't."

Paterson and Robinson had travelled different paths to their activism. Paterson had grown up in Orangeville, Ontario, and at age thirteen he'd organized a student walkout in support of striking teachers. He studied Indigenous environmental movements while an undergraduate at Laurentian University in Sudbury; what he learned there, and during a summer job as a gold prospector in James Bay Cree territory, radicalized him. "I was totally cool with industrial production at the time. But it was seeing the prospecting from fifty years ago, and how it scarred the land, that made me question what industry does to the land." During an academic conference, he was recruited to come to Winnipeg to pursue a master's program in Indigenous governance.

Robinson was from London, Ontario, and had lived in British Columbia, Prince Edward Island, and Saskatchewan before ending up in Winnipeg. She got involved with the Council of Canadians when it fought a city plan to let a private company run its waste-water plant. "I was just looking for something to do," she said. "There was a clear need for people, for someone who would do things." She chuckled brightly from behind thick-rimmed glasses. "I was the kid in my classroom out in the hallway for telling the teacher things I was right about. So I wasn't a stranger to this sort of discourse."

The council's split from the coalition wasn't bitter. Paterson urged me to speak to Robinson and gave me her number. Their differences were "mostly around messaging," he said. A few coalition members "who have professional degrees" weren't comfortable with Paterson's style of noisy protest, including what he called the "bird-dogging" of politicians—the disruption of Fontaine's speech, for example. They worried that that kind of action "would make their professional designations less worthy in front of the National Energy Board," he told me. "They were a barrier to us doing the bombastic, edgy things we wanted to do." But if the split was amicable, it did leave some bruised feelings. In 2015 the coalition released a report by biophysicist Dennis LeNeveu on Energy East's risk to Winnipeg's water supply—the right-of-way crossed a key aqueduct—but after the split, LeNeveu and the Council of Canadians were granted intervenor status by the NEB while the coalition was denied. "It was our organization that had been the only one to produce research in Manitoba," Paterson said. "There's definitely things that our organization offers in terms of research and perspective that they don't offer."

These divisions were nothing new on the left, which, like most political movements, was often torn between seeking tangible, incremental gain and demanding sweeping change—between working within existing processes, such as the NEB, and boycotting them. Calgary writer Chris Turner observed that starting with Rachel Carson's call to action in her book *Silent Spring*, the environmental movement had tended to focus on specific goals such as banning DDT, saving the whales, and stopping clear-cuts—"discrete phenomena that could be assessed, addressed, maintained." But climate change was different: the real cause, the reliance on fossil fuels, was everywhere, and hence not as easy to target. So activists went looking for tangible objectives, symbols they could take down. Symbols like pipelines.

Alison Redford, the former Alberta premier, blamed Barack Obama for turning the Keystone XL permit into a political issue. "When the president of the United States says, 'I'm interested in this pipeline,' everybody's got an interest in that pipeline," Redford said. "Activists learned that it was possible to do this work in a political arena and that it would garner a different kind of attention than if it was only being dealt with in a regulatory sphere." In an industry magazine, John Soini, TransCanada's vice-president for Energy East, pleaded with pipeline supporters to be just as vocal as opponents. "If you're not out front, actually supporting the oil and natural gas industry," he said, "quite frankly, your message is not getting out there." In December 2016, the *National Post* listed thirty-five major energy projects, worth $129 billion, that it said had been stymied by activists. The *Globe and Mail* lamented that extremists were dominating the debate and declared that "the moderates have to get off their butts and storm the barricades."

Instead, industry supporters attacked environmentalists with language that was anything but moderate. Harper's natural resources minister, Joe Oliver, denounced the "radical ideological agenda" of environmentalists funded by "foreign special interest groups." Vivian Krause, a Vancouver writer, took up the crusade against those foreign organizations, particularly the Tides Foundation of San Francisco. "If the activists marching in protests and storming NEB hearings make the anti-pipeline campaign look like an amateur, grassroots movement, the reality is it's anything but," she wrote. In *Alberta Oil* magazine, Krause accused Tides of funding Leadnow, an anti-vote-splitting group, which she said helped defeat the Conservative government with strategic endorsements of non-Tory candidates in the 2015 election. "To be sure, there is nothing wrong with Leadnow being part of an international network of progressive organizations," Krause admitted, but its funding and its U.S. connections "need to be out in the open."[*]

"I just find that another straw man," Mary Robinson told me. "It's something you can throw out there to get riled up and screaming things without a clue." An industry that supported cross-border trade and an integrated continental oil market was hypocritical for wanting to block climate activists from doing essentially the same thing, she said. American oil companies generating profits in Canada, like ExxonMobil, had funded climate denial research.

Polling by the Canadian Association of Petroleum Producers had revealed another effective argument to be used against Energy East opponents: respondents were receptive to the idea that although activists were crusading against Alberta oil—extracted and regulated where democratic governments protected workers' rights and the environment—they showed no similar concern about the foreign oil refined in eastern Canada, imported "from different places that have lower regulatory and environmental standards than Canada," said Chelsie Klassen, the organization's spokesperson. Alex Paterson experienced this tactic firsthand: "I actually had someone show up at a meeting and start screaming at me, 'Why are you supporting the House of Saud?'" But Energy East wasn't going to displace all the foreign oil coming into Canada, Paterson said. It was primarily an export pipeline: the world price for oil was key to its business case. Refineries in eastern Canada would still import crude

---

[*]   Among the groups Krause listed as having received funding from Tides in 2015 are several I spoke to for this book, including Greenpeace, Equiterre, Ecology Ottawa, the Council of Canadians, Manitoba Energy Justice Coalition, and Transition Initiative Kenora.

and still enrich those regimes. And Bronwen Tucker, from Greenpeace's Alberta office, pointed out that Canadian activists were most effective in taking on Canadian fossil fuels. "You do what you can in the community you're in," she said.

Stopping a pipeline wasn't going to stop climate change, of course, but it might shift the debate. Two social scientists who studied the effect of a fossil fuel divestment campaign on American university campuses concluded that while the financial standing of oil companies was unaffected, the campaign did push concepts like carbon taxes and cap-and-trade from the fringe into the political centre. Rachel Notley's calculation in Alberta was that her climate plan would make pipelines more acceptable to mainstream opinion; some activists felt their anti-pipeline protests had forced Notley and Trudeau to introduce climate regulations.

Paterson believed that the Alberta cap fell short and that Notley's government was racing against stricter greenhouse gas restrictions. "They want to build this pipeline because they want to get their assets out before climate policy is cutting into maximization of profit," he said, arguing that if Canada wanted to meet its Paris targets, more aggressive activism of the kind he championed was needed. "Obviously it would be really great to do it in a planned, democratic, equitable way," Paterson said ominously, but "the deadline's going to hit and we're going to have to do something or we fail."

This carried risks, because the industry and the activists were fighting for the middle ground. Bruce Anderson of Abacus Data reported in 2016 that most Canadians rejected arguments that were "overly binary: right or wrong, moral or immoral, now or never. They are far more drawn to ideas about how to marry their environmental aspiration with their economic goals and to achieve economic renewal and growth based on cleaner forms of energy." That explained why anti-pipeline activists didn't rely solely on broad climate arguments: people also had to feel a direct risk to their daily lives. Energy East was "a target that would be a game changer for the way climate change and energy politics is approached," Paterson said, but it was also easy to persuade people there was a local risk. "There's nothing else in the province that would threaten the water supply of 850,000 people."

Pragmatism still ruled in Winnipeg. Riel's rebellion led to a watered-down compromise on Manitoba's obligations to its minorities; he won and lost at the same time. Once considered a violent insurrectionist, he was eventually commemorated with a statue at the Manitoba legislature. Mary Robinson acknowledged that progress was slow, and that opinion had to be nudged gradually. "Climate is definitely the main place where we speak from, but that's not where you reach people," she said. "The pipelines [are] suddenly hitting the news, it's a thing that's happening here. It's a clearer thing for people to grasp, yeah, and we're in an era of thirty-second little snippets. People need something they can hang on to."

In Winnipeg, there were signs the strategy was working. The city council had hired a consultant who identified "high-level concerns" about Energy East's risk to the municipal water system, and planned to intervene at the National Energy Board hearings. The city's decision wasn't about the wider issues of climate change, Robinson said, but it was a start. "You end up gathering people who don't have any other concern except, well, 'NIMBY' [not in my backyard], or 'not my water' or 'not my farm, or my horses,'" she said. "Maybe that's their big concern, but you start to teach them, and they shift."

8

BACKYARDS

SOME OF THE BACKYARDS Mary Robinson was thinking of were south of Winnipeg's urban core—past the Perimeter Highway, which routes Trans-Canada traffic around the city, and on a stretch of farmland just beyond the last batch of new subdivisions. Where most people saw only farms and fields, Peter Tines imagined a new kind of life, and a new kind of backyard. Dozens of them.

"We're a wonderful transition zone between urban and large-farm rural," Tines said as he drove around the land he was buying. "We're very much interested in encouraging alternative uses." He already owned almost a hundred and fifty acres nearby, and was buying Sagehill Stables, another sixty-nine acres, so that he could build a hybrid residential development with modern homes among riding trails and green space. He wanted to create communities with "some densification, so you can have not necessarily urban sprawl the way that typically happens, [but] more village-type-plus uses, denser senior housing, multi-family use, setting aside certain lands and trails forever for people to enjoy."

Tines, who sported a lavender golf shirt, sunglasses, and a Bluetooth ear-piece, talked at a rapid clip. He got into real estate development, he told me, by building retirement homes and commercial plazas in London, Ontario. Next came Vancouver, but the cost of land there was "insane"; that's when friends from Manitoba suggested Winnipeg. And now, close to the city limits, he was mapping out six hundred acres of walking paths, community centres, eco-villages, garden homes, and an equine centre "with a canine component." His venture reflected a changing market demand: people felt disconnected from the land, "so if we can provide them a community here that gives them more of that, but very close to the university and some of the bigger shopping centres in the area, it'll be very well received."

Tines had one problem, though. "See that light patch there?" he asked as we sat in his parked truck behind the stables. "That's where the pipeline goes through." The TransCanada gas mainline cut diagonally through the fields in the distance. Tines worried how potential buyers might feel about a pipeline carrying bitumen near their property. "We're concerned about the potential safety impact—the potential market impact as well."

Here was one of the people Mary Robinson had spoken of, someone who needed "something to hang on to" to shift him to an anti-pipeline view. Tines had attended an open house organized by an anti-pipeline group and heard about the risk to the city aqueduct. He applied to the NEB for intervenor status so that he could ask the board to order TransCanada to reroute the oil line. "From a philosophical perspective, shouldn't they?" he said. "It's amazing these pipelines have gone through some of the most dense urban areas of the nation. You'd think that with all the money that's being made from moving the oil, they could pick some better routes."

Of course, when TransCanada had first selected the route through these fields, Winnipeg's sprawl hadn't reached nearly this far south. Tines wasn't developing bucolic eco-villages back then. But if the city could creep south, if the nature of home living could change, perhaps the pipeline's route should, too. "Maybe the time is now, when you want to switch to bitumen," he said. "Maybe now's the time for them to start to think about it. Use that as a catalyst to start that discussion about where they might best be relocated."

Tines was definitely—literally—a NIMBY, but had he been "shifted"? He wasn't sure. Just as his proposed development didn't fit easily into either an urban or a rural model of living, he was still sorting out which pipeline camp he was in. "I don't have definite opinions on this yet," he said. Oil is used "in a zillion things, everything from plastic bags to kitchen utensils to the clothes we wear." Even if all cars were electric, Tines reasoned, fossil fuels would still be in demand. "We have to figure out what's the smartest way to move them," he said. "So I'm not necessarily against it. I'm not necessarily for it, either. I really don't think they should be going through densely populated urban areas. They shouldn't be in cities."

Tines drove a bit farther south, across the La Salle River. We took a look at Duff's Ditch, the spillway built under Premier Duff Roblin in the sixties to reduce the danger of flooding in the city. I told Tines about the Harbour Landing subdivision in Regina, and the municipal setbacks the developers had left around the pipeline right-of-way. "What's your understanding of that?" he asked. "You said you're trying to find what the different perspectives are. You haven't been able to formulate your opinion on that?" He seemed desperate for an indication of how radical he should be, how far he should shift on the issue of pipelines and oil.

From Peter Tines's property, the pipeline route passed under the La Salle River and the Red River, then moved across fields south of the city to a TransCanada compressor station at Île-des-Chênes, where two of the six natural gas lines turned south toward the United States. The remaining four met up with the four-lane Trans-Canada Highway, zigging and zagging parallel to it, crossing back and forth, heading east. Pine and birch trees closed in along the highway, as did the increasingly rocky terrain of the Canadian Shield. The physical contour of the land was so distinct from the prairie that it made real how large and diverse the country was.

I felt it, literally, the afternoon after my visit with Tines: while tearing through another backyard—the pipeline's—on a mountain bike, I wiped out; the hard rock of the Shield cut a four-inch gash below my knee.

It happened on Falcon Lake, a popular cottage area for Winnipeggers near the Ontario border, where Gary Turnbull faced the prospect of Energy East running close to home. Two of the gas lines were just over a small ridge from his cottage overlooking the lake; two others ran through woods not far away. Turnbull was a director of the South Whiteshell Trail Association, which had built a network of trails around the lake, and he'd convinced me to join him on a bike tour of the right-of-way. We pedalled through damp brush and careened down rocky ravines. "I love to ride a bike and I love to be in the bush," said Turnbull, a small, wiry man. "I'm not a spiritual person from a religious perspective, but being in the woods and nature like that is an uplifting experience for me." Trees were cleared and shrub trimmed back on the right-of-way, allowing us to follow it along the north shore of the lake. "We like the pipeline," Turnbull continued. "We feel it adds a bit to the property. It's used as another access to the wilderness."

The gas pipeline, yes, but not a converted line carrying bitumen. "That's a problem," Turnbull told me back at his modern cottage, which had a large deck with a sweeping view of the lake. "I don't want to be pigeonholed as NIMBY . . . because I recognize that pipelines probably have a place." He knew when he bought the land for the cottage that two of the lines were just a few hundred metres away—but that was gas, a risk "so small it's insignificant." Bitumen, though, "that's a whole other game." A gas line break might explode and cause localized damage, like a fire. "It's not everlasting or decade-lasting." But Turnbull was convinced that a leak of dilbit—the diluted bitumen—would be a disaster.

The land near the gas lines slopes downhill to the water. The lines cross multiple brooks and streams. "It would be impossible to keep it out of the lake. They could never shut off the valves fast enough." Rerouting would be better, Turnbull said, except it would be impossible to get around Whiteshell Provincial Park, which occupied this entire corner of Manitoba. The planned pump station would be within the park. "They'd have to be far north, and the cost would be prohibitive. I hate to say that's what needs to be done, because I don't think it's a realistic possibility."

Turnbull didn't count himself among the political activists trying to stop the project. He held a master's degree in environmental biology and had worked for an agricultural science company, where he researched disease management, weed control, and genetics. "I feel I have a more scientific, grounded opinion," he said. "I have an understanding of what benzene is, what toluene is," two of the chemicals used to dilute the bitumen. Benzene, he said, was "kind of nasty," a carcinogen that had required lots of precautions in his lab. "Whereas a lot of light oils will float on the surface of the water, the bitumen sinks," Turnbull said. "We have a deep lake here. If it got in, we'd never get it out." This was, in fact, still a matter of scientific inquiry: in 2017, federal researchers were conducting experiments in an Alberta laboratory on whether spilled dilbit would float or sink. They concluded, tentatively, that it would often float—but that density, viscosity, and temperature affected to what extent, and that dilbit sitting on the surface of a lake was still "all bad."

The day was overcast and Falcon Lake was the colour of pewter, but it was easy to grasp why Winnipeggers considered the place a haven. Turnbull's family's connection went back three generations, to when his wife's grandfather bought a cottage on the south shore—"more of a plywood shack," away from the water—for fifteen hundred dollars. In 1957 Turnbull's future in-laws were visiting friends at their cabin on the north shore when a crew from TransCanada asked them to leave because they were blasting rock for the first gas line. When they came back, "there was a rock lying on the centre of the living room floor that had come through the roof."

His in-laws inherited the family cabin and eventually transferred it to Turnbull and his wife, but they wanted lakefront and eventually bought their own land on the north shore. Their children spent all their summers on the water. "Some of their best friends are the kids they grew up with out here," he said. In one room of the new place, there was a windowpane from the old cottage that Turnbull had converted into a picture frame holding snapshots of four generations of his family relaxing at the lake. In the summer of 2016, Turnbull's daughter got married at an eco-resort on the opposite shore. He organized a weekend of golf, hikes, lawn bowling, horse rides, and biking, and rented pontoon boats to give tours of the lake. "The weather really cooperated and everyone had a great time."

When Turnbull first heard about Energy East, he thought immediately of Falcon Lake. At a TransCanada open house in Winnipeg, "I was aghast at how poor the information was that they were ready to provide," he said. "They couldn't answer my questions, and my questions weren't that scientific." Since then, his questions had multiplied. Manitoba Hydro was building a new hydroelectric dam, Keeyask, with 40 percent of its generation committed to power pumping stations for Energy East and Enbridge's Line 3 replacement. The electricity would be sold at discounted industrial prices, Turnbull said, meaning that ordinary Manitoba ratepayers would be subsidizing the pipelines. "We're actually using clean energy to pump a not-so-clean energy."

This was where Turnbull's NIMBYism shifted to a larger perspective, and he wasn't the only one shifting on Falcon Lake. We drove from his cottage to the home of Barbara Hamilton, a fellow member of the trail association and the owner of Falcon Trails Resort, where Turnbull's daughter got married. She was in her kitchen chopping zucchini for a ratatouille-style dish she called Zucchini Surprise. "It's what I have in the garden that's ready to be used," she said.

Hamilton worried about leaks, too—the lake was her livelihood—but the pipeline didn't make sense for other reasons. "Aren't we going a bit backwards by investing in more gas and oil instead of more alternative energy?" she asked. Rerouting "would be better," but that would still allow more fossil fuels to be burned. "It would make me feel better, but it doesn't really solve the problem. It solves it [only] for us."

Hamilton considered herself an environmentalist. "I'm not a hard-core activist but I'm certainly someone who takes my environment seriously." She and her husband operated the resort as sustainably as possible, and off-grid cabins were available. But she wasn't against the oil companies. "I've got investments. I want them to do well, right? I have some ethical investments, and they always do poorly," she said with a laugh. Her business relied on fossil fuels, like the diesel that powered the engines on the boats for her guests. "I want to be reasonable about this. I know there are all sides to this story and I'm trying to understand the other side too. We all use gas and vehicles and boats and motors, but I think our direction should be towards limiting that, not increasing or maintaining that."

For Turnbull, too, Energy East began as a backyard issue but was turning into something else. "I'm not concerned about how it's going to affect my property value," he said. "I'm concerned about how it's going to affect our environment around the lake. It would change the whole environment here." He was also thinking about the Paris agreement on climate change. "I haven't really crunched all those numbers, and there's so many ways of cutting that one." But he was convinced that the oil sands were a dead end. "Maybe we should be keeping this oil in the ground, versus other oil that takes less energy, less refining, that's closer to markets."

Gary Turnbull didn't see himself as a radical, but he had shifted, as Mary Robinson hoped he would: his backyard had become significantly—even radically—larger.

To finish the story of Winnipeg's pipeline activism, to complete the exploration of the city's political backyard, I had to cross into Ontario. From Turnbull's cottage it was a fifteen-minute drive through another cottage community, West Hawk Lake, and back onto the Trans-Canada Highway and the provincial border. The road, just two lanes, cut through deep rock as it entered Ontario. The turnoff for Route 673 came up soon, and the road went south, crossing the TransCanada gas line right-of-way again. The land was green and wet.

The road led to a ramshackle toll booth operated by the Iskatewizaagegan No. 39 First Nation. A brightly coloured road permit cost twenty-five dollars. The streets had no names, but the kid who took the money said the cell tower would be a reference point for the small ferry dock. There I drove onto a rusty barge for three or four cars. The boat's noisy motor coughed. The sun was out and the leaves were turning colour as it crossed a narrow channel of water. Shorn of what it represented, the voyage could not have been more idyllic. A sign taped to the barge advertised an upcoming public meeting to discuss the Freedom Road.

This was how you got to the Shoal Lake No. 40 First Nation in the summer of 2016. The reserve, separated by water and by the federal Indian Act from its cross-channel neighbour, No. 39, was isolated because it was poor, and poor because it was isolated: located on a peninsula jutting out into the lake and over the Ontario line, it had only one land connection—its most natural link— to the west, to Manitoba, but there was no road that way. A visitor had to come by ferry in summer and by ice road across the frozen channel in winter.

The reserve's dirt roads were winding and had no road signs. The houses were small and weather-worn. "Shoal Lake is my home," said Preston Redsky, part of a crew tearing down the old band council office, which had been condemned because its floors were sagging. "I don't want to live in any other place in the world."

On the spectrum of injustices imposed on Indigenous communities in Canada, Shoal Lake No. 40 was a particularly vivid and tragic example of a broken colonial relationship that had yet to be mended. Winnipeg's clean drinking water—the same water that activists said was threatened by Energy East—was drawn from Shoal Lake, and the engineering that made that possible had also doomed the reserve to live under a boil-water order that would soon enter its third decade.

A century ago, Winnipeg needed a modern water supply, so it built an aqueduct from the edge of Shoal Lake to the city, a distance of more than 135 kilometres. The city also built a dike to divert murkier water entering the lake away from the aqueduct intake; this sent it toward the reserve. "The majority of the natural spring water is taken out," said Daryl Redsky, the band's consultation officer. "But at the same time it's getting mixed up with the water that's being drawn in from Lake of the Woods." When cryptosporidium was detected in Shoal Lake in 1997, the city began treating its water, but the reserve couldn't afford to build a treatment plant of its own: the lack of road access made the project too expensive. "Until about fifteen or twenty years ago, you could walk down the hill from here, stick your head in the lake, and drink right out of the water," Redsky said. "That's how clean and fresh it was. That doesn't happen anymore. You go down there, you'll get sick." Children were getting rashes when they took showers and baths, he added.

The source of the contamination is disputed. Shoal Lake is part of Lake of the Woods, and Redsky told me that industrial and cottage waste flows from that direction; a University of Manitoba report said Indigenous fishermen "perceive" that inflow from both Lake of the Woods and Falcon Lake was "degrading" the water. In Winnipeg, Alex Paterson also blamed sewage from the cottages on Falcon Lake flowing down the Falcon River into Shoal Lake. But Gary Turnbull told me that everyone on Falcon Lake either has a septic field or a connection to a sewage system, or pays to have their tanks pumped out. "No cottage owners or businesses are allowed to put waste water into the lake," he declared. The entire area was a provincial park, and the authorities were "quite strict" about it, he insisted. The city of Winnipeg's website said that "darker river water" from Falcon Lake was getting into Shoal Lake, but asserted that it "would flow to the First Nations communities with or without the diversion."

Regardless of the source, Shoal Lake No. 40's water was contaminated while Winnipeg enjoyed clean water from the same lake. Perversely, in the eighties the city had blocked the band from building a cottage development on its territory—a chance to generate some economic activity—because of the supposed risk it represented to the municipal water supply. In 2014, the Canadian Museum of Human Rights, a modern and monumental $350 million project spearheaded by the Asper family, opened in the city. It catalogued just about every human rights struggle in the world, large or small—with one notable omission. In the Indigenous Perspectives gallery, a large circular theatre made of wood played a 360-degree film of Aboriginal women speaking about their rights. "Everything we do is interrelated and has an impact on the world," one of the women said. "We are all in this together. We are connected." But there was no mention of the connection to Shoal Lake No. 40—no mention that the clear water flowing abundantly through the museum's shimmering reflecting pools was drawn from a reserve without clean drinking water.

But 2014 was also the year Shoal Lake became a *cause célèbre* for activists. Winnipeg's Council of Canadians chapter brought its national president, Maude Barlow, to the community. The organization saw links between the pipeline, the aqueduct, and the reserve: the threat from Energy East was "tied into the oppression and colonization that happened to the Shoal Lake community," Mary Robinson told me. "So it's a double whammy." Activists from nearby Kenora joined the effort, and the pressure paid off in December 2015, when the Canadian, Manitoba, and Winnipeg governments announced funding to build the Freedom Road, a twenty-four-kilometre link between the reserve and the Trans-Canada Highway. This, in turn, would make the construction of a water treatment plant more feasible. "The fix is the road," Daryl Redsky said. "Once the road is built, the possibilities are endless." Four months after the announcement, Prime Minister Justin Trudeau visited the people of the reserve, another sign of recognition.

The chief and council were doing fewer media interviews now, because the attention—though it had galvanized governments into action—was a time-consuming distraction. "It helped to create that awareness," Redsky said as he sat in the temporary band office in the reserve's arena. "But at the same time it's put our community in a place where they've had to reflect on all the negative things that have happened in our lives," like seeing family members die when their cars went through the ice crossing the channel. "But if it's part of a process where you're trying to create a better future, trying to deal with these issues, reconcile and move forward, that's a good thing, I believe. Now we want to talk about what lies ahead of us."

And that included Energy East. After struggling so long over water, Redsky did not want to see the lake further endangered by a potential bitumen leak. TransCanada had posted a "Myths Debunked" article on its website pointing out that the Energy East route was twelve kilometres north of Shoal Lake, and that oil would have to travel twenty-five kilometres or more "through still lakes and slow moving rivers that act as natural barriers to contain an unlikely release" before reaching the lake. But Redsky, a cousin of the Shoal Lake chief, said that no safety assurances from TransCanada would persuade him. He mentioned the recent Husky spill in Saskatchewan. "I'm sure people in those communities that have had the bursts and the breaks and the ruptures have been told the same thing, and have been convinced of that," he said. "But you ask them now." The band government had not yet taken a stance. It was part of Treaty Three, another of the numbered treaties signed after Confederation, and the treaty chiefs were still conducting their own collective, quasi-judicial review of the pipeline. "I've told our leadership that I'm not in favour of this," Redsky said. "That's my position and that's the position of a lot of people in the community: that we can't compromise the water."

Redsky's temporary office was in one of the arena's locker rooms, which also contained what he called the Canadian Museum of Human Rights Violations, an ironic riff on the gleaming Winnipeg museum. The reserve version was a series of laminated news clippings and documents taped to the walls, telling the story of the aqueduct construction, Winnipeg's blocking of the cottage development, and the increased activism in support of the community. Aboriginal power had changed a lot over that period: court rulings had given Indigenous people more legal clout, from having their oral histories recognized as valid courtroom evidence to imposing a "duty to consult" on governments reviewing resource projects on traditional territory.

I asked Redsky if he felt he had the power to stop Energy East. "You have to define power," he said. "Power in the Western mindset is different from the way we see power. Power is that water. That is life-giving. That's power. You can't get any more power than that. But if the question you're asking me comes from the Western world in terms of power and authority, we have no place in that world. We have five hundred years of existence that proves that." When he agreed to answer the question on my terms, though, he pointed to the museum displays, the taped-up clippings and photos, the diagrams of the Freedom Road now so tantalizingly close to being built. A community of fewer than five hundred people had accomplished that after a century-long battle, he said. "I don't know if you consider that power, but I consider that influence. We have done everything possible within our limits. And this is just daily survival."

Energy East wasn't just another example of NIMBY here, because Shoal Lake was no ordinary backyard. "Once we're able to get out of survival mode, can you imagine how effective we will be once we turn our focus to the pipeline, to treaty rights, to all these other violations that are happening?" Redsky said. "Our record should stand for itself here. Once we're able to see the light, get out of the darkness and fight, and join all the rest of the First Nations and Canadians who are fighting this thing, we'll be a good ally."

PART FOUR

ONTARIO

9

PINCH POINTS

KENORA WAS AN HOUR'S drive from the Shoal Lake barge. The two-lane Trans-Canada Highway sliced through more rock and forest and ran alongside shining lakes toward the city. Signs for cottages and boats sprang up. The road wound its way spectacularly along Lake of the Woods, across four bridges spanning the mouths of four bays, and traced a long arc into the compact downtown. Vacant storefronts, the signs of economic decline, were mixed with businesses catering to upscale cottagers: yoga studios, art galleries, "solar solutions."

Kenora, according to a book of local history, was "a link between the East and West, the railroad and the highway; a link between the North and South, the waterways; a link between civilization and the wilderness, the airways." With the large lake to the south and other waters to the north, this was the only feasible route for the CPR. When the railway line was completed, the town that grew around it, then called Rat Portage, had a thousand residents, outnumbered by three thousand Ojibway in the area. It has remained a crossroads for settler descendants and Indigenous people. Manitoba claimed the area until Ontario won an appeal to the Judicial Committee of the Privy

Council in London in 1884, but the town's orientation remained toward the prairies. Closer to Winnipeg than to any Ontario metropolis, it prospered thanks to flour mills that processed grain coming by train from the west. The city's very name springs from that connection: in 1905, after the Maple Leaf Flour Company said it didn't want "Rat Portage" on its packaging, civic leaders blended the names of three local communities, Keewatin, Norman, and Rat Portage, to create "Kenora."

"It's a natural, physical bottleneck," said Cuyler Cotton. He was leaning over his mug at HoJoe's, a coffee shop on Main Street. "You can't avoid the damned place. You've got the TransCanada pipeline, the Trans-Canada Highway, two railroads, and they're all at the top of the lake, which is why it was always the stage on which the Indigenous relationship was playing out." In 2006, 16 percent of Kenora's population was Indigenous, the highest percentage of any Ontario city. It also once had the highest concentration of residential schools. Thirteen First Nations bands in the area were part of Treaty Three. "It's like a microcosm," Cotton said. "The displacement, the appropriation of rights, Shoal Lake—all of those get played out here, literally on the streets. And that's going to play out again with Energy East."

Cotton wore a rumpled denim jacket; his hair and beard were almost white, and deep lines fanned out from behind his glasses. He arrived here from his hometown of Thunder Bay in 1970 to open an office of the Ontario Human Rights Commission. "Kenora had the reputation of being the racist capital of Canada," Cotton said. "I was going to solve all the problems." Indigenous people were barred from local restaurants; many men were beaten and many women were raped. The father of the Anishinaabe writer and broadcaster Wab Kinew was one of the first to fight back, in the streets. "Their rage in response to racist attitudes and aggression," Kinew wrote, "eventually grew into an important part of the Indigenous rights movement in that part of the country." This drew media attention, and activists like Cotton, to the city. He later worked for the Canadian Civil Liberties Union, visiting First Nations reserves, including Shoal Lake No. 40, to do "shit-disturbing 101"—teaching people how to use tribunals, the Ontario Human Rights Code, and employment standards legislation to resist discrimination. In 1974, Cotton supported an armed occupation of Kenora's Anicinabe Park by the Ojibway Warriors Society to protest living conditions, poor education standards, and lack of access to traditional land. Burnt out, Cotton turned to carpentry for a living, but when he went to Shoal Lake to help build houses there, he learned the saga of the Winnipeg aqueduct. "The rest, as they say, is history."

Cotton was still advising the band. "In terms of the idealism, nothing has changed," he said. "I fiercely love the concept of this country, the idea of this country, the principles espoused by this country: fairness, equity, inclusion, respect for treaties, all those things we tell our children." But, he added, "we ain't doing it." Still, his anger was tempered in 2016 by his sense that the country was at a turning point. "There's a growing group of people in Canada who actually believe in the words of the country, who are saying, 'What does it mean to be treaty people?' What it means to be treaty people is to share place. And those alliances between Indigenous people and settlers are different now." That alliance had helped the people of Shoal Lake No. 40 win the Freedom Road, he said.

Something else has changed since Cotton's early activism: the power of Indigenous people in the courts. Around the time of the Anicinabe Park occupation in Kenora, Thomas Berger, a Vancouver judge appointed by Ottawa, was beginning three years of travels in the Mackenzie River Valley and the Western Arctic. He went to listen to the Dene, Inuit, and Métis people about a proposal to build a gas pipeline through their lands. A consortium that included Exxon, Shell, and TransCanada wanted to bring gas from Alaska through the Yukon to the Mackenzie and then into Alberta. Before that, Berger had represented British Columbia's Nisga'a people in a landmark 1973 case on whether their title to their land had been legally extinguished by Canada. The Nisga'a lost on other points of law, but the Supreme Court acknowledged Aboriginal title, prompting Ottawa to establish a land claims process for Aboriginal people.

The Indigenous people of the north "still rely on the land," Berger would say after completing his inquiry. "It wasn't a nostalgic thing, it wasn't a lament for a lost way of life." His report, released in 1977, recommended a ten-year moratorium on any pipeline. "The social consequences of the pipeline will not only be serious—they will be devastating," he wrote. The gas line would surely be followed by an oil line, roads, maintenance facilities, airports. "We look upon the North as our last frontier," he continued. "It is natural for us to think of developing it. . . . But the native people say the North is their homeland. They have lived there for thousands of years. They claim it is their land, and they believe they have a right to say what its future ought to be." Berger was giving the rights of Aboriginal people priority over the extraction of oil, a watershed moment. "Defining the relationship between Canadians and the native people in our midst is as much of the essence of the Canadian experience as defining the relationship between English and French," he said. "It has to be addressed again and again."

Five years later, Berger joined the campaign to have Aboriginal rights included in the 1982 Constitution, an intervention described as "instrumental" in enshrining those rights. Section 35—"the existing aboriginal and treaty rights of the aboriginal people in Canada are hereby recognized and affirmed"— would reshape Canadian society, including the politics of pipelines. Starting in 1990 with the Supreme Court of Canada's *Sparrow* decision, which created new thresholds for governments seeking to infringe on Aboriginal rights, First Nations carved out a greater role for themselves in Canadian law. The *Badger* case, in 1996, strengthened treaty rights, holding that "the honour of the Crown is always at stake" in living up to its obligations, that ambiguities should be resolved in favour of First Nations, and that the onus was on government to prove treaty rights had been extinguished. A year later *Delgamuukw* allowed the admission of traditional oral evidence, and in 2004 *Haida* created a "duty to consult" Indigenous communities on resource development projects, a duty strengthened a decade later by *Tsilhqot'in*.

In Treaty Three territory, these new legal powers explained TransCanada's consultations with the Grand Council—the political body representing twenty-four First Nation signatories—about Energy East. Cotton likened the process, held under *Manito Aki Inakonigaawin*, the Great Earth Law, to "their own mini-NEB." Treaty Three guaranteed the Indigenous people the right to maintain their own economy, to fish, hunt, and cut trees—and to sell what they harvested. To exercise those rights, Cotton said, "they need the land to be secure."

There have been other purported turning points for Indigenous people, most recently after the Oka crisis of 1990 and a subsequent royal commission. The dynamic was different now because of those court rulings, and a growing and impatient youth population. "The line in the sand is here," Cotton said. "You met it yesterday." He was referring to my drive to Shoal Lake to see Daryl and Preston Redsky. Daryl had been wearing a ball cap with the word "Army" emblazoned on it and a T-shirt with an archival photo of four nineteenth-century Indigenous men carrying rifles. The text said "Homeland Security: Fighting Terrorism Since 1492." Redsky had joked that the two messages—the hat symbolizing the military, the shirt resistance to it—contradicted each other, but Cotton told me there was more to it than that.

Redsky had been in the military. "Daryl's a professional," Cotton said. "He's a Warrior. He's been on the front lines at Burnt Church and Caledonia and Grassy Narrows," three communities that had seen collisions between Indigenous rights and federal authority. "If you want a logistical person to run some kind of action, Daryl's your guy. He's called upon right across the country, almost as a first responder." When I told Cotton I'd covered the Burnt Church dispute, he said Redsky "would have had a balaclava on. You may not have recognized him."

Cotton predicted that if Energy East was approved, Redsky would be on the front lines again. "That skill, that power, that talent, that experience is there. So when Daryl says, 'That's not going to happen,' he's not just blowing smoke." This border area between Ontario and Manitoba—Treaty Three territory, the corridor from eastern Manitoba to the city of Kenora—was a "pinch point," Cotton said. "When they come to build the pumping station between Falcon Lake and here, they're going to be up against Daryl and Preston and the coalition."

Teika Newton was part of that coalition: non-Indigenous, raised in Kenora, and the daughter of a pipeline welding inspector, she threw herself into the Energy East battle in 2013. She and Cotton greeted each other warmly when she arrived at HoJoe's, then Newton drove me out to see the large TransCanada compressor station and the gas pipeline right-of-way cutting through residential neighbourhoods. The day was cool, the sun was shining, and everything looked sharp. At the corner of Ritchie Road and Canfield Drive the gas line passed the former home of Dave Canfield, the city's mayor. Elsewhere, it came within metres of more houses.

Newton's role in the coalition involved fighting city hall. In April 2014 she learned that the Northwestern Ontario Municipalities Association, of which Kenora is a member, had passed a motion at its annual meeting endorsing Energy East. The rationale was that the pipeline was safer than oil-by-rail; the CPR ran through the centre of many member municipalities. "Of course it got a lot of support and passed," Newton told me, "because who wants an exploding bomb train through your town?" But there had been no discussion of the environmental implications, and no chance for local councils to consider the issue first, she said. "The member municipalities never had a chance to discuss it." Mayor Canfield was the president of NOMA at the time.

Newton made a presentation to Kenora council a month later to refute the pro–Energy East arguments. "The basis of the resolution is ill-informed and flawed," she told them. "It's wrong to ship petroleum by rail or pipeline." When she called the NOMA process anti-democratic, "the mayor exploded," Newton recounted. "He got so angry with me in council chambers. He called me an ideologue and a hypocrite." But several councillors had reservations about the NOMA resolution—and they passed a motion asserting Kenora's right to make its own comments to the National Energy Board.

Taking on the mayor was complicated in a small municipality. Rory McMillan, a councillor Newton considered an ally, chose his words carefully when he talked about Energy East. "I can't speak for council," he said. "I would answer it this way: I have some concerns about it and there are some things I'm still trying to learn about it." He worried about the water crossings in the area. But taking a bold stand wasn't easy. Although the council had asserted its right to dissent from NOMA on the pipeline, it did not officially oppose the project. "That would be so divisive and awkward in a small town that that is just something that doesn't happen," Newton said. "There are a lot of issues that are back-burnered to not cause a conflagration, to be able to get along and get other things through council."

Teika Newton's great-grandfather was a labourer on CN's Grand Trunk Railroad when it was built north of Kenora. The CN and CP lines were key to the city's development, as was water: rivers and falls provided hydroelectric power for sawmills, flour mills, and later pulp and paper mills. "The town really does have its origins in resource-extractive industries," Newton said. Raised by parents who opposed the paper mill—Kenora's economic lifeblood for decades—Newton studied ecology and environmental biology in Vancouver, then returned to Kenora with her husband, built an off-grid house, and founded Transition Initiative Kenora, a renewable-energy advocacy group. In 2012 she protested the Harper government's omnibus Bill C-38 and its cuts to the nearby Experimental Lakes Area, a federally run network of lakes and watersheds used as a natural research laboratory. When she heard about anti–Energy East protests in North Bay, "we decided we needed to do something similar."

Newton read William Kilbourn's *Pipeline*, the 1970 book bankrolled by TransCanada that told the story of the first gas line's construction. When Newton's father worked for the company as a welding inspector, "all the employees were given this book on the glorious history of TransCanada— how it was such a success story and it was the little company that fought all the odds," she told me. "To read it now, you realize how much that company and its proponents manipulated government." Energy East, she said, "has used the same playbook, exactly the same tactics used to push the Canadian mainline through in the fifties."

TransCanada representatives appeared at Kenora city council in the spring of 2016. Outside presentations are normally limited to five minutes, but, Newton said, Mayor Dave Canfield gave the company a half-hour. She recorded the session and captured Canfield talking about not being able to "make that Calgary meeting, but Iain was there. . . . I kind of wish I could have been there because it was pretty interesting stuff." The mention of "Iain" was a reference to Iain Angus, a Thunder Bay city councillor and the vice-chairman of NOMA. The trip to Calgary by municipal leaders raised alarm bells for Newton. "They look like good guys, but they've been working with TransCanada all along," she said. "It's very cozy."

The company was aggressive in building support for the pipeline, waging what its public relations firm, Edelman, called a "perpetual campaign" to promote the project and respond quickly to critics. According to documents leaked to Greenpeace in 2014, that involved gathering background information on environmentalists and distributing it to friendly think tanks, academics, and others, who could then write opinion articles and give interviews. TransCanada spoke often of its wish to "engage" with communities along the route, but the leak's revelations struck a discordant note, confirming for activists that the company would use bare-knuckle tactics to overcome opposition. (A TransCanada spokesperson said that some of the strategies in the documents weren't implemented.)

TransCanada's communications person told *The Globe and Mail* that the company had learned from the brutal public relations setbacks with Keystone XL; in the Energy East debate, it wanted to "get into that conversation space better than we ever did in the last four years." Edelman also recommended recruiting "supportive third parties to put pressure" on opponents. Identifying potential project supporters, then using "targeted messaging and behaviour" to "appeal to the individual's trigger points," would turn them into champions of the project, the leaked document said. They could then speak at public meetings or appear in advertising, providing "a rich base of advocates who passionately understand and support our cause and are willing—more often than not—to do what's asked of them." Online videos featured endorsements from figures ranging from local mayors to the owners of companies that were potential subcontractors. This use of "third-party advocates," Edelman said, "is often much more effective in establishing connection with the public."

In places like Kenora, where the decline of the old manufacturing economy was acute, the message leaned heavily on spinoff jobs, and the mayor, Dave Canfield, was receptive: he was among the four hundred employees laid off when the Abitibi mill closed in 2006. "That threw everybody into a tailspin," Cuyler Cotton recalled. There had been temporary closures over the years, but "this was the shock. It was gone." Lake of the Woods shifted its focus to growing its existing tourism sector, but "there is desperation for the old," Cotton said. "It is construction industry; it is extractive industry. That's what people here know." Canfield, Newton told me, was "a very vocal proponent for resource industry. That's his background and he's good at that. He's trying to be a champion of the local economy, and that's very admirable, but we're into a new era and it's time to embrace that." Kenora was now gambling on an oil pipeline at a time when the long-term prospects for fossil fuels were in doubt: prices were low, oil sands projects were being shelved. "The investment capital to sustain a project of this size and duration is just not there," Newton said. "The economic need for this project is eroding rapidly."

In May 2015, Newton's local fight against Energy East earned her a meeting with officials from the National Energy Board, including Peter Watson, the board chair appointed by Stephen Harper. With polls showing that a majority of Canadians lacked confidence in the NEB, officials arranged the public "engagement" tour to repair its reputation. But a discussion of Energy East was off-limits, Newton was told, to avoid influencing the board's future deliberations. "They explicitly said, 'We're not here to talk about projects.'"

Still, Newton took the measure of the NEB officials. "The sense that I got from Peter Watson was that he was honestly overwhelmed with the scale of the task before him," she said. Harper's Conservatives were in power. "He said, 'We have a lot of flexibility in our mandate—what we can study, what we can undertake—but you have to understand, we also have to be able to sell ourselves politically. We can't put forward recommendations that aren't going to go anywhere—what would be the point? So we have to make points that are politically salient, given who's in office.'"

The board, established in the wake of C.D. Howe's gas pipeline fight in the fifties, had been intended to take politics out of the process. Now the board itself was politically compromised, Newton believed. "I came out of that meeting with a much better set of insights about how the NEB works within the political system," she said, "and it isn't an easy fit for them." She concluded that it was "a really broken system." Little did she know how her short meeting would give her the chance to strike a blow against that system.

The Northwest Ontario Municipalities Association was meeting in Thunder Bay during my trip along the pipeline route. The morning after my interviews with Cotton and Newton, I set out from Kenora on the five-hour drive to the city on the shore of Lake Superior.

Route 17 wound through more sheer rock cuts and along more lakes. On the shore of Little Joe Lake, a marker from the Ontario Heritage Trust bore the heading "The Last Spike at Feist Lake"—a different "last" spike than the better-known one at Craigellachie: in June 1882, in the forest nearby, crews completed the six-hundred-kilometre section connecting Thunder Bay to Red River at present-day Winnipeg, "an essential link in the building of a transcontinental nation." The first shipment of western grain came through a year later, "the fulfillment of the dream of central Canadian western expansionists."

That other essential west–east link—TransCanada's Canadian mainline— also sliced through the woods here. I glimpsed the telltale no-dig warning signs several times where the line criss-crossed the highway to Thunder Bay. A large compressor station squatted by the side of the road outside Vermilion Bay. All three of Canada's sinewy symbols of commercial unity—gas lines, railway, Trans-Canada Highway—closely paralleled each other for long stretches of the drive. Near a bend in the road called Upsala, "Pipeline Road" led to another compressor station. A series of eleven large grey tanks resembling robotic elephants were suspended on metal grating, each with a tube emerging from the base and running underground. The entire facility was humming loudly, the sharp metallic sound piercing the air.

Electricity was another local concern about Energy East: northwestern Ontario had surplus power in 2016 because so many forestry mills had closed, but the new pump stations on the converted pipeline would consume a lot of it, and that would complicate the goal of attracting new manufacturing. "When that next big industry wants to come to town, there's not going to be any of that lovely hydro power left, because it's going to be used to pump bitumen to China," Cotton said. "All of the risk goes to the people who live here."

Near a spot named Raith, a road sign marked the ninetieth meridian; soon after that, a large billboard with silhouettes of a moose and a bear informed drivers that they were crossing from the Arctic watershed to the Atlantic watershed. "From here all streams flow south into the Atlantic Ocean," it said—down to Lake Superior and through the Great Lakes into the St. Lawrence River, the defining feature, and thoroughfare, of "Canada" before the opening of the prairie. This was the true end of the west and the start of the east: the sprawling, vital, infuriatingly middle-of-the-road, watershed-straddling province of Ontario, that national linchpin and honest broker of consensus where the country's existential struggles often sought resolution.

Thunder Bay was once two cities, Fort William and Port Arthur, and although they'd amalgamated almost a half century before, their dual legacy was apparent: two urban cores along the lakeshore, with a vast area between them—"Intercity"—filled in with box stores and light industry. Changing patterns in global trade had shrunk the port where western grain was loaded on ships for Europe. The forestry industry, though still vital, had also shrunk. The city bore the familiar signs of taxpayer-funded transformation: regional offices of government departments, a young university, and a downtown waterfront revival development with a pedestrian walkway, landscaped skateboard park, restored train station, restaurant, and arts centre.

But at the lake, if you walked to the very edge of one of the wharves, you could believe this was still the top of things, that "Superior" referred to more than just the lake's size—that in its wide, shimmering openness to the world, it offered connection and greatness.

Delegates to the NOMA convention, mostly men in jeans and button-down shirts or golf shirts, milled around a long corridor of meeting rooms at the Victoria Inn Hotel and Convention Centre, a low-rise hotel near the airport. These mayors and councillors saw each other several times a year, and the atmosphere was clubby: many were blue-collar guys with a knack for local politics, like-minded fellows in a hard-luck region facing industrial decline and a shrinking population. Outside one meeting room, I overheard a session on the federal plan for a carbon tax. "This is going to be a burden for poor people," one said. Another called it futile: "Canada's such a small player." A third: "This sickens me." A new voice said residents of his small, isolated municipality had no choice but to burn gas: "We don't have transit systems." Another delegate said, "There's new technology out there. Let's embrace it." That got a round of applause. Tough times called for common sense.

That also applied to pipelines, according to Kenora's mayor, Dave Canfield. "I take a very pragmatic approach to things," he told me between sessions. "When you take a look at Energy East, and you take a look at the alternatives, and you take a look at the future—yes, we're going into different types of technology like the electric car or whatever, but we're still going to be using a lot of petroleum products for the foreseeable future. And when you look at transporting them, bar none, pipelines are the safest way."

The tanker car explosion at Lac-Mégantic had been bracing for mayors like Canfield with rail corridors running through their downtowns. "The oil's gonna go," he said. "What's the safest way for it to go?" I told Canfield that I'd seen his old house next to the gas line. "People used to say, 'Are you crazy?'" he laughed. "I said, 'You know, my odds of getting killed just walking across the street are a lot higher than that pipeline blowing up and killing me.'"

Canfield was like everyone's favourite uncle, relaxed and amiable, explaining Energy East over Thanksgiving dinner. "It's all about practicality and reality," he said. "Activists are activists, and they do things because they think they're doing it for the right reasons, but when you're a political leader, you have to be a little more pragmatic than that. You have to look at the whole picture." Smiling patiently, he brushed off Teika Newton's complaint about the lack of a local vote in Kenora before the NOMA motion. The "vast majority" of delegates to the 2014 meeting voted for it, but it wasn't rammed through, he said. "There were people opposed to it. Some of the people who were opposed to it, including Mayor Hobbs of Thunder Bay, now have changed their minds."

Kenora's tourism industry—even more vital after the Abitibi mill closed—was based on Lake of the Woods remaining pristine, Canfield told me. "Nobody's more concerned about water than me," he said. "I live on the lake." So it was better to work with TransCanada than fight them. "I look at it as being part of the solution, not part of the problem." Consultations would lead to improvements that might otherwise "fall through the cracks," he continued. He was confident that Kenora could "hold their feet to the fire and make sure they're doing the job that we're asking."

Another mayor, Richard Harvey of Nipigon, was pressing TransCanada to add double walling to the line that would be converted for Energy East. It crossed the Nipigon River upstream from the city's water intake and traversed other rivers and wetlands. Still, the risk of an oil leak was small compared to a tanker car derailment, he said. In 2008 a CPR train had derailed near Nipigon, sending two boxcars of nurdles—tiny plastic grains destined to become plastic products—sliding into Lake Superior. "Ten years later, we're still trying to clean that mess up," Harvey noted. And, he added, articulating a theme common among NOMA delegates, eastern Canadian refineries should be processing Alberta crude, not "dirty oil, bloody oil, unethical oil" from overseas. Harvey had done missionary work in Nigeria, a major oil producer. "I know how horrific their environmental record is there." This echoed the industry's communications strategy.

Canfield outlined other benefits of Energy East that aligned with TransCanada's message. "These are really good-paying jobs, for the construction, the upgrades of some of the pipe to a better standard," he said. Chambers of commerce in the region were endorsing the project, citing a study, commissioned by TransCanada, that predicted four thousand jobs in Ontario during construction and fifteen hundred when the line was operating—the kind of industrial, country-linking jobs of old that the region knew well. Kenora would also gain new property tax revenue from a new pump station. And Canfield cited the national interest: "If we're going to be using oil, I'd sooner that Canadians benefit from that, right across the country from Alberta to New Brunswick." People he'd met who had worked in oil overseas—"say, in the Middle East"—told him that those places "have no environmental guidelines at all, [whereas] we're world leaders at environmental guidelines."

Canfield seemed very reasonable, very common-sense, very Ontario. But other comments he made had a darker edge, echoing the more aggressive arguments from pipeline supporters. He mentioned a documentary about Patrick Moore, a co-founder of Greenpeace. Moore later left the group, questioned whether climate change was caused by humans, and became a Greenpeace critic. "It wasn't about saving a world anymore, it was more like a religion," Canfield summarized. He also dismissed the conclusion of the Ontario Energy Board, a provincial regulatory body, that the environmental risks of Energy East outweighed the benefits. That conclusion, he said, was "probably from pressure."

In 2015 Canfield had seen the oil sands firsthand, thanks to a trip sponsored by the Canadian Association of Petroleum Producers. Friends who'd left Kenora to work out there told him, "That stuff you see on TV, Dave, is wrong," he recalled. The Federation of Canadian Municipalities was meeting in Edmonton that June, so Canfield suggested to CAPP that it organize a field trip. "I said, 'Lookit, I don't want a guided tour of all the nice stuff. I want to see the good, the bad, and the ugly.'" One morning at six o'clock, twenty-eight mayors and councillors from across the country boarded a Dash 8 for a daylong tour. "From the air you see everything," Canfield said, "and I was pleasantly surprised." He saw land that once produced oil being remediated; one parcel had a buffalo ranch. "These are the stories that never get out there," he said. One oil industry CEO had told the group that "nobody anywhere in the world, even in the United States, compares to what they have to do, the technology and the safeguards, in the oil sands," he added. "I didn't know that."

The trip changed a few minds. "There were a lot of people that weren't in favour of Energy East when we went up," Canfield said. "When we got off that plane, everybody understood."

Although Dave Canfield was NOMA's president, it was one of its vice-presidents, Iain Angus, a city councillor in Thunder Bay, who'd chaired the committee in 2014 that brought the Energy East resolution to the floor for a vote. Nothing in NOMA's rules, Angus explained, allowed member municipalities a pre-emptive vote on such an issue. "That's not something we can do," he said.

Burly and outwardly gruff-looking, Angus was, in conversation, candid and affable. He was more realistic than Canfield about the economic benefits of Energy East: there would be construction jobs in the short term, "and up here, that's always important," but the long-term impact would be minimal. He also acknowledged accepting free travel from the oil industry: "that Calgary meeting" Canfield had mentioned on Teika Newton's audio recording was convened by the Canadian Pipeline Association for municipal leaders "to talk about the reality that pipelines are seen as bad, and what can we do that is better?" He saw nothing insidious in accepting the free trip. "Those who know me know I'm my own person," he said. "No matter who buys me lunch, I'm still going to have my opinions." And Angus's opinion of Energy East was positive.

Iain Angus had been a New Democratic member of the Ontario legislature for two years in the seventies under leader Stephen Lewis—who more recently had backed the anti–oil sands, anti-pipeline Leap Manifesto—and later served two terms as an NDP MP in the House of Commons. "I know exactly where they're coming from," Angus said of the Leap crowd. "They see the oil sands as a major contributor to global warming, and they see [stopping a pipeline] as an easier fix than moving to electrical cars and hybrids." But "there's a naïveté to some of it. To think that we can run entirely on renewable fuels, that soon, indicates a lack of understanding of how the system operates." The Ontario government had phased out coal, even though, Angus said, scrubbers would have reduced emissions at two coal-power plants to the equivalent of natural gas—and at a lower cost than what had been paid to convert one, Atikokan, to burn wood pellets.

"Sometimes people grasp on to very simple solutions without understanding how complex the real answers are. And quite frankly I was one of those at one point," Angus said. The Ontario Energy Board had studied Energy East in isolation, and hadn't "looked at the railway side of things in the way that they should have, understanding what the alternative is." In a Lac-Mégantic–style explosion, "some of the towns would be wiped out," he said. "Our choice is between that or a pipeline that already exists, and that is almost totally underground." Although emissions from the oil sands and global warming were important issues, NOMA said in its submission to the Ontario Energy Board, "we must be as concerned with the health and safety of our residents as we are of the natural environment!" Climate change was literally not part of the equation. "We've just looked at what's good for our municipalities," Angus said.

To the extent that climate and energy policy were on the radar in north-western Ontario, it was from a profoundly local and utilitarian angle. Cuyler Cotton had pointed out that the new Energy East pump stations would require a lot of electricity; Angus agreed that demand would be an issue and that "TransCanada is part of that." But he saw solutions in the vast forests that would have been cut by now if not for the decline in the forest industry. If those trees were left to die and rot naturally in their own time, they'd give off their stored carbon dioxide, Angus said. Instead they should be harvested and turned into wood pellets to generate electricity at two underused power plants, Atikokan and Thunder Bay, already converted to burn them. "Ontario forests are underused," Angus said: more cutting would pre-empt the release of more CO_2, address the looming demand for electricity—and create more forestry jobs in an economically battered region.

There seemed to be a strong consensus at NOMA for sticking with the resource economy, for wringing from it every last bit of wealth that could be wrung. One delegate, however—Angus's Thunder Bay council colleague, Mayor Keith Hobbs—questioned the prevailing view. Canfield had told me that Hobbs was an opponent of the 2014 Energy East resolution who'd since changed his mind, but Hobbs corrected that: "I said my mind *could* be changed, but not yet," he said. "I get it that transportation by rail is danger-ous, but I don't think the pipeline is going to lessen the traffic of crude oil through Canada. . . . That's a growing industry and that will continue to grow even with this pipeline, so that argument doesn't wash with me."

Hobbs was elected mayor in 2010 after retiring from the Thunder Bay city police. "Accidents happen," he said. "We all know that. I was a cop for thirty-four years, so I know all about accidents happening." As mayor, he became a board member of the Great Lakes Cities Initiative, a grouping of more than 120 municipal leaders in Canada and the United States along the shores of the lakes and the St. Lawrence River. The group dealt with such water issues as pollution and invasive species. "I can't support the pipeline until I have a guarantee that those waters will be protected," he said. The mayor's backyard—or front yard—was the great waterway at the heart of Canada. "The Great Lakes provide drinking water for probably thirty million people, and we have to protect that at all costs." NOMA's resolution in 2014 was premature, he felt, and ought to have come after proper research.

TransCanada had promised extra safety measures for "significant" water crossings, but NOMA was still waiting to hear what the company meant by that. Common Voice Northwest, a policy think tank set up by NOMA with Angus as its executive director, eventually issued a report that found "deficiencies" in TransCanada's assessments "that led to questions about the credibility and thoroughness" of its approach. "We suggest it is not of sufficient depth to satisfy the public that all reasonable measures have been taken" to protect watercourses, the report warned.

"I was evidence-based my whole career," Hobbs said. "I didn't lay a charge until I had all the evidence. . . . I wanted to make sure I had a hundred percent. We don't have a hundred percent. We don't have anywhere near the evidence we need as an organization to say yes."

When Thunder Bay council voted in 2017 to endorse Energy East—contingent on Common Voice Northwest's conditions being met—Angus supported the motion and Hobbs opposed it. If Ontario was Middle Canada, and if this stretch of the pipeline route between Kenora and Thunder Bay represented the straddling of the country's diverse regions, economies, and opinions, then Hobbs's dissent revealed the challenge of finding a consensus on Energy East, even in this most moderate, compromise-for-the-good-of-the-country province.

At the eastern edge of Thunder Bay, where traffic from the city accelerates to highway speeds along the shore of Lake Superior, stands a monument to Terry Fox, whose cross-country run to raise money for cancer research ended nearby after the disease returned. Perched on a dramatic outcrop of rock overlooking the lake, the rendering of Fox, his artificial leg and curly hair silhouetted against a late-afternoon sun, was instantly recognizable.

The statue was unveiled in 1982, a year after Fox's death, when Quebec separatism and western resentment were flaring. The inscription on its base, shaped like a bridge, felt like an effort to span the country's differences. "He united Canadians as they have never been united before," it declared. "It is for such a reason this monument was designed, joining east with west, depicting all provincial and territorial coats-of-arms and the Canadian emblems of the maple leaf and beaver." It was an admirable and stirring sentiment—but it was easy to unite the country behind a courageous athlete testing the limits of his endurance to fight a killer disease. A fossil fuel pipeline was far less inspirational, and far less unifying.

"There are hard-liners on both sides," Iain Angus told me. "There are those who say no pipelines, never. They automatically jump onto whatever campaign is out there, whether it's in Canada or the United States. It's become part of the language: pipelines are evil. On the flip side, you've got the industry that is very adamant that they need these: it's a form of transportation, it's efficient, it's energy-efficient. And they're locked into it.

"So I don't think there's a national consensus that's out there," Angus said. "I don't envy the prime minister and his cabinet having to do the balancing act on this one."

10

THE DIVIDE

FROM NEAR THUNDER BAY, the Energy East route traced an 1100-kilometre arc across northern Ontario, following Route 11, the Trans-Canada, through dozens of remote communities where there was little opposition to the pipeline. "A lot of the communities north of us are based on mining or forestry," said Peter Bullock, a resident of North Bay. "There's a dominant industry. They're accustomed to using the resources of the land for economic purposes." In several towns, the compressor stations for TransCanada's gas lines provided the biggest share of the local tax base. "If the company gets in trouble, the town gets in trouble," Bullock said. In the township of Black River–Matheson, population twenty-four hundred, the $1.1 million in property taxes TransCanada paid in 2014 represented 18 percent of municipal revenues. The council there endorsed Energy East. "We badly need the tax revenues and the new jobs that will be created in our municipality," Mayor Mike Milinkovich told the Ontario Energy Board in 2014.

"They can't say no," said Marc Tessier, another North Bay resident, who'd grown up in Wawa. "'Railroaded' is a strong term, [but] you can't bite the hand that feeds you. That's what's happening in northern Ontario."

Only in North Bay did substantial opposition appear again. TransCanada's large compressor station was just one of many industrial sites lining Route 11 at the northern entrance to the city. The company's relatively small economic footprint—it employed sixty people out of a population of more than fifty thousand—changed the politics. "We're somewhat detached," Tessier said. "That's why we can stand back and say no." Just before the station, a large billboard on the side of the road proclaimed, "Clean Water, No Pipeline, Stop Energy East."

North Bay's slogan, "Just North Enough to Be Perfect"—the product of "one of those branding exercises about twenty years ago," Mayor Al McDonald explained sheepishly—seemed apt. Indisputably north of larger cities like Toronto and Ottawa, less hectic and crowded and a degree or two cooler, North Bay is nonetheless economically and philosophically closer to those places—more southern, more urban, more diverse—than the towns farther up along Route 11, a road people in North Bay call "the north highway." But the city also cherishes its connection to the wilderness. As environmental services manager at city hall, Bullock dealt often with the provincial environment ministry. "They said North Bay is totally different than their other jurisdictions. They said if a creek runs red in Timmins, there's not a single phone call, and if a creek runs red in North Bay, their phone rings off the hook."

North Bay is also a dividing point. Two major highways run south from the city, one to Ottawa and one to Toronto. On the west side of the downtown, Lake Nipissing feeds into Lake Huron, while to the east, Trout Lake flows toward the Ottawa River and the St. Lawrence. And TransCanada's mainline gas system divides there, too: from the compressor station on Route 11, two lines carry gas to a compressor station in Vaughan, north of Toronto, and two others run southeast to a station at Iroquois, Ontario, near Cornwall. At both locations, the gas is fed into lines owned by local distributors, who sell it to their customers.

TransCanada has been in North Bay since the first gas line was built in the fifties. "It's a fairly reputable company," Bullock said. "My uncle worked there. It's been an outstanding company." But, he added as he drove along the shore of Trout Lake, "our understanding of TransCanada today is far different than what it would have been when we first started, because we've had a lot of things revealed to us."

Bullock, wiry and slight, was driving to the gas line right-of-way. The line to be converted to carry bitumen as part of Energy East ran close to Trout Lake, putting the eleven-kilometre-long lake at the heart of the pipeline debate in North Bay. The water was metallic grey, foreboding but magnificent, stretching long and narrow on a west–east axis. Near the western end, an intake valve drew water for the municipality; at the eastern extremity, the lake emptied into the Mattawa River, near where the gas pipeline passed beneath it.

Between those two points several major creeks flowed into the lake, and Energy East would carry bitumen close to them. This worried Bullock, a member of the Trout Lake Conservation Association's board. At the right-of-way clearing, spring runoff gushed down a muddy track, forming a channel several feet wide rushing into the woods, headed for the lake. Nearby, Four Mile Creek was moving fast with the May melt to Four Mile Bay, part of the lake. "This is the main conveyor path from the TransCanada pipeline that could carry oil very rapidly," he told me.

Bullock had printed images of two front pages from the local newspaper, the *North Bay Nugget*, one from 1961 and one from 1977. Both featured stories and photos of gas explosions from breaks in the line. "Pipeline Rupture Spawns Evening Spectacle," blared the 1977 headline. Damage was minimal, but a large fireball attracted enough gawkers to snarl traffic. Gas explosions are dangerous, Bullock said, but they don't spill on the ground. Oil would be different. "They say the probability of having a spill with the oil pipeline is one in seven thousand years." He pointed to the front pages. "But in the last fifty or sixty years, we've had two."

A boom in cottage development on the lake, with no corresponding tightening of water regulations, prompted the creation of the Trout Lake Conservation Association in 1987. Now North Bay residents were building year-round homes there; Bullock estimated that they'd come to outnumber cottages two to one. He got involved with the association because he felt his experience as the city's environmental manager would contribute; the board also included a scientist, a geologist, and an engineer. When they quizzed TransCanada officials, he said, they weren't satisfied with the answers. "We've slowly gone from wanting to work with TransCanada" to minimize the risk "to slowly becoming against it. . . . We were finding out information over time that was eye-opening for us." A former TransCanada employee, a whistleblower embraced by the Council of Canadians, had told the association about a washout during the construction of the newest gas line near the lake—the one to be converted for Energy East. "He told us that in that accident, the integrity of the pipe was compromised." TransCanada did not respond specifically to the claim, but spokesperson Tim Duboyce said that the company "would not put the pipeline into service without the assurance it will operate safely. That includes testing the integrity of the pipeline being converted from gas to oil service."

Like the highway and the water and the gas pipeline themselves, the pipeline fight in North Bay split in different directions. The association wanted Energy East moved out of the Trout Lake watershed, but "because TransCanada successfully got the city to only worry about their water supply . . . this is not on their radar as a significant issue to be concerned about," Bullock told me. Mayor McDonald said he was being realistic: "If we just say, 'Move it somewhere else,' it sounds like 'not in my backyard' and we're just putting it in somebody else's backyard." The city instead proposed that TransCanada move the route farther north, away from the lake but still within city limits. "It gives us more time to react," McDonald said. "We would be comfortable they're taking the risk away from us." Duboyce said that the company had ruled out either scenario. "We are not looking at the option of re-routing the line farther north," he said in an email. "However, discussions with the city continue on other solutions."

———

The mayor's stance frustrated another group of pipeline opponents, a group of citizens called Northwatch, comprising veteran social justice advocates, anti-poverty campaigners, and environmental activists. Some of them attended TransCanada's first public meetings back in 2013. "The maps, to me, were astonishing," said Jane Howe, one of the first members. "None of the watercourses were named. The lake wasn't named. . . . That was a big shock to people, that they didn't seem to have answers to some pretty pertinent questions." For one early meeting, a local organic farmer, Yan Roberts, arranged for activists to wear golf shirts that closely resembled TransCanada corporate attire: the logo read "SaveCanada" instead of "TransCanada." They handed out anti-pipeline leaflets to citizens who mistook them for company staff. "People were pretty galvanized, and it was a lot of fun to dress up like them and go into their space," Howe said.

That spirit of mischief took root: once a week, some members of the group donned gas masks and hazmat suits and held "Oil and Water Don't Mix" signs at a busy intersection in North Bay's downtown. "There is an overwhelming positive reaction," said Bunty Swanson. "People go by with their thumbs up and they honk their horns." The members I met, at a gathering at Average Joe's, a restaurant on Trout Lake, were mostly senior citizens. They cheerfully acknowledged the skewed demographics. "We have the time, the energy, the contacts, and the passion," Swanson said. Another woman in the group, Brennain Lloyd, added, "And we can't be fired. If we get arrested at a protest, what does it matter if we lose a security clearance?"

The group also packed municipal council meetings to demand that the city take a position against the project on climate grounds. The mayor demurred. "He was pretty clear from the very beginning that the only way we were going to convince people in this community to oppose the pipeline was to oppose it on the basis of the threat to the watershed," Howe said. "He didn't think [climate change] was going to fly" as an argument. Elizabeth Frazer, a United Church minister, said the council was "what I describe as a 'chamber of commerce' council," eager to show that the city was open for business. But Lloyd said the mayor was probably right. "That is what he has evaluated to be the strongest card to play with that kind of a council," she said. "That's just him being pragmatic." Jim Sinclair gestured out to the centre of the lake, to where the water intake ran, invisibly, beneath the surface: "The strategy of the mayor is, 'Where are people most anxious?' It's easy to identify that right here is where people are going to get the most upset."

North Bay city hall is a functional mix of glass, red brick, and concrete. Mayor Al McDonald is big and gregarious, a formidable presence. For him, the lake was the entire argument: although modelling showed that only the most severe spills would reach the intake, that was still too high a risk. The city would have only nine hours of water if the valve had to be closed. "There is no science to clean it up," McDonald said. The fire department would also be without water. "The question becomes, What do you do with a city of fifty-four thousand people if there's no water?"

In the leaked strategy document from TransCanada's public relations consultants, Edelman, North Bay residents were described as more concerned than most Ontarians about Energy East, but also more willing to listen to arguments in favour of it. One-quarter of the five hundred residents surveyed were "strongly opposed," the report said. McDonald had his own measure: when the pipeline was in the headlines in 2015, "I couldn't go anywhere without people stopping me to say they supported the position the city was taking," he told me. But that support was based on water concerns, not climate change or the oil sands. "As Canadians, they understand that this has a bigger impact on our country than just our local issue," he said. "I think the vast majority of our citizens will have an opinion one way or another on the pipeline itself, but I think a bigger majority would say that we need to protect the only source of drinking water that we have."

McDonald was briefly a Progressive Conservative member of the provincial parliament, and ran federally for Stephen Harper in 2004. He identified with parties that supported oil pipelines. But unlike Dave Canfield in Kenora, he didn't see the case for working with TransCanada. "Anything that we've said, they've tried to discredit it," he told me. "They're not offering any studies to us showing that it's safe." The company's only real duty, he said, was to its shareholders: "It's how they can make more money per quarter than they did the previous quarter. They have armies of communications experts and people trying to convey the message that it's safe, and we're a small city of fifty-four thousand trying to do everything [we] can to get our voice out there. There's no question they have a bigger budget."

A vivid example appeared online in 2016, when TransCanada's communications team posted a series of videos with municipal fire chiefs along the route in northern Ontario. The company met regularly with the chiefs for mock disaster exercises for the gas line, and that was ostensibly the subject of the videos, though on YouTube they carried the label "Energy East—Committed to Safety," blurring the distinction. "They've gone above and beyond in trying to show us exactly what it is that they want to do and how they would do it," North Bay's then fire chief, Grant Love, said in his video, shot before he retired but released afterward. "And if we have any questions, they're always open and honest with their answers."

Fire chiefs were ideal "third-party advocates," to borrow Edelman's phrase. Other TransCanada videos featured Love's counterparts from towns like Cochrane, Kapuskasing, and Englehart, but in North Bay, the video—and the resulting headline on a local news site ("Former Fire Chief Throws Support Behind Energy East Pipeline")—provoked controversy. Love wasn't paid to appear in the video, nor had he sought the city's permission; he later pointed out to the local CBC station that the message "doesn't say 'I support Energy East.'" The point of the video was that TransCanada had been good to work with. "It doesn't matter whether I'm for it or against it."

Even so, McDonald was unhappy, and TransCanada apologized and took down the video. Duboyce told North Bay media that it was "never our intention to surprise or offend anyone" with the video, which he described as the perspective of an emergency responder "who has had a long-term relationship with our company regarding our commitment to safety." Duboyce added: "We always strive toward positive relationships with municipalities, including the mayor and council in North Bay." In its strategy document Edelman had described North Bay as a place where residents had heard "positive things" about the company. "We can perhaps leverage TC brand in North Bay to counter negative noise around the EE brand." But the effort backfired: McDonald was more skeptical than ever of the company. "There's no question that they're using their communications to separate, conquer, and divide."

Mayor Al McDonald wasn't the only politician whom pipeline opponents wanted to see come out more strongly against Energy East. Northwatch members hoped Ontario premier Kathleen Wynne and her Liberal government would lead the fight in the province. But "they've been very guarded," said Frazer at the gathering of activists on the lake. "Mum's the word." Although pipelines that cross provincial boundaries are regulated by Ottawa alone, Brennain Lloyd said that Wynne could slow the issuing of road permits for Energy East or the approval of new power lines to pumping stations. "They'd have to reach to do it, because it is a matter of federal jurisdiction, but they could reach."

Early on, Wynne seemed likely to reach. In 2014, after winning her majority government, she aligned herself with Quebec premier Philippe Couillard on the project: they didn't explicitly oppose it, but they did agree on a set of conditions, including measuring its effect on greenhouse gas emissions, consulting Indigenous people, and assessing environmental and economic risks. "We have to protect people in Ontario and Quebec," Wynne said after a meeting with Couillard. Less than a month later, however, Alberta premier Jim Prentice persuaded the pair to drop their insistence that regulators assess potential increases in oil production from new pipeline capacity. Larger climate issues could be addressed separately, Wynne said: "The Energy East project is not the whole discussion." Wynne asked the Ontario Energy Board to study the project, and it concluded that the risks outweighed the benefits for the province, highlighting Trout Lake as one of four water sources that warranted "special attention" from TransCanada. But Wynne "never actually responded," Lloyd said. Instead, Ontario told the NEB it would ensure that the pipeline's pump stations got the electricity they needed to operate.

Wynne was making political calculations, Frazer told me. "What really halted Ontario coming out one way or another was when Rachel Notley was elected," she said, "and Rachel Notley wanted to have the Liberals support her proposals around energy." Notley needed political cover for her climate plan, and that meant persuading other premiers to accept pipelines. "Kathleen Wynne's main MO is to promote climate leadership," Teika Newton had said in Kenora. "The way to do that politically is to say, 'We will lend our tacit support to Energy East if you do these good things in Alberta.'" After meeting Notley in January 2016, Wynne declared that the Alberta NDP's plan "makes the national conversation about climate targets and pipelines easier." Ontario's concerns were "starting to be addressed," she said. "The people of Ontario care a great deal about the national economy and the potential jobs that this proposed pipeline project could create in our province and across the country."

A provincial election was looming, and the Northwatch activists hoped to make Energy East a campaign issue for Wynne's Liberals. "She needs to be pressed about what their position will be around the pipeline," Frazer said. Other issues would bedevil Wynne in the 2018 campaign, however—issues that, though not tied directly to Energy East, illustrated how politically dangerous climate and carbon politics had become.

Kathleen Wynne's green-energy headaches could be traced back to her predecessor, Dalton McGuinty, whose government had passed the Green Energy and Green Economy Act in 2009. The law let entrepreneurs generate renewable electricity with windmills and solar panels and then sell it to Ontario's provincial power grid at inflated rates—in effect, subsidizing the launch of their companies. The trade-off for the higher energy cost was forcing the companies to buy their materials in Ontario, stimulating "green jobs" in the manufacturing of windmills and solar panels. But after the World Trade Organization ruled that the Ontario-first provision violated free trade agreements, there were fewer jobs to justify the artificially high cost and the corresponding increase to residential power bills. If the overriding goal was more renewable energy, said one industry insider, the Liberals should have let the free market decide where companies bought their materials. "The moment politicians say, 'I might be able to get some jobs out of this green energy'—that's the problem," he said. "It's been a major cock-up in this province."

At the same time, the province phased out coal-fired generating plants, a 2003 election promise. To replace them, the Ontario Power Authority signed contracts with TransCanada Energy to build natural gas–fired plants in Oakville and Mississauga. But in the face of strong opposition in both cities, McGuinty cancelled the agreements. After the 2011 election reduced the Liberals to a minority government, the opposition Progressive Conservatives and NDP used their control of legislative committees to investigate the true cost of the cancellations. It emerged that Liberal staffers had scrambled to cover up thousands of pages of documents and delete emails from government servers. With the opposition closing in, McGuinty prorogued the legislature on October 16, 2012, and resigned as premier.

TransCanada Energy emerged unscathed from the gas plant episode. The province's auditor general said that the Oakville cancellation alone would cost Ontario an estimated $675 million, largely because McGuinty had promised to keep TransCanada Energy "whole" despite legal mechanisms to cancel the contract at a lower cost. TransCanada built a plant in Napanee instead; the power authority and ratepayers had to pay for gas line upgrades to the new location, which was farther from the Toronto market and thus from gas supplies. The company would have borne those costs under the Oakville contract; with the plant in Napanee, it would save money and therefore enjoy "a higher rate of return," the auditor general said. "We believe that the settlement with TCE will not only keep TCE whole but may make it better than whole." The total price of the gas plant fiasco was estimated at $1.1 billion.

Wynne won the leadership race to replace McGuinty and led the Liberals to another majority in 2014, but other consequences of McGuinty's green plan began to hit Ontario pocketbooks. The Thunder Bay and Atikokan generating stations, converted to burn wood pellets, were found by the auditor general to be inefficient; the cost of creating electricity at Thunder Bay was estimated at twenty-five times that of other biomass plants. Despite a glut of electricity in the province, Ontario Power Generation announced that it would spend $13 billion to upgrade its aging fleet of nuclear reactors; at the same time Bruce Power, a private-sector operator, was spending the same amount to refurbish its reactors—two staggering expenses that also had to be passed on to consumers.

By 2016, power rates were double what they'd been in 2005. Wynne's popularity plunged, and her government desperately introduced legislation to force bills down, which added an additional $21 billion to an eventual fiscal reckoning sometime around 2027. "People are rebelling, and people know this isn't just market activity," said the energy insider. "It's the politicians. . . . There is no more wiggle room, and the future is not bright and green and sunny."

Green energy supporters were glum, but tried to see the positive side. "The government has done a fabulous job bringing in green energy," Peter Bullock said, insisting that renewables were only a fraction of the problem. "The nukes are what have caused these huge, huge costs." Tom Adams, a well-known energy consultant in Toronto, disputed that: wind and solar generate high-cost electricity only intermittently, he wrote, requiring expensive gas plants for backup generation—in effect forcing ratepayers to pay twice for infrastructure. Wynne fixed some of the problems, but her cut to electricity rates punished people like Bullock, who'd invested thousands of dollars to lower the carbon footprints of their homes. "We've done all of these things based on a payback, based on electrical rates," he said. "It discourages people from taking steps to manage their load."

When Bullock worked at North Bay city hall he'd led a project to lower municipal methane emissions, on the expectation that Canada would adopt a system of emissions-credit trading under the Kyoto Protocol. But the Harper government pulled Canada out of the agreement. "All of a sudden one of the means for us to pay for this capital project dried up," Bullock said. "I almost lost my job over this. I was hauled in [front of council]. . . . I was the one who wore it." Bullock wasn't fired, but his credibility was damaged. "My opportunity to bring another project forward like that wasn't possible."

The same kind of reaction was now being felt across Ontario. The Liberal flirtation with "radical greenism," wrote financial columnist Terence Corcoran, had been "a monumental failure. . . . Instead of being a worthy model for other nations and states, the province's energy megaproject stands as a cautionary tale." The Ontario experience had damaged the credibility of climate initiatives, particularly Liberal climate initiatives. "People can't help but notice that this government has done good things badly," Brennain Lloyd said. "And that's a problem. It takes up all the political space. So now, how do you do those things effectively?"

The political damage was hitting its peak just as Justin Trudeau's federal Liberals were ramping up their climate plan. Corcoran noted that one of McGuinty's key environmental advisers, Gerald Butts, had moved on to Ottawa and was "working on turning Prime Minister Justin Trudeau into a global political celebrity and carbon taxer."

"They've created all this political enmity. The job still needs to be done, but it now is much harder to do it for them or for successive governments," Lloyd said. "The rhetoric against the Green Energy and Green Economy Act is really going to be hard to recover from."

A small outpost of Kathleen Wynne's green revolution stood near the highway on the way out of North Bay. Bur Oak Resources, a company advertising solar power services on signs along Route 17, had set up shop there. A few sample panels sat in a spartan showroom downstairs. Upstairs, in the office of owner Lance Johnson, a map on the wall showed Canada's energy sources in a series of provincial pie charts and arrows.

Johnson had worked in mining for two decades before a major downturn cost him his job. "I decided if I was going to make a change, I might as well make a change for the better," he said. "I decided that renewable energy was the best industry to get into. I think it's a fairly noble cause." The company built wind and solar generation for general contractors, buying windmills and panels manufactured elsewhere and assembling them wherever the customer wanted to generate power to sell to the provincial grid.

Bur Oak had twenty-five employees, was moving into Manitoba, and had just established a subsidiary in Mexico—a success story that Johnson traced back to the green policies of Dalton McGuinty and Kathleen Wynne. "A lot of people say they're paying too much for the power, but the way I explain it—right or wrong, I'm not the one who came up with the policy—is before they came up with the Green Energy and Economy Act in Ontario, there was no real solar economy." Contrast what the Liberals had accomplished, Johnson said, to old-fashioned job-creation spending on roads. Highway jobs vanish the day the road is finished, and taxpayers are stuck with the cost of maintenance. Bur Oak was creating fewer jobs, but they were in it for the long term—and they were lowering carbon dioxide emissions. "They kick-started the industry by offering these high contract rates to start off with," he said, "and the industry grew."

Ontario's green plan didn't look like a fiasco to Johnson. Clad in overalls with the company logo on the shoulder, he explained that many of his customers weren't hippie idealists but rather pension funds and investment funds run by savvy capitalists. Those guaranteed rates were attracting investors to solar power. "You know you're going to get this investment back through a revenue stream for twenty, twenty-five years," he said.

Johnson was equally businesslike about Energy East. "I'm not for it, of course, but the oil's going to find its way there one way or another. If I had to pick truck, train, or pipeline, I would have to suppose it's probably the least risky." Johnson lived on the water in North Bay, so he worried about spills, but he worried more about another Lac-Mégantic. "It's the least of the evils," he said of Energy East. "If we say no to the pipeline, we're going to have tanker cars going through on the rail line."

Even renewable energy had to deal with NIMBYism, Johnson told me. "People don't want a solar project next to their property," he said. "I'm like, 'Why?' It's a thing of beauty. It collects energy from the sky and it makes power, quietly." Some other solar developers had made bad site choices, he acknowledged, but mostly he found local objections hypocritical. "If you don't want that, take the power meter out of your house and live without power, because you're part of the problem. We are all part of the problem. If we don't work together to find a solution, it's never going to come."

Twenty minutes outside North Bay, Highway 17 crossed the gas line right-of-way where it came down from Trout Lake. Snow flurries whipped the highway leading into the town of Mattawa. Soon I was alongside the Ottawa River, which lurked behind the trees.

Despite the cold, I indulged my curiosity with several stops along the road. I crunched through snow to see TransCanada compressor station 1204, at Deux-Rivières, pushing two lines of natural gas south. Just before Deep River, I stopped for a glimpse of Ontario Power Generation's Des Joachims hydroelectric dam straddling the river. A historical marker commemorated Canada's first nuclear reactor, a prototype built nearby that paved the way for a carbon-free but controversial way to generate energy. Farther down Route 17, closer to Ottawa, solar panels appeared more and more frequently on homes and in fields.

The drive down the Ottawa Valley was a journey through a diversity of energy sources: natural gas, hydro, nuclear, and solar. But there was no crude oil—at least, not yet.

II

TORQUED

NEAR THE TOWN OF Cobden in the Ottawa Valley, a historical marker stands near the spot where in 1867 a local farmboy discovered an astrolabe bearing the date 1603. The plaque says that the instrument, used to calculate latitude, "is believed to have been lost" by Samuel de Champlain when he was portaging during his expedition up the Ottawa River in 1613. Some scholars believe that the astrolabe, eventually displayed at the Canadian Museum of History, more likely belonged to a Jesuit missionary. The belief that it's Champlain's rests in part on how deeply this area is felt to be part of Old Canada, the territory of the country's founding narrative, in which the St. Lawrence River and its tributaries represent vital links for nation building.

To the dismay of Robert Dewald and Gary Sayer in Czar, Alberta, and many others in western Canada, it's also where the modern nation's political power still resides, and where the fate of Energy East would be decided.

At the town of Arnprior, Route 17 became the four-lane Highway 417. Thicker traffic raced into Ottawa. The Energy East route passed under an interchange and entered Stittsville, a former village amalgamated into the larger capital city in 2001. Box stores, fast food places, and modern town-houses were pressed against the highway, but farther down the main road was the historic heart of the community, with quaint red-brick buildings, elegant old houses, a village square—but even there Ottawa's sprawl, in the form of strip malls and condos, was encroaching.

Mike Fletcher knew Stittsville well. Fletcher estimated that he'd knocked on about six thousand doors in the area to gather signatures on a petition against Energy East. "I start off talking about the local issues, but assuming I don't get cut off by whoever I'm talking to, I'll also mention the climate change implications and the mess being made in northern Alberta," he said as we walked west on the Trans Canada Trail, away from the edge of metropolitan Ottawa. The pipeline right-of-way was twenty-five minutes out on foot. "I'll reference this trail," he said, a popular spot for walking and cycling. "I've always thought I should lead with the local issues because I thought that would get more traction." But the big picture was effective, too. "They get it on climate change and they're ready to sign." Out of every ten people he met, about six signed.

Fletcher's campaign, covering about fifty streets each year between spring and fall, was no lonely crusade. He was a member of Ecology Ottawa, the city's leading environmental group. Maybe it was the thick layer of national politics draped over the city, but the organization used professional, disciplined, election-style mobilization. "We had a weekend course in activist training," Fletcher said. One lesson was that face-to-face contact moves people's opinions more than emails or robocalls. "I thought, 'If I want to fight this thing, I'm going to do the thing that's the most effective,' so I started knocking on doors and I've never really looked back."

Ottawa was a very particular place to campaign: behind any door on any street, you might find a departmental employee or ministerial staffer who knew your issue. "I do knock on a lot of civil servants' doors," Fletcher said. "Very few of them refuse to sign because they're civil servants." Some even pass on intelligence: "I've bumped into a couple of people on the doorstep who've told me things that are happening in government." The first summer that Justin Trudeau's Liberals were in power, Fletcher was told that the prime minister's office was hands-on with Energy East. "Everything about it was being buttoned down very tightly." The pipeline was "a priority issue that needs to be managed."

Fletcher got involved in environmental activism at the University of Guelph, and he stuck with it after he moved to Ottawa for work. He lived in Munster, a hamlet farther out from Stittsville, where he and his family tried to practise sustainable living. He was the very personification of Canadian activism: firm in his views, polite about advancing them. "Probably the best question I get on the doorsteps is 'What are your chances of stopping it?'" he said. "If I thought it was a lost cause, I'd move on and do something else, but I don't think that's the case."

In the 2015 federal election, Fletcher stepped up his door-to-door canvassing. He quizzed candidates in his riding about Energy East during a local debate and created a handbill summarizing their views, which he distributed in areas where people were most concerned about the pipeline. At one point in the campaign, Ecology Ottawa decided that its overriding goal was to defeat the Harper government, and diverted canvassers to ridings around Ottawa where Conservative incumbents were considered vulnerable. "I broke off doing some work in this riding and went and supported that." In 2015, that meant voting Liberal. "I get that with politics," Fletcher said. "You try to swing the best deal you can. I'm not a purist."

In the next federal election he said he might be less accepting of that logic, particularly in Ottawa Centre, the downtown riding held by Trudeau's environment and climate change minister, Catherine McKenna, who Fletcher believed should categorically oppose pipelines. "I don't think that much of her," he said. McKenna narrowly defeated a popular New Democrat incumbent in 2015, and Fletcher was thinking ahead. "In my dreams, in the next election, if the NDP are doing well enough and the Liberals are doing poorly enough, we do some mobilizing in that riding to try to get the NDP back," he said. This was another facet of the Energy East debate: even the Liberal Party of Canada—the ultimate straddler of the political centre—was finding it difficult to forge a consensus on oil, climate, and pipelines.

Within a month of being sworn in, Justin Trudeau and Catherine McKenna were at the Paris climate change conference, COP 21, where McKenna helped broker the final agreement. It was seen as Canada's return to the world stage as a supporter of multilateral action, including on carbon emissions. At home, however, McKenna had to reconcile the Paris agreement—to limit global temperature increases to less than 2 degrees above pre-industrial levels, with an ultimate goal of 1.5 degrees—with her conditional support for new oil pipelines. Canadians would support such projects, McKenna said, if they faced a more rigorous and credible environmental review, and if the government brought in real climate measures. "I think what Canadians are looking for now is real action," she told the CBC.

Conservatives disputed that the Liberals had a mandate for stricter emissions rules. "I don't think it's tied to climate," Lisa Raitt, one of Harper's former ministers, said in an interview. "Justin beat my party leader in an election, and he is now trying to say that everything he said in the election was the reason. But the reason was we were a ten-year-old tired government, and the Canadian populace didn't like Stephen Harper anymore."

Harper's tenure in office began with his promising action on climate, too. "Despite the mythology, it wasn't a government that came in and from day one started kicking sand at environmentalists," Andrew Leach had told me in Edmonton. The Conservatives declared upon taking power in 2006 that emissions targets developed by the previous Liberal government under the Kyoto Protocol—a reduction of 6 percent below 1990 levels by 2012—were unachievable, and they set a new, less ambitious goal of a 20 percent cut below 2006 levels by 2020. They also said they would force large emitters to cut carbon "intensity," which measured carbon relative to production: if emissions per barrel of oil produced went down, "intensity" was deemed to be reduced even if overall production, and emissions, still rose.

The plan was never implemented. Harper won the 2008 election by opposing a proposed Liberal carbon tax, and seemed to calculate that more political benefit could be gained by opposing aggressive emissions measures. "As global climate policy momentum began to increase, Harper adopted the strategy of limiting policy change and castigating proposals for greater ambition," wrote George Hoberg, a political scientist at the University of British Columbia. Leach imagined a Conservative strategy session: "'The wedge issue here is no longer taking action on climate change. It's a whole bunch of people who are frustrated with NIMBYism and environmentalists standing in the way of economic growth, and there are potentially more votes on that side of the equation.'"

Raitt, Harper's natural resources minister from 2008 to 2010, argued that the Conservatives were reacting to circumstances. "Don't underestimate the impact that whole Keystone XL debate had upon the mindset of the minister at the time and the desire to move pipelines," she said. The long approval process for a second bid to build the Mackenzie Valley pipeline had undermined the project's financial viability. And as Obama began stalling Keystone, Enbridge faced opposition to its $7.9 billion Northern Gateway project to carry oil from Edmonton to an export terminal on the Pacific coast at Kitimat, British Columbia. Ottawa established a joint review panel of the National Energy Board and the Canadian Environmental Assessment Agency; environmentalists adopted a "mob the mic" strategy, swamping the 2011 hearings with thousands of participants and forcing the panel to extend the process by a year. "There was actually no time limit" for environmental assessments, Raitt said. "It was an infinite amount of time. . . . [Whereas] industry was asking for a finite amount of time, which I think is reasonable. You want some certainty and some clarity."

The following year, the government introduced Bill C-38 and Bill C-45, which shortened the timelines for project reviews, limited participation to those who were "directly affected" or had "relevant information and expertise," weakened protections for fish habitats and watercourses, and narrowed the definition of "environmental effects." They also gave the prime minister and his cabinet new powers: until C-38, the NEB could send only the projects it was recommending to the cabinet for approval; now rejections would be sent on as well, and the cabinet would be allowed to overrule them. "Elected officials are always going to be the ones to wear the blame when something is approved or not approved," Raitt said, "so if you're going to wear the blame, you might as well be part of the decision making."

Activists were enraged, labelling the legislation the "environmental destruction act." A former senior adviser to Harper chuckled at that. "Only in the public sphere would a thirty-month study of something . . . be considered so massively fast as to not be able to give it proper scrutiny," he said. Moderate critics argued that Harper was needlessly provoking environmentalists to adopt even more hard-line strategies, but his former adviser scoffed at that, too. Limiting intervenors to those directly affected upset the "very well-funded industry" of activists, "international people whose livelihood is intervening," and groups that fundraise off them, but they would never be satisfied, he argued. "The opposition to oil sands development is fundamental. It doesn't go down by 10 percent if you increase the consultation period by 10 percent."

The Conservatives introduced other environmental measures, such as new emissions standards for cars and a ban on any new coal-fired electricity generation that did not sequester carbon—the regulation that led to the construction of the carbon-capture plant at Boundary Dam in Saskatchewan. But Harper never brought in regulations for the oil and gas sector, despite its being the fastest-growing source of emissions and, Hoberg wrote, "the single biggest symbol domestically and internationally of his government's climate evasions." Harper's explanation shifted. First he was waiting to harmonize Canada's measures with those in the U.S., although American legislation was unlikely while Barack Obama faced a Republican Congress. Then, after the crash in oil prices in 2014, Harper declared that it would be "crazy economic policy to do unilateral penalties on that sector."

Officially, Washington insisted that it was treating Keystone XL and greenhouse gases as separate issues. The evening of June 2, 2013, Obama's new ambassador to Canada, Bruce Heyman, made his Ottawa debut at a soirée hosted by a progressive think tank. Heyman took questions onstage from Frank McKenna, a former premier of New Brunswick and former Canadian ambassador to the United States. McKenna, also a member of the board of Canadian Natural Resources Ltd., the largest oil extraction company in Alberta's oil sands, pressed Heyman on Keystone XL. The ambassador said there was no "quid pro quo" between the pipeline and climate action. But he noted that the State Department had received "a very, very large and significant number of comments" from citizens during its review of the project. "For whatever reason, people are very emotional and excited about this issue on all sides of the spectrum, those for it and those not for it." Heyman turned in his seat to look at the audience, but cast a cool glance at McKenna. "We understand this is a serious issue for Canadians, and those who participate in the oil fields," he said. "This is also a really serious issue for Americans."

In the final years of Harper's government, its frustration with climate activists deepened. The Canada Revenue Agency began auditing environmental groups on whether their political activities violated the terms of their charitable tax status. Raitt's successor as natural resources minister, Joe Oliver, accused them of receiving funds from foreign organizations. But on other fronts, the Conservatives seemed to shy away from the fight: the cabinet approved Northern Gateway, but no Conservative minister would even comment on the day of the decision. "There was zero political capital," Andrew Leach said. "Nobody [was] taking that and saying, 'We're going to sell this pipeline in B.C. or make any investment in it politically.'" Harper had twenty-one seats on the line in British Columbia, where Premier Christy Clark was holding fast to her conditions and Indigenous nations were vowing a court battle.

The pipeline battle had reached a stalemate. Environmentalists concluded that their best strategy was to defeat the Conservatives in the upcoming election. The only question was the one Mike Fletcher had posed: how best to do it?

Early in the 2015 election campaign, Stephen Harper stopped in Saint John for an invitation-only rally at the Irving Oil refinery, which had committed to buying fifty thousand barrels of bitumen a day from the Energy East pipeline. "Our Conservative government supports projects that get our natural resources to market and create good jobs as long as they are safe for Canadians and safe for the environment," Harper said. He was careful in his comments: because the National Energy Board was a quasi-judicial body, the prime minister could not be seen as influencing its review. But he added that new rules promised by his Liberal opponent would kill the project. Energy East, he said, "is subject to an independent review, and whether it goes ahead or not should be based on the facts, not on political expediency."

He was referring to Justin Trudeau's vow to "put some teeth" into the NEB. The Liberal leader was promising to require more consultations with Indigenous people during its reviews and to examine whether a project would cause more emissions. Trudeau described Harper as "a cheerleader instead of a referee," who had "torqued" the process in favour of industry. But he also blamed Harper for the fact that pipelines weren't being built. Bill C-38 was "why we can't get our resources to market right now." This was an early articulation of Trudeau's horse-trading strategy: tougher regulations would yield greater public acceptance of pipelines. "We need to get those resources to market, whether it is Energy East, whether it is a western pipeline, whether it is Keystone XL, because the alternative is more rail cars carrying oil, which nobody wants across the country," he said. It was classic Liberal middle-of-the-road equivocation, a promise of everything to everyone.

Trudeau soon displaced the NDP as the best vehicle to oust Harper, and he won a majority government that included four MPs from Alberta and forty from Quebec. Within weeks he was at the Paris climate summit, where he posed for a photo with two of his ministers and four premiers—including Quebec's and Alberta's—as well as NDP leader Tom Mulcair, former Conservative cabinet minister Ed Fast, Green Party leader Elizabeth May, and Perry Bellegarde, national chief of the Assembly of First Nations. The image oozed harmony and consensus, as if bitter partisan battles over energy and climate had come to an end in Canada.

Early in 2016, Catherine McKenna and the new Liberal natural resources minister, Jim Carr, announced independent studies on overhauling the National Energy Board and the Canadian Environmental Assessment Agency. Because that would take years, they also announced interim measures for two pipeline applications already before the board, Energy East and Kinder Morgan's expansion of its Trans Mountain pipeline from Edmonton to Burnaby, B.C. Ottawa itself would organize "deeper" consultations with Indigenous people, and would assess how the two projects would affect upstream greenhouse gas emissions. That would require more time for the NEB review of Energy East and for cabinet's final decision on the project.

This satisfied no one. Because the NEB hadn't yet declared the Energy East application complete—the legal trigger for the start of the review—environmentalists argued that Ottawa could have forced TransCanada to wait while it reformed the NEB first. But McKenna suggested that the Liberals had little choice. "It is not fair to ask a company that has been through a process—and it raises other considerations, legal considerations—to go back and wait a number of years before they get there." TransCanada, meanwhile, claimed that a review of greenhouse gas emissions was unnecessary. "There's millions of miles of pipe around the world," said Russ Girling, the CEO. "If you took a thousand miles of it out, would it change GHG emissions? The answer is no." Opponents argued that the very existence of the pipeline—and the need to pay off its construction costs over decades—would spur the extraction of more oil to fill it. But Girling countered that TransCanada's Keystone XL studies had found that "a single pipeline doesn't change upstream development or downstream development."

The Liberals had succeeded in displeasing both the builders and the opponents of pipelines. Trudeau himself sent mixed signals on the issue. "My predecessor wanted you to know Canada for its resources," he told delegates to the World Economic Forum in Switzerland in January. "I want you to know Canadians for our resourcefulness." It sounded like post-carbon utopianism—and was immediately seen in Alberta as an insult to the oil industry, which the prime minister apparently viewed as unskilled and backward. Two months later, however, at an oil industry conference in Houston, Trudeau declared that "no country would find 173 billion barrels of oil in the ground and just leave them there." At a public forum at New York University, where he was accused of campaigning against pipelines but embracing them once in power, he called the effort to block them "a simplistic solution" and "a shortcut to being concerned about climate change."

The prime minister may have been reflecting public opinion: a poll commissioned by CBC News suggested that more than half of Canadians had little or no confidence in the NEB, and Abacus Data found that Canadians, though increasingly less enthused about pipelines and more supportive of a shift to renewable and low-carbon energy, preferred "a transition, rather than an abrupt stop when it comes to the development of domestic oil." The Liberal Party had a long history of trying to have it both ways on polarizing issues. Pipelines were only the latest example.

The balancing act would become increasingly difficult. The same week McKenna announced the ad hoc NEB process, the mayor of Montreal, Denis Coderre, a former federal Liberal minister, announced on behalf of eighty-two municipalities in the metropolitan area that they would oppose Energy East. "It still represents significant environmental threats and too few economic benefits for greater Montreal," Coderre told a news conference, citing the fear of a spill expressed in public consultations. The pugnacious mayor was speaking for an urban region representing half of Quebec's population;

Saskatchewan premier Brad Wall responded with his tweet asking the province to "politely return" $10 billion in equalization payments.

Coderre had turned "a challenging issue for Justin Trudeau's government into a highly toxic one," wrote one columnist, speculating that Energy East could revive Quebec's separatist movement. Other national reporters compared it to the constitutional crises they had covered a quarter century before. "Instead of pouring oil into a pipeline, we have poured [in] all our national unity grievances," said the *Toronto Star*'s Susan Delacourt. "We've got western alienation. We've got the indigenous issues. We've got Quebec separatism. We've got the tension between provinces and municipalities. East and west. It's all in there."

The growing polarization complicated Trudeau's effort to convince the provincial premiers to agree to a price on carbon, a market incentive for lower consumption of fossil fuels. At their first meeting to discuss the idea in March 2016, he couldn't get a deal; the premiers would only endorse examining it. In July, with still no sign of a consensus, Trudeau threatened to impose a federal regime on any province that didn't develop its own. "We're going to make sure there is a strong price on carbon right across the country, and we're hoping that the provinces are going to be able to do that in a way for themselves," he declared.

Carbon pricing was, in part, another way to be seen as acting on climate change and thus obtaining "social licence" for pipelines. But social licence, a suddenly current phrase having to do with public consent, was an amorphous concept, vague and unquantifiable. And Russ Girling told the *Financial Post* that Trudeau's efforts, and Alberta's climate plan, weren't obtaining it from pipeline opponents. "It doesn't appear to be affecting their decision making," he said. "That doesn't mean we shouldn't encourage conservation, reduce emissions. Those are good policies we should be pursuing. But for particular folks like this, there doesn't appear to be any compromise." This cast climate policy as a mere transaction—a way for industry to buy approval—but that, after all, was how Trudeau himself had defined it.

With tensions increasing, the pipeline debate shifted to new terrain: the National Energy Board had declared TransCanada's Energy East application complete, starting the clock ticking on the legislated timeline of a twenty-one-month review. Cross-country hearings would open the second Monday in August, in Saint John; the board would issue a recommendation by March 2018, and Trudeau's Liberal cabinet would make its decision that fall.

The process, torqued or not, was finally underway, and would now move inexorably toward a conclusion—or so it was believed.

Four blocks from Parliament Hill in downtown Ottawa sits 123 Slater Street, one of dozens of mid-sized office buildings in the centre of the city that house the associations, lobby groups, consultants, and news organizations that orbit the seat of government. On the sixth floor is Impact Hub Ottawa, a co-working space where freelancers and start-ups come and go—the trappings of office space at a fraction of the cost. This was the workplace of Mike DeSouza, the journalist who single-handedly threw the National Energy Board's review of Energy East into disarray.

DeSouza arrived in Ottawa in 2006 from Montreal, landing at the Postmedia bureau on Parliament Hill, where he took on a beat not particularly coveted: energy and the environment. "I didn't want to step on anyone's toes, and there was this one area that wasn't being covered," he told me. But Stephen Harper had started promoting Canada as an energy superpower. "The government made it a big political story," he said.

In 2011, DeSouza was part of the press pack following Harper's annual trip to the Arctic. He filed a story on the government's decision to let a gold mine in Nunavut dump its waste in a nearby fish habitat. "Obviously, when you dig holes here, you know, you create some environmental issues and those have to be addressed," Harper said, "but that can't stop development, any more than we would let that stop development in Toronto, Montreal, or Vancouver." DeSouza saw the story as reflecting larger issues. When Bill C-38 was passed the following year, he reported on how the oil industry had influenced the legislation. "It's important as a journalist to ask questions about why this is happening," he said. "Is it truly a question of eliminating doubling up and red tape, or is it a matter of cancelling oversight and scrutiny that would have been there?"

DeSouza and four other reporters in the Postmedia bureau were laid off in a round of cuts in February 2014. The same day, he got a call from Linda Solomon Wood, the owner of the *Vancouver Observer*, a progressive online news site that was expanding nationally. She wanted DeSouza to join the *National Observer*, a new site she was launching to cover energy politics; the launch would be funded through an online campaign. "I decided this was a good opportunity to build something," he said. "I knew I was taking a leap, but I knew this was one of the solutions to help the media survive." It was a fateful decision.

In early 2016, DeSouza submitted an access-to-information request to the National Energy Board for documents about its new satellite office in Montreal and the meetings board officials were holding there with local mayors and other stakeholders. He received "scenario notes" for each meeting, including the name of the person and some briefing material. One note was for a January 15, 2016, meeting between Jean Charest, the former premier of Quebec; Peter Watson, the NEB's chair; and Jacques Gauthier and Lyne Mercier, two of the panel members hearing the Energy East application. "The first moment I saw it, I thought, 'Maybe it's okay for them to meet with a former premier,'" DeSouza recalled. Then he remembered a *Globe and Mail* story that said Charest, a corporate lawyer after leaving politics, was working for TransCanada and—though not a registered lobbyist—had tried to arrange a meeting between company officials and staffers in Trudeau's office. "I thought there might be a story there," DeSouza said.

He filed another access-to-information request, this time for notes taken at the Charest meeting and for emails sent before and after it took place. While he waited, he asked the NEB whether board officials had known that Charest was a consultant for TransCanada. The answer: Energy East had not been discussed. DeSouza filed a story on that and kept waiting.

A month later, the second batch of documents was sent to DeSouza, this time by email in a PDF file. Included was an email from Gauthier to Charest's office ahead of the meeting; Gauthier wanted to discuss "the major oil industry issues that will affect Quebec (Energy East, etc)." DeSouza called that "unusual." In another email from Gauthier, he said they would talk about "the upcoming hearing process" and would "engage in an open discussion with Mr. Charest on these topics." Notes from the meeting showed they discussed that "the economy needs investments" and, next to a reference to Lac-Mégantic, that "pipelines [are] safer."

This clearly contradicted the NEB's earlier assurance to DeSouza that the project hadn't been discussed. Spokesperson Craig Loewen apologized: "While there was no ill intent in our response, the Board deeply regrets that our search for records at that time was not comprehensive and that our response did not accurately reflect the meeting." The NEB said that its officials hadn't known Charest was a consultant for TransCanada when they sought the meeting, and that there had been no "inappropriate" discussion of "the substance" of the application.

But the revelation was sensational. Board members had also met with environmental opponents of the pipeline during a cross-country tour "to understand what was at the heart of the debate, and to be prepared to respond," Watson had written. An example was the session with Teika Newton in Kenora, but at that discussion, she recalled, "they explicitly said, 'We're not here to talk about projects.'" Newton tried to bring it up herself, of course. In the Montreal meeting with Charest, however, an NEB panellist raised it. "The difference with the Charest meeting was that Jacques Gauthier contacted Charest and asked him to come and meet," Newton said. "It was a meeting specifically about Energy East that was made at the behest of an Energy East panellist."

Steven Guilbeault of the Montreal-based environmental group Equiterre had also met the NEB panellists in Montreal. "We were a bit taken aback" by the invitation, he said. "From a legal perspective, it was very unusual." The panellists told him, too, that they weren't there to talk about Energy East.

"My colleague said, 'From a legal perspective, this is very awkward,' and they said, 'No, no, it's all good,'" Guilbeault recalled. The notes from Charest's meeting indicated that he'd talked about how the NEB should approach public opinion in Quebec. "Even if they were meeting with opponents," DeSouza said, "I think they were trying to figure out their bottom line: 'What will it take to get this group of people to say yes?'"

The two panellists who met Charest, Jacques Gauthier and Lyne Mercier, had been appointed by the Harper Conservatives. Gauthier was the former CEO of a geotechnical and energy services company; Mercier, the board's vice-chair, was a former executive at Gaz Métro. They were among forty-nine federal appointees reappointed to boards and agencies by the federal Conservatives in early 2015, with extensions postdated to take effect after the election. Gauthier's new term began in December 2015 and would run until December 2018; Mercier's would last until 2022. "Particularly with the National Energy Board, they were trying to tie the hands of the future government," a Liberal senator said.

Lisa Raitt, Harper's former natural resources minister, said in an interview that the postdated extensions were a matter of efficiency. "Getting appointments through the process is long and difficult, and Liberals notoriously—" Raitt caught herself mid-sentence. "I'm not going to say 'Liberals' because we never thought we were going to lose," she said. "We assumed we were going to win, so [we thought,] 'Let's put in place the appointments that we would normally do anyway' and continue on as business as normal when you pick it up on the other end." The panellists' meeting with Charest, Raitt acknowledged, was a mistake. "The NEB is there to make sure they do everything legally, by the book," she said. "If I were the minister in charge, I would read them the riot act."

DeSouza's story broke on August 4, a Thursday. Gauthier and Mercier, along with the third member of the panel, energy lawyer Roland George, were scheduled to be in New Brunswick the following Monday to start the Energy East hearings. But now the credibility of the process was in jeopardy— because of their role in it. "From the moment I saw the meeting notes,"

DeSouza said, "I knew that was an inevitable conclusion, that these people could not stay."

From downtown Ottawa, I returned to the Energy East route by taking Highway 417, the city's central artery, to the interchange with Highway 416 heading south. Off one exit was Fallowfield Road, a country road of farms and rustic old houses still untouched by the growing metropolis. TransCanada's compressor station No. 1217 was hidden down a long driveway. Another exit led to the Baxter Conservation Area, a park, beach, and campsite on the Rideau River that was popular with residents living in the city's southern periphery. The sun was low in the sky, and the spring grass and foliage were aglow. The remaining two lines of the TransCanada mainline passed under the park and the river. A small valve station surrounded by a fence was tucked in behind some trees. Nearby, a little panel display explained how the two lines carried natural gas from Alberta—a four-day journey, it said—to Quebec and New York. There was no mention of Energy East and diluted bitumen.

The park was flooded. Near the riverbank, trees, picnic tables, and some cabins, golden in the late-day sunlight, were reflected in the river that had risen to surround them. The water was calm and flat, the effect peaceful, but elsewhere in the Ottawa River watershed that week there were evacuations, damage, and one death. The flooding was described as a once-in-a-century event, and although no scientist tied a single flood to the warming planet, "these are the types of events brought by climate change that climatologists have been predicting for thirty years," Adam Fenech of the University of Prince Edward Island told *The Globe and Mail*. "They're just starting to show themselves now."

From the Baxter Conservation Area, the Energy East route continued south through farmlands and across country roads. Big red-brick houses dotted the well-paved rural roads; other homes were freshly painted, and there were new cars in many driveways. I crossed the CPR tracks in a flat hamlet called Mountain. Near another small community, Dixon's Corners, large windmills silently whisked the dusky air as a nearly full moon rose over the fields. Finally I turned left on Zeron Road and pulled up to the final compressor station of my pipeline journey.

The Iroquois station, built far back from the road, was difficult to make out in the gathering dark. Past the field on the other side of the road, transport trucks were roaring down Highway 401, the busiest highway in Canada. The Iroquois plant was three thousand kilometres by pipeline from the first station I saw outside Burstall, Saskatchewan, and it was the last compressor on TransCanada's Canadian mainline—the end of the segment that would be converted from gas to oil for Energy East, and the spot from which eleven hundred kilometres of new construction through eastern Ontario, Quebec, and New Brunswick would begin.

The Iroquois station also formed the bottom-right corner of a large gas triangle created by the splitting of the mainline at North Bay. Two lines came here; two others ran to a compressor station in Vaughan, Ontario, north of Toronto. Both stations connected to local gas distributors, who sold the gas to customers along the densely populated corridor between Montreal and southwest Ontario. A third TransCanada line, running parallel to Highway 401, connected Iroquois and Vaughan, completing the triangle and allowing gas to move around it in any direction to meet demand. (The triangle also reflected the continental integration of the gas market: in southwest Ontario, cheap American gas crossed the border and entered TransCanada's system at Vaughan, competing with Alberta's gas; from Iroquois, a line ran under the nearby St. Lawrence River, allowing Canadian gas to be sold into New York State and New England.)

In 2014, three local gas distribution companies supplied by the triangle, Gaz Métro, Union Gas, and Enbridge, said they would oppose the conversion of the North Bay–Iroquois line to oil for Energy East, worried that the reduction in gas capacity would compromise their reliable supply at peak demand times—and that the cost of conversion would be reflected in the distribution fee their customers would pay to recoup the capital costs of pipelines. "This is a fool's errand," Gaz Métro's CEO, Sophie Brochu, said in an unusually blunt critique delivered to the Board of Trade of Metropolitan Montreal. "Removing transport capacity between North Bay and Ottawa will put a stranglehold on our gas supply and push up the price of natural gas distributed in Quebec and Ontario. . . . Asking Quebec and Ontario natural gas consumers to subsidize oil exports makes no sense."

The following year, TransCanada signed an agreement to placate the three companies. It included $100 million to keep those bills down, and it guaranteed that TransCanada would add enough capacity to new gas line segments between Iroquois and Vaughan to allow additional gas imported across the border from the United States to replace any lost supply. The agreement demonstrated to what lengths TransCanada would go to remove obstacles to Energy East—even if it took American gas to save an ostensibly all-Canadian project.

Across Highway 401 from Zeron Road was the town of Iroquois, where one could observe another example of commercial infrastructure on an epic scale: one of the locks in the St. Lawrence Seaway that let large freighters bypass rapids and dams between the Great Lakes and the outer reaches of the river. From a small parking lot overlooking the locks, I gazed out over a two-hundred-metre-long bulk freighter, the *Federal Kivalina*. A town firefighter had brought his young daughter to watch. We listened to the crew talking on the deck and to the sound of water rushing out of the lock, lowering the ship to the level of the river downstream. Imperceptibly at first, the freighter began inching forward. The little girl gasped when she saw it moving.

Commerce always finds ways to overcome barriers, I reflected, whether it's cargo travelling by ship or oil by pipeline. But Energy East had more obstacles in its path.

Like the *Federal Kivalina*, I resumed my journey eastward.

PART FIVE

QUEBEC

12

REVERSALS

ROUTE 18 RAN EAST toward Quebec through a stretch of Ontario's history: in St. Andrew's West, near Cornwall, the Quinn's Inn, built by John Sandfield Macdonald, the province's first premier, was at the main corner. Farther along the idyllic two-lane road were the haunting stone ruins of St. Raphael's Church, once the administrative base of Upper Canada's first Roman Catholic bishop. Behind the grey husk of the church, gutted by fire in 1970, a cemetery tells of the area's Scottish history—graves marked McGillis, MacDonald, McDougall—and also, with names like Dupuis, Renaud, Viau, Richer, and Lajoie, of the intersection with another culture.

Stéphane Levac was stacking sausages in his butcher shop in Dalhousie, the first village over the border. The tiny community sat in a little notch of Quebec that protruded across Ontario's Route 23. Two hulking guys were buying meat. A bread delivery truck had parked outside Levac's shop, the only retail store left in Dalhousie. "It's like every other small town," he said. "One business dies and everything follows. People move away." He was sustained in part by Quebec's looser liquor laws, which let him sell cheap beer to his Ontario neighbours.

Across four provinces, pipeline supporters had spoken of the anti-pipeline sentiment in Quebec. But Levac told me that Energy East wasn't a pressing subject among the few dozen remaining residents of Dalhousie. "I've never seen anybody say anything negative about it," he told me. The best argument for the project was the CP rail line running behind his shop, where oil tanker cars had passed in the hundreds. "My main thing is that explosion in Lac-Mégantic," he said. "Once you've seen that, you can see it might happen somewhere else and the pipeline might not be a bad thing. . . . People are afraid of the unknown, but to me this is a safer way of doing things."

Near Dalhousie, the proposed Energy East route turned northeast and ran through farm fields. There were no longer any compressor stations or gas line right-of-way signs to look for. The new line would be built here, across rural farmland and then under the four-lane Trans-Canada Highway near the village of Pointe-Fortune, on the Ottawa River. Then TransCanada would tunnel under the riverbed to the opposite shore. To follow the route, I'd planned to take the ferry that crossed at Pointe-Fortune, but the road into town was blocked by a yellow wooden barrier: the same flooding I'd witnessed on the Rideau River had shut down the town.

Energy East's trajectory across the Ottawa River was also fraught. In 2014, TransCanada filed a study with the National Energy Board by Entec, a Calgary consulting firm. It concluded that the "horizontal directional drilling" method, or HDD, the company proposed to use to get the line under the river was "not feasible" at the company's chosen location. It predicted "higher costs, delays, and an increased environmental impact, with a heightened risk of failure."

By February 2016, TransCanada still hadn't filed a new study on how to get across. The company blamed a local municipality and the Quebec government for refusing to issue permits for more testing. "Energy East is aware this river is of interest and important to many stakeholders, and is seeking to determine the crossing method as expeditiously as possible," the company said, promising to report on what it called "an expanded approach" by the fall. But that self-imposed deadline came and went. Meanwhile, another consulting firm working for TransCanada, Golder Associates, revised the river's hazard rating from high to moderate, saying that the crossing wouldn't require a customized tunnel after all, only "regular monitoring." Duboyce told me in the summer of 2017 that the company was again looking at horizontal directional drilling—a pipe "dozens of metres beneath the riverbed" with entry and exit points "far away from the shorelines on each side of the river in order to minimize any disruptions to sensitive animal and plant habitats"—but in a new location on the river. He did not say where.

Pipeline opponents called the uncertainty alarming. "The Ottawa River has enormous ecological, commercial, historical, and recreational value," noted a report by two environmental groups in 2017; it was "difficult to understand" how TransCanada still couldn't explain its plans for crossing the river "at this late stage in the game—two and a half years after the original filing of the Energy East application." A study by the greater Montreal regional government concluded that if there was a major spill, the fast-moving current in the river would carry oil to the city's drinking water intakes within hours. (TransCanada's own studies disputed the calculations, asserting that it would take two or three times as long as the city's estimates.) A lawyer for the nearby Mohawk First Nation of Kanesatake called it "mind-boggling" that details were still lacking.

I crossed the river by backtracking from Pointe-Fortune into Ontario and using the bridge at the town of Hawkesbury. Near the span, residents on the south bank gazed at the swollen current. On the other side, Quebec's four-lane Route 50 hugged the pipeline path past the Mirabel airport and into the northern reaches of Greater Montreal. The landscape was industrial, then rural, as the Energy East route swung around the top of the city.

TransCanada would have preferred a straight west–east trajectory from Iroquois, Ontario, along existing gas line routes to reach the Suncor refinery in Montreal, one of its NEB filings said, but "the high-occupancy density" on the islands of Laval and Montreal left it with "few options." A labyrinth of residential areas, wetlands, a planned industrial park, a national park, vegetable crops, and new development along existing gas line right-of-ways forced engineers to trace a long arc north of the city to Mascouche, straddling the boundary between farmland and spreading sprawl. A small seasonal fruit and vegetable stand sat within sight of a grain silo at the three-way intersection; across a field stood newly built homes, and in the middle of the field another control point of Energy East would be built: a pump station where a lateral line would branch off and head south to Montreal.

Here, as in Dalhousie, anti-pipeline outrage was hard to find. Four residents were chatting in the middle of the intersection, their cars and trucks idling, but they didn't want to talk about Energy East. One of them pointed to the home of the man who owned the field—"*Il chiâle,*" they said, "He whines"—but at the doorstep, he said no to an interview. So I left Mascouche and drove down to Highway 40, merging into six lanes of metropolitan traffic to follow the lateral's route onto the island and into the city. Within minutes I was driving alongside the Suncor refinery. The company logo was painted in large blue letters on the white storage tanks. Behind them, a web of steel towers and pipes, reminiscent of Hardisty, stretched southward.

Six refineries were once packed into this industrial landscape in the east end of Montreal. In 2017 only Suncor remained—a decline that was also part of the debate about where Alberta's oil should go and how it should get there.

Jacques Benoit wanted to explain something about the Suncor refinery. "We talk a lot about gas, but that's only 50 percent," he said. The refinery processed 137,000 barrels of oil a day, not only into gasoline but also into asphalt, fuel oil, petrochemicals, and solvents, among others, said Benoit, the president of Unifor Local 175, which represented Suncor employees. Other companies were crammed in around the refinery, siphoning byproducts through smaller pipelines to create a range of goods. Plastic bags, detergents, patio furniture, cell phone components—they were all made with oil products, Benoit pointed out. "Even makeup for women often has a petro-leum base," he added. "They say we don't need it, but we need it."

And the refinery needed *Canadian* oil, Benoit said: its profit margins were smaller because it was forced to buy more expensive crude imported from abroad. Shell's nearby refinery, once the company's largest in Canada, closed in 2010, a decision the union blamed on higher world oil prices cutting into profit margins. "The same refinery using western crude would have been profitable enough to justify substantial investments in its growth," Daniel Cloutier of the Communications, Energy and Paperworkers Union—later merged into Unifor—said in 2013. A Deloitte study the same year estimated that based on a hundred thousand barrels a day, Energy East's supply would save Suncor between $92 million and $336 million a year on oil. For Benoit, this was an existential question. The company's Sarnia refinery processed fewer barrels per day than Montreal, he told me, but it was more profitable because it received cheaper western oil by pipeline. "They have diversity of supply," he said. "We are restricted. . . . If a company's making money there, and losing it over here, which will they close?"

Benoit had long hair swept back from his forehead, and with two chains around his neck and a bright striped shirt, he looked more like a fading Belgian pop singer than the president of a refinery union. But he was every inch a loyal employee of the fossil fuel industry, frustrated by the crusade against oil and his national union's reluctance to endorse Energy East. Unifor was debating how to reconcile a project that would benefit workers with its support for Indigenous rights and climate action. Benoit understood that, but this was his livelihood. He recalled anti-pipeline delegates—from unions not in the energy sector—at a meeting of the Quebec Federation of Labour. "I'm an environmental guy," he said, "but you know, I was looking around at every-body, and I asked myself, 'Does anyone here have an electric car parked out-side?' Nobody."

The Suncor refinery employed about five hundred people, half of whom were in the union. Benoit, a petrochemical technician, had been the local's president for five years. During that time he'd whittled down a backlog of twelve hundred grievances to a hundred and fifty, and relations with the company had improved, he said.

His tenure had also been marked by pipeline debates: before Energy East, the *oléoduc du jour* was Enbridge's Line 9B, a project that raised the same dilemmas of west–east nationalism and north–south commerce as TransCanada's proposal. The only thing that made Line 9B different, as Benoit put it, was that "it was already there."

When the United States restricted oil imports in the late fifties, Alberta producers studied a west–east pipeline to shift their shipments to refineries in Montreal. But then the Eisenhower administration exempted Canada from the restrictions on national security grounds—because Canadian oil came not by ocean-going ships but by pipelines from safely contiguous territory. Wary of jeopardizing the exemption and wanting to ensure that prairie oil moved south, the Diefenbaker government said it wouldn't allow an Alberta-to-Montreal pipeline.

And Diefenbaker went further: Ottawa created a de facto trade barrier between Ontario and Quebec. Alberta could supply Ontario refineries via the existing Edmonton–Sarnia line, but processors farther east wouldn't have access to Canadian crude; they were forced to keep importing foreign oil, including through a pipeline from the ocean at Portland, Maine, to Montreal. "The new policy would have the effect of drawing Canada closer to the United States," wrote scholar Tammy Nemeth. "The U.S. would become the major outlet for crude oil from the Canadian west, and national policy was establishing a continental, north–south trade pattern." It also dealt a blow to the notion of a shared Canadian energy market. "Western Canada and Eastern Canada might as well be different countries," lamented *Alberta Oil* magazine.

In 1973, Pierre Trudeau tried to undo Diefenbaker's decision. As part of a push for energy independence, his government subsidized the Interprovincial Pipe Line company in extending its Edmonton–Sarnia line to Montreal. But foreign oil was cheaper than Alberta's, so the line was unprofitable. The company stopped using it in 1991 and six years later asked the NEB for permission to reverse the flow—to bring imported crude through Montreal to refineries in Sarnia. Then, in 2013, after Canadian oil had become the cheaper supply, the company, now renamed Enbridge, applied to reverse the line again to bring Alberta oil to Suncor. The west–east link that Pierre Trudeau had tried to impose by state fiat was now needed to respond to market forces.

Unifor endorsed the Line 9B reversal for reasons harkening back to Trudeau's economic nationalism: "We have to safeguard our energy independence," Cloutier said in 2013, "by ensuring that oil moves from west to east." Four union locals allied themselves with a consortium of business groups to push for approval, which the NEB gave in 2015. The oil began flowing to Montreal that December.

Line 9B also represented a potential link to export markets. Suncor had already sent oil shipped by rail to Montreal to Europe via the port of Sorel-Tracy, downriver from the refinery. Another option was to relay crude from Line 9B onward to Portland, Maine, by reversing the existing pipeline connecting the port to Montreal. But neither option was ideal: only small tankers could dock in Sorel-Tracy, which meant poor economies of scale, and in Maine, activists won a municipal "Clear Skies" ordinance to block oil sands exports through Portland.

Energy East would not be afforded the relatively easy ride Line 9B was given. As early as 2013, Cloutier warned that the union might oppose it, given that most of the bitumen would flow past domestic refineries to export terminals for shipment overseas. Benoit disputed this: most of the oil coming from Alberta through Enbridge was refined in Sarnia, he said, with only ninety thousand barrels reaching Suncor in Montreal—only two-thirds of the refinery's capacity. It was still importing the rest of its supply, so western crude had a market here.

Benoit was hardly alone in supporting Energy East, even in a city and a province where opposition was strong. Robert Coutu, the mayor of Montréal-Est, said that a pipeline that was good for Suncor was also good for his city, which was adjacent to the refinery and home to many of its workers. "It's a big player on the island of Montreal. The businesses, the families—everyone benefits." Montreal's mayor, Denis Coderre, claimed to speak for all eighty-two municipalities in the region when he came out against the project, but "he didn't call us before he made his declaration," Coutu said.

Coutu had worked in New Brunswick for the Irving group of companies; one branch of the billionaire family was a partner in the proposed export terminal in Saint John. For Coutu, this lent the project more credibility. But ultimately, the pipeline was justified by market demand. "I understand people are against it, but these are people who still get around in cars," he said. And there were the dozens of idle tanker rail cars amid the industrial streetscape around the refinery, a grim reminder that without a pipeline, the industry could ship oil by train. Thousands of those tankers had passed through Coutu's municipality en route to Suncor. "If [Energy East] happens or doesn't happen isn't the question," Coutu said. "The oil has to get from Point A to Point B."

The Lac-Mégantic disaster remained seared in Quebec's consciousness. The train that exploded in July 2013—one example of the fiftyfold increase in oil-by-rail between 2009 and 2013—had come through the American Midwest, crossed into Canada at Windsor, then passed through Montreal before heading toward the Maine border to cut across the northern part of the state, the shortest route to the Irving Oil refinery in Saint John. The derailment released six million litres of oil, and the resulting inferno killed forty-seven people and destroyed thirty downtown buildings. The Transportation Safety Board concluded that the disaster was the result of human error, a "weak safety culture" at the railroad, "limited" government regulation, and tank cars that did not meet "enhanced protection standards" for shipping flammable liquids.

The oil that ignited there wasn't bitumen from Alberta but a lighter, more volatile crude from the Bakken fields of North Dakota, but it still transformed the debate about pipelines. Anti-oil activists argued that any transit of fossil fuels through Quebec was a safety and environmental risk. "People see oil, and it's 'dangerous,'" Benoit said. "It scares people. That's normal. We need strict standards. I completely agree." Others grudgingly acknowledged that a pipeline would be safer. "That doesn't mean you're enthusiastic," said Yves-François Blanchet, a former Quebec environment minister. "It means it's less bad." Ghislain Bolduc, the Liberal member of Quebec's National Assembly representing Lac-Mégantic, supported Energy East. "If you want to supply Irving Oil or Valero in Quebec and you don't have a pipeline, you have to railroad," he said.

As a former businessman and chemical engineer who'd worked in the United States, Bolduc saw Energy East through other prisms, not just that of the rail explosion. The U.S. was laced with pipelines, he said, pointing to one that ran from Houston to New York to supply parts of the eastern seaboard with gasoline. "I don't want to say the pipeline is the solution to everything," he noted. "I'm using it as an example where you have huge infrastructure and it allows a lot of savings if you invest for the long term. And TransCanada's Energy East pipeline is one of those that will last decades." Bolduc knew there was a transition to renewables coming, but "we're going to be dependent on oil for another thirty years," he said.

Even with Energy East, there was no guarantee that Suncor would buy Alberta bitumen if the price of foreign oil went lower. "You could force them," Benoit said. "The important thing for me is to get [Alberta] oil to refineries in Canada—it's our country—and not send it overseas where value will be added there. . . . You have to create jobs for your people." Benoit's logic sounded familiar: it echoed what the industry was saying in those office towers in Calgary. "If you say you don't need to use oil, great," Benoit said. "If you need to use oil, let's do it here."

But as I would be reminded, "here"—Montreal—wasn't Calgary.

The urban landscape around the Suncor refinery in the eastern end of Montreal hardly matched the city's image as a chic, classy metropolis: freight containers were stacked in a yard to the right, the vast Lafarge quarry yawned on the left. Farther on were vacant warehouses, parked tanker rail cars, discount mattress stores, more Suncor storage tanks, tire retailers, and the Resto-Bar Larry advertising *"Serveuses Sexy."* Near Shell's former refinery, now a storage terminal, a series of small pipelines passed over the street.

Hip, artsy, sophisticated Montreal was only a subway ride away. Near Place des Arts, the city's ultra-modern downtown performance venue, at an upscale bar packed with a well-dressed after-work crowd sipping cocktails, I met Audrey Yank and Marie-Ève Leclerc, two young women leading the fight to stop Alberta's oil from reaching Montreal. I mentioned the flooding on the Ottawa River. "It's a preview of the nightmare that's to come," Leclerc said. "You can't look at one event, but when you put all the events together, it's clear." People in Quebec were realizing that climate change wasn't just happening elsewhere, she said. "They're seeing the consequences. It's not one cause, one effect, but it's the accumulation of effects."

In early 2014, Yank, an environmental engineer from the Outaouais, and Leclerc, an activist from Quebec City, helped create Coule Paz Chez Nous, a loosely organized grassroots campaign against oil pipelines. Equiterre, a long-established environmental lobby group based in Montreal, had held public meetings in smaller communities along the Energy East route, but there was no organization on the ground for local residents. Coule Pas Chez Nous— "Don't spill in our home"—was designed for them. "It's to empower the local groups, to give them tools they can use for their own citizen campaigns," Leclerc said. "It was very organic."

Leclerc and Yank were also trying to fill a void left by Quebec's elected politicians. Environmentalists traditionally had the support of the left-leaning separatist Parti Québécois, but while Premier Pauline Marois had campaigned on a green energy platform, once in power she'd supported the Line 9B reversal and hadn't opposed Energy East, either. It ought to have been easy: polling by TransCanada's communications consultants, Edelman, had shown that Quebecers were more "environmentally concerned" than other Canadians, and that although they preferred Alberta oil to foreign oil, they did not "link the success of Canada's oil and gas industry to economic growth in their region." A pan-Canadian pipeline in particular would have been a convenient target for a separatist government.

Instead, Marois's government was divided on the issue. An early symbol of that division was Daniel Breton, Marois's first environment minister. A longtime, well-known activist, Breton used his environmental bona fides in 2012 to defeat a star candidate of the left-wing upstart party Québec Solidaire in a Montreal riding. Within weeks of his swearing-in as minister, he spoke out against the Line 9B reversal. "Alberta wants to bring its oil on our territory without our consent," he said, evoking a provincial election fought and won fifty years earlier on the nationalization of Quebec's hydroelectricity sector. "Are we *maître chez nous* or not *maître chez nous* on our territory?" Breton asked, borrowing the defining phrase of that campaign. "We'll see."

Breton's linking of nationalism and hydroelectric power—the emissions-free source of 99 percent of the province's electricity in 2016—was politically potent. "There's a history in Quebec with hydroelectricity and clean energy that I think people are proud of," Yank said. "That has an impact—that these kinds of [pipeline] projects aren't our way of doing things." Hydro-Québec, she added, "is seen as part of the Quebec nation, and that association is being challenged by oil projects from western Canada."

Breton's comments against Line 9B, however, put him at odds with the political exigencies of job creation. The natural resources minister, Martine Ouellet, said her goal was to help Suncor diversify its crude supply. Marois told me she shared this view: "We knew very well that there were risks, but at the same time our petrochemical industry in Montréal-Est needed that raw material to work. We said, 'Let's consult people,' but we were inclined to be favourable."

Breton soon had bigger problems than a public disagreement with his cabinet colleagues. Just weeks after taking office, the PQ fired the Liberal-appointed chair of the Bureau d'audiences publiques sur l'environnement (BAPE), the arm's-length provincial agency that conducted environmental assessments;

Breton had said he held a pro-industry bias. When it emerged that Breton had also visited the BAPE offices and asked staff for their phone numbers, he was accused of violating the agency's independence. Because Marois had a minority government, the Liberals and the third party in the legislature, the Coalition Avenir Québec, were able to schedule committee hearings into Breton's actions. But before that could take place, newspapers revealed a series of minor legal infractions from his past. He resigned the next day.

In the same week as Breton's downfall, Marois met with Alison Redford, the premier of Alberta, to discuss Energy East. During a summer gathering of Canadian premiers in Halifax, the two premiers agreed to set up a joint working group to examine the project. "There's certainly an economic advantage given the jobs that could be created in Quebec," Marois told reporters. "We have a significant petrochemical industry." It looked like the PQ would not try to block Energy East. "She was a very reasonable supporter of the project, I will say," said Dallas McCready, an adviser to David Alward, then the premier of New Brunswick. "She knew it would be met with environmental concerns, but she also understood the economic importance and was approaching it with the best of intentions, and appreciated the position New Brunswick was in and wanted to be as supportive as she could in the most prudent way."

Marois told me, however, that too much was read into her comments. "If you review the coverage . . . you'll see that journalists said 'It seems' or 'The Marois government would have a favourable view,'" she said. "We never, ever said on the public stage that we would eventually accept that project." To prepare for our interview, the former premier told me, she'd reviewed media coverage of her comments and consulted advisers from that period. She insisted that the record showed she never endorsed Energy East outright. "We always had doubts," she said. "I wanted to maintain good relations with my counterparts in Alberta and New Brunswick, who were very interested in the project. But my own reaction was I had great doubts."

———

Daniel Breton was replaced as environment minister by Yves-François Blanchet, a second-term MNA from Drummondville. Though Blanchet was smoother and more polished than his predecessor—his background was in music management—his environmental credentials were limited to organizing Quebec's Earth Day activities for three years.

Sitting in the cafeteria at Radio-Canada's Montreal studios, where he frequently appeared on a television panel of former politicians, Blanchet described himself as a pragmatist—a not-too-subtle critique of Breton. "If you arrive at the environment ministry and you say you're going to impose your principles without compromise, you're not doing anything for society because you're going to lose your department within a week," he said. "So you seek the maximum gain according to your convictions."

Blanchet said he had "no sympathy" for fossil fuel projects, and found Energy East particularly hard to swallow; he recalled seeing figures that told a different story from Jacques Benoit's—that Suncor's refinery, and Valero's in Quebec City, received almost enough oil from Line 9B and so didn't need Energy East. Quebec would be a mere transit corridor for the export of dirty oil. "But your job as environment minister is not to block everything that moves," he said.

In May 2013 Blanchet announced that Quebec would allow drilling for gas on Anticosti Island, which many environmentalists saw as a PQ betrayal. "I'm not here to denounce, to condemn, to reproach," Blanchet told reporters, calling himself a "partner" of the business sector. "There are people who want us to block things outright," he said. "That's not my goal. That's not my job. That's not my mandate." Breton, relegated to the backbench, struggled to rationalize his continued fealty to the PQ when he would encounter his one-time activist allies, though he eventually endorsed the Anticosti drilling, arguing that natural gas would serve as a transitional fuel during the shift away from oil.

The pipeline issue remained divisive within the PQ. Line 9B was still before the National Energy Board in mid-2013, with Quebec journalists reporting that ministers were divided on it and on Energy East. The finance minister, Nicolas Marceau, declared that cheap western oil was going to come to Quebec and New Brunswick "one way or another, so a pipeline is inevitable." Marois told me that "some were favourable" to Energy East, "but I remember the debates we had, and others were fiercely opposed. . . . There were tense debates."

Blanchet asked TransCanada to voluntarily submit its proposal to a review by the BAPE, Quebec's environmental assessment agency, but the company said no. This put the PQ in a bind: because the pipeline would cross provincial boundaries, it was by law subject to federal oversight alone; Quebec lacked the power to block it. Using the province's geographical position to disrupt commerce between two other regions of Canada risked making Marois's government look like a band of left-wing radicals in the eyes of world markets. The PQ had to be "good players in the North American economy to help the eventual transition to a sovereign Quebec," Blanchet said.

But Marois had a different account. "In my immediate entourage, it had been decided that we would not accept the project," she said. Even Lac-Mégantic, a vivid illustration of the alternative to pipelines, did not sway her. Rail could be safer "if we took the proper safety measures," she said. And, she added, "the railroad was already there—a railroad that's already there versus a pipeline that we have to build." If the PQ had been re-elected in 2014, Marois said, "we definitely would not have accepted it. We would have rejected it."

And yet Marois was never forced to act. She called an early election, hoping to secure a majority, but lost to the Liberals. The PQ was suddenly unburdened of the Energy East dilemma, just as the debate around it began to intensify.

The pipeline battle in Quebec entered a new phase the night of November 23, 2014, when one of the province's best-known activists appeared on television screens around the province.

Gabriel Nadeau-Dubois had become a household name in Quebec in

2012 as a leader of a mass protest movement by university students against tuition increases proposed by the Liberal government of Jean Charest. He wrote a memoir of the protests, *Tenir tête*, which won the Governor General's Award for French-language non-fiction. A few days after the announcement, he appeared on Radio-Canada's *Tout le monde en parle*, an interview program watched weekly by more than a million viewers. Nadeau-Dubois, a separatist, said that the Governor General's Award was "not exactly the institution I had in mind when I wrote the book."

The charismatic twenty-four-year-old had a knack for showmanship and symbolism. "I decided to take this money that comes from a federal institution"—the award had bestowed twenty-five thousand dollars—"and put it at the service of a cause that represents Quebec's historical ambition for self-determination," he said on television that night. "I chose the struggle that, at the moment, best represents Quebec's desire to choose our own destiny." The beneficiary would be Coule Pas Chez Nous, the grassroots group formed to stop the Energy East pipeline, which, he said, would "make Quebec a highway for the oil sands." And, he added, he was challenging Quebecers to match his donation.

Audrey Yank, one of the leaders of Coule Pas Chez Nous, couldn't believe the response. "Donations were coming in for thousands of dollars," she said. Nadeau-Dubois's pledge was matched the same night. Four hundred thousand dollars poured in over the next week. The Energy East debate had been simmering for months in Quebec, but now it caught fire. "The issue was already known," Yank told me, "but Coule Pas Chez Nous allowed [people] to do something." The organization used the money to incorporate as a non-profit foundation and start funding local anti-pipeline projects along the route.

One of Coule Pas Chez Nous's most effective stunts would be an anti-pipeline beer. All twelve thousand bottles sold in one night, and the launch generated international media coverage, but for Yank the most telling aspect was that twenty craft breweries around Quebec supported the campaign. "It's the first time in Quebec that there's been a mobilization of the private sector against a project," she said. Anti-pipeline sentiment was going mainstream.

Blanchet wasn't persuaded that the groundswell of support for Nadeau-Dubois was based on anything real. "I think Quebecers are complacent about being green," he said. But politicians quickly adjusted to what seemed to be a hardening of public sentiment against Energy East. Quebec's new Liberal premier, Philippe Couillard, had favoured the project during the spring 2014 election campaign, saying that the pipeline would spur development of the port in Cacouna, a village on the lower St. Lawrence River where TransCanada planned to build an Energy East export terminal. He also argued that Quebec, a beneficiary of equalization payments, owed it to other provinces to help sell their products. Later that year, however, Couillard attached conditions to his support, demanding that TransCanada hold more consultations, take responsibility for all environmental risks, and assess the impact on emissions.

As Couillard became less decisive, the Parti Québécois became more stridently anti-pipeline. The interim leader, Stéphane Bédard, denounced the Liberal premier as too acquiescent. "British Columbia said no, the United States said no, but Philippe Couillard said yes," he told a party convention. For the Liberals, the St. Lawrence River was "nothing more than a highway for oil exports," Bédard declared, but for the PQ, "it's the heart around which Quebec was built." He tied this to the party's raison d'être: "It's up to us to decide what happens on our territory," he said, calling Energy East "the best argument to achieve sovereignty. As a country, we can retake control of our river." The party, out of power, was suddenly playing a nationalist card it had refused to play when it was in government. Yves-François Blanchet, who lost his seat in 2014, attributed it to potential leadership candidates' cultivation of the party's base as they jockeyed to replace Marois: "Ministers who had supported the government's position because it was their job . . . became environmental heroes and took very strong positions against TransCanada."

Jacques Benoit, of the refinery union, found the growing opposition frustrating. "It's their right, except I think they've got bad information," he told me. He blamed TransCanada's early missteps, which included preparing its 39,000-page NEB application in English only and skipping public consultations held by Montreal's regional council. "Energy East didn't start well," he said. "They're not transparent, and that makes people doubtful."

Audrey Yank and Marie-Ève Leclerc from Coule Pas Chez Nous took some credit for the shifting party positions, but they didn't see electoral politics as their vehicle. "If the party in power is against it, great, but we're not counting on it," Yank said. "People have tried all kinds of conventional ways—petitions, meeting their elected members, public consultations—and there's a lot of disenchantment with that, a lack of confidence that those methods can represent their views. . . . When those means don't work, when institutions aren't listening, people are prepared to use other methods, to escalate." And activists in Quebec, she added, could escalate in a manner that their counterparts in other provinces could not: "The pipeline is already there in English Canada. Here they still have to build it."

13

THE RIVER

STEVEN GUILBEAULT NEVER EXPECTED to be where he found himself on November 22, 2015: at a podium in Edmonton, applauding the climate and energy policies of an Alberta NDP government. Rachel Notley was announcing her climate plan, including a carbon tax and an emissions cap, and Guilbeault—on behalf of Equiterre, the Montreal-based environmental group he helped found in 1993—was nodding his approval, in tandem with executives from four oil sands companies standing nearby. "I supported that plan—we supported that plan—because we felt it was a significant step forward," Guilbeault told me.

Yet there were flaws in Notley's plan, he continued. "The cap is not as absolute as people would like us to believe. We feel it's too high." Oil sands emissions were at seventy megatonnes in 2016, and Canada wouldn't be able to reach its Paris targets if Alberta let them climb to Notley's cap of one hundred megatonnes. But if Equiterre and others managed to block pipelines, Guilbeault said, Paris might be achievable. "If they don't have pipelines, they won't increase production. It is another cap by default." Notley drafted her policies to make pipelines more politically palatable;

Guilbeault said they could work only if pipelines were halted. They were operating at cross-purposes, but in the short term, the premier's plan was better than none.

Bathed in the natural light of his Montreal office, dressed in a crisp white shirt and sporting a short haircut and beard, Guilbeault described the lessons of a quarter century of activism, including the failure of the Kyoto Protocol. "Countries thought they could tackle climate change by just doing more of the good stuff, the better stuff, that we needed: more renewables, more transit," he told me. "But what became very clear was we weren't going to tackle this unless we tackle our dependency on fossil fuels." If society couldn't wean itself quickly, he said, it should at least use less of the high-emissions bitumen from the oil sands. "We figured if we could stop enough proposed pipeline projects, by default the production would stop increasing."

Other environmentalists saw a contradiction in Guilbeault's purported goals and his willingness to stand with Notley, but Equiterre had a long record of partnerships with corporations and the political establishment. The organization received 10 percent of its budget from the Quebec government, and its modern headquarters in downtown Montreal had been built with donations from major Quebec corporations, including a large forestry company, on land leased from Hydro-Québec for a dollar a year. In 2010, Jeffrey Simpson, *The Globe and Mail's* national affairs columnist, gave Guilbeault his mainstream stamp of approval, applauding his pragmatism and quoting him approvingly on the need to "enlarge the tent and work with business." He predicted a bright future for the activist, including a possible career in politics.

This benediction, and the disapprobation of more strident climate activists, didn't earn Guilbeault a pass from the oil sands' most vocal defenders. Vivian Krause, the Vancouver writer who criticized U.S. funding for Canadian environmental groups, noted that in 2015, Equiterre received $100,000 from the anti–oil sands Tides Foundation in San Francisco. "It's a very small percentage of our budget," Guilbeault said. "If we can't receive money from outside of Canada, neither should TransCanada or Enbridge.

If it's okay for these guys to get money from all over the world from investors, why can't we? If we can't, they can't either."

Guilbeault was decidedly mainstream in his tactics. He wanted to win the pipeline battle with sound arguments, not with street protests. He asserted that Energy East wasn't needed to feed Suncor's Montreal refinery, as Benoit had argued; Suncor was already exporting much of the oil that came through Line 9B rather than refining it locally. He also told me Suncor had actually cancelled the purchase of a coker it would need to process bitumen at the refinery, and hadn't committed—as Irving had in Saint John—to refining a fixed amount of oil from Energy East.*

Guilbeault was similarly moderate in his approach to the National Energy Board. No matter how flawed the board was, he wouldn't support boycotting it or blocking its Energy East review. "Different groups have different opinions," he said. "We thought it was better for us to participate in a deficient process while demanding changes than to not be there at all." Equiterre had appeared at Line 9B hearings by a Quebec legislative committee, and some of the committee's recommendations "were taken directly from the work we'd done." Guilbeault hoped to have the same influence on the NEB—to use the regulatory mechanisms, as weak as he said they were, to wage his battles. "We don't like the strategy of the empty chair."

To leave Montreal, I drove back through the industrial periphery of the city, past the giant white storage tanks of the Suncor refinery. Highway 40 crossed the Rivière des Prairies and met the Energy East route where it came down

---

*   Guilbeault never sent me the documentation he'd promised to back up these assertions, and Suncor did not respond to my request for a clarification of how much of Line 9B's oil it was refining in Montreal and how much, if any, was exported. In 2016, a TransCanada official estimated that 55 to 60 percent of Energy East's dilbit would be exported, with the balance to be refined in Montreal, Quebec City, and Saint John.

from the lateral point in Mascouche and continued east. Parallel to the highway, and to the pipeline route, was a two-lane road hugging the St. Lawrence River called the Chemin du Roy.

Completed in 1737, the road was the first in eighteenth-century Quebec, the nation-building infrastructure project of its time. A dirt track a few metres wide, it allowed the French colonists to travel the 280 kilometres between Quebec and Montreal by carriage in summer and sleigh in winter. Crossing thirty-seven of the land grants known as *seigneuries*, the Chemin du Roy united the disparate communities of Lower Canada economically and politically. Today, provincial Route 138 follows roughly the same path through the towns and villages along the river and is marked with tourist-route signs bearing the words "Chemin du Roy" and the image of a crown.

About fifty kilometres east of the Suncor refinery, the Chemin du Roy runs through the town of Lanoraie. On a small boardwalk on the river, I found the Senate in session—a gathering of some of the town's oldest and wisest men, who shuffled onto the benches most days to watch the St. Lawrence and discuss the latest news. One of them, Jean-Guy Bonin, had carved a little wooden sign into the railing, marking the spot in red letters as "Le Sénat."

Energy East was a subject that Lanoraie's five senators knew well: the route would pass about five kilometres north of the village. "Honestly, I'm in favour," Bonin declared. "We're going to consume oil one way or another, and to consume it, we need to transport it. And it's the safest way to transport it." He understood the environmental concerns, "but how long will it take us to get off oil and switch to electricity?" he asked. "It could take fifty years."

These men had little time for the noisy activists of downtown Montreal. "They're against everything," Jocelyn Brazeau said. "If there wasn't a pipeline, they'd find something else to protest." A gas pipeline had been built near the village half a century earlier, Yvon Bonin said, and there had never been an incident; a helicopter flew over a couple of times a week to inspect it. "If that were today, everyone would say, 'We can't have a gas line, it'll explode,'" Jean-Guy Bonin added. "But it's been there for fifty years."

This was a Quebec that didn't subscribe to radical politics. In the heart of Montreal, urban environmentalists were fuelling the growth of Québec Solidaire, a party that was cannibalizing the Parti Québécois's left-wing base. But Yves-François Blanchet, the former PQ minister, considered them out of touch with reality. "You can promise an ideal world because you're never going to have to deliver an ideal world," Blanchet had told me. "They have a lot of support among young people, and those young people have strong support for the environment." But, he said, "in Montreal, people, notably those who use public transit, are not very sensitive to people in Abitibi who would not be able to go work without their cars that consume gas." Jocelyn Brazeau cocked his head over to where I'd parked my car. "How did you get here?" he asked. "Did you walk?" His fellow senators chuckled in agreement: end of debate.

The aging senators, of course, did not have to fret over what the planet would look like in 2030 or 2050. But a vision of that future wasn't far away. Past Lanoraie, the Chemin du Roy hugged the banks of the St. Lawrence. Near Berthierville, sandbags began to appear, packed around houses to hold back the river steadily filling their backyards. This was more of the unusually severe flooding I'd seen on the Rideau River and at Pointe-Fortune. Past the town, water filled fields on both sides of the road, leaving the Chemin du Roy a narrow lifeline of asphalt amid nature's revolt. This was Canada's climate destiny, Prime Minister Justin Trudeau told reporters after surveying the flooding. "We're going to have to understand," he said, "that bracing for a hundred-year storm is maybe going to happen every ten years now, or every few years."

The pipeline route continued east along Highway 40 toward Quebec City. The last major interchange before the provincial capital was at Saint-Augustin-de-Desmaures, a bedroom community that stretched from the highway down a steep hill to flat lands running along the St. Lawrence. The municipal road there included nine kilometres of the old Chemin du Roy of 1737, now paved in asphalt, the longest stretch of the original road in the province.

The name fit here. Past the farmhouses and fields stretching out to the banks were several large modern houses closer to the river. Some were tucked down tree-lined driveways or behind trimmed hedges; others, close to the road, were regally visible to passing traffic. Greater Quebec City was booming thanks to well-paying civil service and university jobs and a growing private sector; senior government officials and CEOs were choosing to live in Saint-Augustin-de-Desmaures, building million-dollar homes on spectacular river-front lots a half-hour from their offices. "It's close to nature and close to the city. It's the best of both worlds," the mayor, Sylvain Juneau, told me. Reliant on fossil fuels for their daily commutes, these high earners were nonetheless suspicious of an oil pipeline in their quasi-rural paradise. "People don't want any additional risk," Juneau said. "People are asking questions."

As it happened, Mayor Juneau was a civil engineer. "That's my world—I know what I'm talking about—and I see no gain for our city," he said. "If there's a leak a kilometre from the river, it goes in the river. That's the concern." If the project was approved, he said he would "symbolically" demand that TransCanada create an emergency response fund for the city and donate a million dollars a year per kilometre of pipe within municipal limits, a total of $6 million. But Juneau knew he had no power to force TransCanada to pay anything other than property taxes—and, he said, even $6 million a year wouldn't win his support.

In other cities in this part of Quebec, there were signs of support for Energy East. The mayor of Trois-Rivières, Yves Lévesque, welcomed the possibility of a pumping station in his city, and mayors in the Quebec City region cheered the prospect of a lateral line to the Valero refinery in Lévis, making the same arguments that applied to Suncor in Montreal—that more supply options would help guarantee the facility's survival. But in Saint-Augustin, Juneau said, "I've had no citizen come up to me and say, 'It's a good project and we have to do it.' I've had a huge number say, 'It can't come through here.'" Energy East had even united the town's fractious council. Juneau won the mayor's seat in a by-election after his predecessor resigned in a tax controversy, but the departed mayor's allies still controlled the council. "I was elected based on my denunciations of the incompetence of those people," Juneau said. "We never agree—except on the pipeline. That's the only issue where we get along. We're all against it, unanimously." He acknowledged that Alberta's oil wealth benefited Quebec through equalization payments—"I see it at the national level. . . . We're Augustinians and Québécois, and we're Canadians, too"—but it wasn't enough to win him over.

A couple of kilometres west of the city's residential neighbourhoods, TransCanada faced one of the most difficult engineering challenges of the entire 4600-kilometre trajectory from Alberta: getting the pipeline under the St. Lawrence. "We don't know what kind of tunnel, what kind of this, what kind of that," Juneau said. "It's still very fluid." As of mid-2017, TransCanada wouldn't, or couldn't, say how it would pass under the river.

In 2014, the local newspaper, *Le Soleil*, obtained a copy of a study by Entec, TransCanada's Calgary consultants, which called horizontal direction drilling here "technically feasible, but high risk." A pipeline tunnel of that length, 3.4 kilometres, with that diameter, forty-two centimetres, "has never been executed," and failure, the study said, "is always a possibility." TransCanada wouldn't send me a copy of the report, but one of its NEB submissions said that it had "thoroughly investigated" its options here. An existing natural gas tunnel was too narrow for an additional pipeline, and TransCanada's first choice for a new tunnel was too close to Saint-Augustin homes. Université Laval objected to a second option that would cut through its experimental farm. The company settled on a third spot farther west, but that resolved only the location, not the fundamental engineering challenges. The May 2016 report by Calgary-based Golder Associates—the same one that lowered the Ottawa River's hazard rating from "high" to "moderate"—warned that the St. Lawrence still warranted a "high" rating. It was also the only crossing along the entire route where Golder recommended a Phase III hydrotechnical hazards assessment, the highest standard. That assessment was still not underway in early 2017.

"All of Quebec was built around this river," Juneau said. "It's the soul and the heart of the province's development. Quebec was founded in 1608, Montreal a few years later, and the river was the axis." A community was established at Saint-Augustin in 1691, but its history with the river ran even deeper. Along the Chemin du Roy, a plaque paid tribute to the Filles du Roy, the women brought from France to marry the early colonists. A seigneury was granted in 1647, and the first settlers came in 1665; the plaque listed seventeen women who helped start the first families. A quotation from the Quebec author Anne Hébert exhorted readers to "call them by name, facing the river from where they came in the seventeenth century, to bring us into the world, and the country along with us."

The St. Lawrence is "our blood system. It's what brings everything everywhere—including problems, when we see these floods," Juneau said. In other parts of the world, people were desperate for water, "and here we're trying to push it back because we're flooded. So it's a powerful symbol. . . . And it's a fine line between having it in abundance and not having any if there were a major pipeline accident."

For drivers of fossil fuel–powered cars, crossing the St. Lawrence was easy. The Pierre Laporte Bridge spanned it near the mouth of the Chaudière River. On the other side, a web of highway interchanges led me to the eastbound Trans-Canada Highway, Route 20. The highway and the pipeline route crossed the Etchemin River, another waterway where TransCanada's preferred method of tunnelling was deemed "not feasible" by its consultants.

In the city of Lévis, the Valero oil refinery's gas flare gleamed bright, even against the clear blue sky. Another Energy East lateral would allow delivery of Alberta bitumen to Valero, although the company said in 2016 that it was getting enough crude from Line 9 to supply the facility and that it would source oil "from where it's most economical to do so," including overseas.

Early in its planning work, TransCanada had intended Energy East to end near here, at a marine export terminal on the St. Lawrence a few kilometres past the refinery, where 285-metre Suezmax tankers would load bitumen for foreign markets. But local opposition was "significant," the company wrote in its NEB filings, and so when the case was made that the deep waters of the Bay of Fundy would accommodate even larger 330-metre tankers—improving the economies of scale for shippers—it proposed extending the project to New Brunswick. The most direct route from Lévis would cut through northern Maine, but given U.S. opposition to Keystone XL, TransCanada never examined that option, choosing instead to go around the top of the state to reach Saint John.

Long green fields to my left sloped down to the shimmering St. Lawrence along Highway 20. Flocks of hundreds of snow geese were making their annual stop on their spring migration from the U.S. eastern seaboard to their Arctic breeding grounds. The proposed pipeline route followed a ridge of hills on my right that rose higher the farther downriver I drove. Gradually the hills pulled farther away, bending over and around the northern tip of Maine toward New Brunswick. At the city of Rivière-du-Loup the Trans-Canada veered south, too, but I kept following the St. Lawrence. The river was opening up—twenty kilometres across now, almost ten times its width at Saint-Augustin-de-Desmaures—and the mountains on the north shore were taller and more ragged. There was a final stop to make in Quebec, the scene of the first major showdown over Energy East.

The village of Cacouna hugs the river's edge just past Rivière-du-Loup. After TransCanada decided to extend the route this far on the way to Saint John, Cacouna was chosen as the location for a second export terminal for Suezmax tankers, complementing the one in Saint John. A federal port, Gros-Cacouna, had been established in the fifties for cement and wood exports, but had never really boomed. In 2007, TransCanada proposed a liquefied natural gas import terminal there so that Quebec distributors could purchase foreign gas and depend less on western Canada. The project was abandoned, but Cacouna's port stayed on the company's radar. A forty-kilometre lateral would run from the main Energy East line to the terminal.

TransCanada had examined eight possible terminal sites along the St. Lawrence. Cacouna was the best choice, but it wasn't perfect. "Despite the longstanding designation of the Port of Gros-Cacouna as an industrial site," the company observed in one NEB filing, "the nearby village of Cacouna is viewed by many to be a quiet, historical south-shore community in a region typically valued for summer holidaying and relaxing." Another passage noted that "the primary challenges that exist for this site are environmental in nature and sensitive marine and avian populations are present." Directly next to the port is the Kiskotuk Coastal Park, a network of bird-watching sites, nature reserves, and hiking trails sprawling along the shoreline, encompassing salt marshes, forests, and rocky bluffs overlooking the river. Beyond it is the Baie de L'Isle-Verte National Wildlife Area. Birds were calling all around me as I roamed the trails through the wetlands, avoiding a few remaining patches of snow. Sunlight glittered in a pond. A large Coast Guard vessel sat silently over at the port.

TransCanada's assessment of the environmental challenges in Cacouna proved prescient. In 2013, two activists from nearby Rimouski, Martin Poirier and Benoit St-Hilaire, heard that TransCanada was negotiating with landowners and working with the municipal council on the marine terminal. "We had to move fast because they were already at 'Yes,'" Poirier said. "The council was already in favour of it." St-Hilaire began attending its meetings. Councillors were "very cavalier" about fielding questions from the public, St-Hilaire said. "It really angered people." Opinion in the village was split. Seven hundred people attended a march that St-Hilaire, Poirier, and others organized in April 2014.

Coming from Rimouski, an hour away, the two activists were labelled as interlopers by local supporters of Energy East. "They said it was just people from elsewhere who were raising it," St-Hilaire said as we drank local craft beer on a picnic table overlooking the water. "Our answer was that the St. Lawrence belongs to everyone." The river's marine life was the key: a community of beluga whales, a species classified as threatened, had its birthing grounds just off the port, near where a TransCanada jetty would extend seven hundred metres into the river. The company had scheduled seismic testing during the whales' calving season. Robert Michaud, a marine biologist and head of the Groupe de recherche et d'éducation sur les mammifères marins, a research institute in Tadoussac on the north shore of the St. Lawrence, declared it a risk to the whales. "We really leaned on that, because opposing for opposing wasn't enough," Poirier said. "We needed an argument. That crystallized the start of the struggle."

TransCanada agreed to precautions, including having its boats honour a maximum speed and keep a minimum distance from the whales. The activists used Facebook to organize a citizens' watch on the bluff at Kiskotuk to monitor compliance. "Anytime there was an anomaly, something that wasn't right, we reported it right away," St-Hilaire said. In September 2014 the Quebec Superior Court granted an injunction against testing until the end of the whales' calving season, the first legal setback of any kind for Energy East. "Professional opponents suddenly think they have a monopoly on the well-being of the belugas, when we've got a department full of environmental engineers," a frustrated TransCanada official told Radio-Canada.

Cacouna turned into a *cause célèbre* in Quebec. A second protest in October 2014 attracted twenty-five hundred people from around the province. In messages published in a community newsletter, Cacouna's mayor, Ghislaine Daris, lamented the "agitation" in the village and emphasized that the council had no say in whether the project was approved—but would meet its "moral" obligation to ensure that safety and environmental norms were respected. She also addressed accusations that she and her council were negotiating with TransCanada behind closed doors. "Rest assured that we are acting professionally and with complete transparency," she said.

In December 2014, the Committee on the Status of Endangered Wildlife in Canada, a group of scientists, issued a decisive recommendation: the federal government should change the beluga's status from threatened to endangered. Ottawa complied, a turning point in Cacouna—"the nail in the coffin," according to St-Hilaire. TransCanada's spokesperson in Quebec, Philippe

Cannon, had told reporters that Cacouna was an "indispensable" part of the project because smaller ships serving different markets would load oil there. But the company halted its work at the port immediately after the beluga decision. "We knew they were going to throw in the towel," St-Hilaire said. "We chewed up Philippe Cannon. He was a little biscotti to us."

TransCanada made it official the following April. "Moving away from Cacouna is the right thing to do," it declared in a statement. The company claimed that it had intended all along to adjust its plans if new scientific evidence required it. Daris called the decision a setback for the village and the port. "We did everything we could, but it didn't work out," she said.

TransCanada said it would look for another export terminal site in Quebec and would have to amend its NEB filings, pushing back the completion date for Energy East to 2020. "It goes without saying but we'll say it anyway," TransCanada added. "Our decision was certainly not made because of opposition from some well-funded groups that want to deny Canadians the right to benefit from a reliable domestic supply of energy that ensures Canadians enjoy the quality of life they've come to expect in this country every day." But St-Hilaire knew better. "There was a sequence of events, a chain of events, all of which worked in our favour, by which I mean in favour of the non-acceptability of the project."

A few months later, the company announced it was abandoning plans for an export terminal anywhere in the province, and would instead build a larger terminal in Saint John. This surrender had the potential to cut two ways: it reduced Energy East's environmental footprint in Quebec, giving opponents a smaller target. But it also meant fewer economic spinoffs, making the project harder to sell on that basis. And perhaps most importantly, it emboldened anti-pipeline activists throughout Quebec, proving that a well-organized protest campaign could have an impact.

TransCanada adopted a new strategy: cooperation—and deference to public opinion. The company hired Louis Bergeron, a chemical engineer who had overseen the construction of a small refined-fuel pipeline from Valero's refinery to Montreal, as its new vice-president for the province. His job was to win over Quebecers. "Maybe they didn't like the way it was presented, didn't like the approach, didn't like the tone," Bergeron said. "And this is exactly what we're changing now." The company signed a contract with a Quebec engineering firm to build electrical units for the pipeline's pump stations, a deal that would create 120 jobs. On social media, it highlighted seven hundred route changes it had made in the province, however small, to accommodate local concerns. TransCanada had agreed to the less onerous of two possible reviews by the BAPE, Quebec's environmental assessment agency, but after anti-pipeline groups and the Quebec government sought court injunctions, it declared itself eager for the more rigorous version. "It's very clear that the government and the people have concerns about sources of drinking water," spokesperson Tim Duboyce told Bloomberg. "That's totally natural and we share that." The BAPE process, he said, was an opportunity "to continue to answer questions about the project, including safety measures and mitigation measures."

But TransCanada had few other cards to play at that point. It could only acquiesce to whatever new requirements Quebec would impose. Steven Guilbeault predicted that the BAPE would set conditions TransCanada wouldn't be able to meet. "It's hard to imagine the report being favourable to the project," he said. "I've been more and more convinced that this project is never going to happen, if only because of the amount of opposition there is in Quebec."

Then came the *National Observer* story on Jean Charest's secret meeting with the NEB. In the wake of a public inquiry about corruption in government construction contracts, the news that the board's chair and two Energy East panel members had met with Charest heightened skepticism about the federal regulatory process. "What Quebecers increasingly detest," Yves-François Blanchet said, "are these little decisions made behind closed doors, with a little pat on the back, and 'When we leave here, we'll pretend we don't know each other and put an official, formal shell on it.' That's what it looked like."

Denis Coderre, Montreal's mayor, called for a suspension of the hearings, and a Quebec environmental group submitted a formal complaint to the board. Transition Initiative Kenora filed a motion under NEB rules; it noted that Teika Newton's meeting with NEB officials in Kenora during its "national engagement tour" was disclosed publicly by the board and hadn't included any members of the Energy East panel. Newton quoted the NEB's own rules: "Decision-makers must base their decisions, and must be seen to be basing their decisions, on nothing but the relevant law and the evidence that is properly before them." The panel members were tainted by bias, she argued, and should recuse themselves.

This procedural drama unfolded as the NEB review was getting underway with two weeks of hearings in New Brunswick. Montreal would be next, and a coalition of Quebec business groups and unions held a news conference to endorse the pipeline, as they had for Line 9B. But the show of support was overshadowed by the controversy over the Charest meeting. The board asked for submissions on how it should deal with the issue. "I was surprised it took them that long to make a decision, and that they tried to let the process continue without doing anything," the *Observer*'s Mike DeSouza said.

The NEB set up shop at Montreal's Centre Mont-Royal conference facility on the morning of August 29, 2016, with Mayor Denis Coderre scheduled as the first intervenor. Almost immediately, a man rushed to the front of the room, yelling, "Fire the National Energy Board!" He and six other activists unfurled a banner, chanted "*Annulez l'audience*"—Cancel the hearing—and refused to heed security guards telling them to sit down. Chaos broke out, and eventually the police removed the activists. The NEB cancelled the day's hearing, citing the need for safety. But when they didn't reconvene the next day, or the next, it was apparent that the board was in crisis.

Environmentalists kept up the pressure. Equiterre was among several organizations that submitted letters of support for Newton's motion. Her lawyer filed a second motion, upping the ante: Gauthier and Mercier had presided over two weeks of hearings in New Brunswick and had been part of dozens of rulings, including on the completeness of TransCanada's application and on who could intervene. If they were recused, Newton argued, the Energy East proceedings up to that point "should be quashed in their entirety" and restarted from scratch. This would delay the hearings and an eventual decision by months, but on September 9, the board mostly agreed: all three panel members recused themselves, and the NEB's chair, Peter Watson, also withdrew from any dealings with the review. While the existing intervenor list would be allowed to stand, a new panel would reconsider whether TransCanada's application was complete.

Radical activism and procedural arguments had combined to reset the clock. A decision by March 2018 was no longer possible. "It was quite a confluence of events," Newton told me. "It sort of became the perfect storm." Mike DeSouza said the protest may have persuaded the NEB that the Charest story "was starting to have serious consequences on public opinion in Quebec that they didn't have that appearance of fairness."

The oil sector and the country's political class reeled. Former prime minister Brian Mulroney called on Justin Trudeau to show leadership by building a consensus for what he called a "grand nation-building exercise." But Quebec's premier, Philippe Couillard, told reporters that the concerns were "legitimate. . . . We do realize that resources have to gain access to markets, but this being said, we will not compromise our people's security and safety as far as water is concerned." Ghislain Bolduc, the Liberal member for Lac-Mégantic who supported the pipeline, seemed resigned. "I hope we build it," he said, "but if the population says no, I won't go against them. If everybody's against it, the government's not going to go forward."

A two-lane provincial country road ran from Cacouna around Rivière-du-Loup to the Trans-Canada Highway, now Route 85, a hundred-kilometre road running straight to the New Brunswick border. The St. Lawrence River disappeared from sight behind a hill in the rearview mirror.

Quebec was an oversized part of the Energy East debate, where opponents had twice won something precious to their cause: more time. Eight months after the NEB recusals, as I followed the route through the province, there was still no date for the start of the new review and the beginning of the twenty-one-month timeline until a board recommendation. "I think this is a significant delay," Teika Newton said. "This delay has really driven a stake into the project."

Since the recusals, the economics of Alberta bitumen had shifted. Stubbornly low prices and the high cost of production saw capital pull back from the oil sands. "The more time passes, the less these projects become appealing," Guilbeault noted. Renewable alternatives were gaining ground: five years earlier, there had been no charging stations for electric cars in Quebec; in 2017 there were eight hundred, and that was expected to double by 2020, he said. "Time is our friend."

More perilous for Energy East was that the National Energy Board had gained time—and a second chance—to adjust to a changing political context. Three new members were appointed in early 2017 to form the new panel. "I think it's going to be better," Mike DeSouza said. "They are fully aware that last time things went off the rails, and I'm sure they're going to be taking extra steps to be totally without any hint of any problems."

DeSouza was right: the day after he made that prediction, during our Ottawa interview, the new panel issued a draft list of criteria that shocked the pipeline world.

The panel declared that it might study the emissions impact of Energy East not just upstream—in oil sands production—but also downstream, where consumers burned gasoline in their cars. The Trudeau government wanted a reformed NEB to assess upstream emissions in future reviews, but for Energy East the Liberals had taken on that task themselves. Now the board might seize it back, and add downstream emissions as well. It might also look at whether government policies—such as emissions caps and carbon taxes—would affect the project's business case. Such issues "may be outside the scope" of Energy East "and beyond the Board's ability to regulate," the panel said, but it pointed out that the NEB Act allowed it to consider "any public interest that in the Board's opinion may be affected by the issuance of the certificate or dismissal of the application." The NEB was flexing its muscles, announcing, in effect, that it might ask whether a 4600-kilometre bitumen pipeline was viable after the Paris accord.

The impact of DeSouza's reporting was clear now. Without the Charest story, the previous panel—made up of Harper appointees—would have continued its hearings under the old criteria. The proposed new rules from the Trudeau-appointed members were "a world away" from that, Guilbeault said. "I think they understood the expectations were different. I imagine that you want to run your operation as independently as possible, but you can't operate in a vacuum either." He went further: "If they do a fair assessment of all these things they say they're going to do, I can't see the NEB making a positive recommendation on a project like that." Canada was not on track to meet its Paris target, a reality he said the panel would have to confront. "I think the NEB may be setting itself up to say no to a project like that for the first time in its history."

In Cacouna, Martin Poirier and Benoit St-Hilaire were still guarded. "Until Energy East is dead, until it's good and buried, we can't take for granted that it will go away on its own," Poirier said. They wanted the NEB fully overhauled before the review began.

They were also guarded about Equiterre's Steven Guilbeault. His endorsement of Rachel Notley's climate plan—including its cap that would allow emissions to grow to a hundred megatonnes around 2030—amounted to cooperating with the enemy, Poirier and St-Hilaire believed. An activist's role was to reduce emissions, Poirier said, not endorse a cap that would make it impossible to ever return to current levels. Guilbeault, he said, was playing "*les deux côtés du patinoire*"—both ends of the rink.

But working within the system also got results: protests had raised awareness in Cacouna and halted the hearings in Montreal. Still, to kill the marine terminal, Poirier and St-Hilaire had also needed a judge to issue an injunction and a committee of scientists to put the beluga whale on the endangered list. And Teika Newton and Steven Guilbeault had needed legal motions citing the NEB's own rules to force the board to restart its review. They'd needed to follow the process to subvert the process.

It was debatable which strategy deserved the most credit in Quebec. But something was working, because pipeline opponents were winning.

PART SIX

NEW BRUNSWICK

14

IRVINGLAND

SOUTHEAST OF THE ST. Lawrence River, the Trans-Canada Highway passes over a range of hills and descends to Lake Témiscouata. The lake, forty-five kilometres long, is where Quebec bleeds into New Brunswick: it drains into the Madawaska River, which flows south across the interprovincial border and into the larger Saint John River to the Bay of Fundy. On the Quebec side of the border there's an Irving gas station, an outpost of the corporate empire controlled by the powerful New Brunswick family of billionaires. They're said to employ one out of every eight citizens of their home province, a place where Energy East was often described not as TransCanada's project but as Irving's.

The first few kilometres of the pipeline route inside New Brunswick posed a particularly difficult challenge: the small city of Edmundston was in the way. To get around it, TransCanada plotted its initial path to follow a power transmission corridor through the watershed of the Iroquois River, north of the municipal limits. But the river supplies the city water system, and the mayor, Cyrille Simard, objected. The company proposed a second route, but the only way to avoid the watershed was to go through the city itself, near a residential neighbourhood up a hill from the intakes from the river and a small brook, the Blanchette. "It's not easy," Paul Dionne, Edmundston's public works director, said as he showed me how, if the line broke, the oil would run downhill into the wells.

Nor could TransCanada pass south of the city, where the Saint John River forms the international boundary with the state of Maine. So the company moved the route twenty-three kilometres farther north, in a more distant, remote area of the watershed. But this third route, included in its revised 2016 submission to the NEB, still wasn't good enough, the city decided: councillors voted to ask the NEB to impose a condition that TransCanada avoid the watershed completely. Simard estimated that the detour would require an extra sixty kilometres of pipeline, but Derek Siegel, TransCanada's manager of facilities for Energy East, told the NEB hearings in New Brunswick that around Edmundston, "no route will avoid all watersheds." The larger detour would double the number of watercourse crossings, affect seventy more hectares of forest, and push the route on the Quebec side into more protected areas. The third route—the final one, TransCanada implied— was "the most appropriate from an overall balance of many contributing factors," Siegel asserted.

The city could ask the New Brunswick government to exercise its leverage, given that a provincial regulation prohibits any activity in a watershed not explicitly permitted. "A pipeline is prohibited in the watershed because it's not designated," Simard said. The province could issue exemptions, but refusing to do so would force TransCanada to heed the city's wishes. New Brunswick's premier, Brian Gallant, a supporter of Energy East, said he'd let civil servants "do the work and give approvals and make exceptions if they deem it to be okay." But he was noncommittal on what he and his cabinet would do if officials left the decision to them.

Edmundston's twenty thousand mostly francophone residents were hardly averse to resource projects. "We have a pulp mill in the centre of a town," Simard told me. "It's a city with an industrial tradition. Blue-collar people,

Joe Average, they recognize that you have to have an environmental impact to grow the economy." Still, the council's position on Energy East had broad support. "Our position is accepted by everyone because we're protecting the water," Simard said. "If we came out tomorrow and said we were for or against the project, people would be divided. People know it will create jobs and be good for the economy, so there's a contingent that supports that. And there's another group that is environmentally minded. And if I had to weigh the two, I couldn't tell you which one is greater."

Another factor made Edmundston's defiance easier. "There's no Irving tradition in Edmundston," Simard said. "People feel an independence from Irving." The industrial giant dominated many communities in the province, but had little presence here other than its ubiquitous gas stations. In 2015, Simard's council feuded with J.D. Irving Ltd., the family forestry company, over which of two small airports should get public funds: the one in the city or another forty kilometres away, near a large Irving sawmill. "I had people around town saying, 'Don't give in, because Irving controls this province and it's not right,'" Simard said. "People here are not Irving defenders." That made Edmundston almost unique in New Brunswick—because in this sixth province of my pipeline journey, Irving defined the terms of the Energy East debate.

"'The Irvings, they'll ruin it'—I hear all these bad things, but I can honestly say I haven't seen it myself," said Alexis Fenner, the mayor of Plaster Rock. "I find there's so much bad feeling, and I don't understand that." Other than a gas station, the Irvings weren't a visible presence in Plaster Rock, but Fenner had met Irving officials at various conferences and couldn't fathom the enmity toward the province's largest private-sector employer. "All I know is they're feeding twenty-two thousand families," she said. "They put these people in the situation where they can purchase houses, vehicles, and have children."

Fenner would have loved a bigger Irving presence in Plaster Rock. Between 2011 and 2016, the village's already small population dropped by almost 10 percent. The major employer is Twin Rivers, a forestry company whose saw-mill feeds logs to its pulp mill in Edmundston. The operation had been saved by government subsidies, but that alone couldn't reverse the exodus of young people. "We have to look at ways to bring them home," she said.

Fenner had grown up in Wales and worked in western Canada before choosing Plaster Rock for her retirement. Wanting to be closer to the ocean, she grabbed a map of the east coast, closed her eyes, and placed her finger on a spot at random. She found a village beset by fatalism. "When I first arrived here, in 2010, people would say, 'I don't know why you even bother. This is Plaster Rock. We never get anything.'" Two years later she was elected mayor, determined to turn things around.

Energy East wouldn't be a magic bullet, Fenner acknowledged. "It may not create thousands of jobs, but it's a start," she said. She didn't consider the pipeline as an environmental risk: growing up near the infamous East Moors Steelworks in Cardiff, she'd seen far worse. "It rained thick red dust," she said. "You couldn't put washing on the line. We breathed that. We lived in that." And, she noted, "I've made it to seventy-three and my mother made it to a hundred and four." As a marine master, Fenner sailed oil tankers on the high seas in an era before environmental regulations, when captains blithely flushed their tanks a few miles from port. "That was what you did then," she said. In Canada, she farmed on land sprayed with 2,4-D herbicide—"We just pumped it out"—and drilled for oil near Estevan, Saskatchewan. "We had wells and fracking no more than a hundred and fifty metres away from the well in the ground that we drew the water from to drink." So she considered the environmental rules for Energy East plenty tough. "We have improved. The world has improved. It has changed."

Fenner had another vivid argument for moving oil by pipeline. From Edmundston, the Energy East route followed a CN rail line southeast to Plaster Rock. In January 2014, just six months after the Lac-Mégantic explosion, a CN train carrying tanker cars of crude oil and propane derailed moments after passing through the village. Sixteen cars left the tracks and spilled a tiny amount of oil, but the risk of a propane explosion forced about 150 people to evacuate their homes. Many residents were unfazed: "The goods have to get transported somehow," Laurie Beaulieu told reporters. "Accidents happen." But Derrick Green, another resident, asked by a reporter how he preferred to have crude oil move past his home, replied, "Right now, today—pipeline, of course."

Like the train that exploded in Lac-Mégantic, the tanker cars in the Plaster Rock derailment were carrying crude oil to the Irving Oil refinery in Saint John. Fenner cited a Fraser Institute calculation that moving oil by pipeline was four times safer than by rail. If the Irvings were going to take crude off the CN tracks, all the better, she said. "As long as they're obeying the laws of the land and do it with a concern for safety and the environment, as well as the people, yes, I'll support them."

The pipeline route continued south from Plaster Rock, moving deeper into Irvingland, the vast tracts of forest the company harvested for timber. TransCanada initially studied a relatively straight route south to the site of the proposed export terminal, but it would have crossed several rivers, including the Saint John. That was "considered risky," the company said in NEB filings. So it opted for a longer but safer route that went around Grand Lake, the province's largest open body of water. That route ran southeast along the CN line and a power transmission corridor, passing near one of J.D. Irving Ltd.'s sawmills and its sprawling tree nursery, where the company cultivated seedlings in more than a dozen greenhouses for its vast plantations. The pipeline would also pass under Route 8, a provincial highway—coincidentally, near the site of an earlier environmental skirmish that many saw as a prelude to Energy East.

In 2011, some residents of the area blockaded a road to prevent SWN Resources, a natural gas company from Texas, from testing for shale gas. The residents were anxious about how hydraulic fracturing, known as fracking, would affect their water wells. It was unusual in New Brunswick to see people insist on placing environmental concerns ahead of economic development, but Stephanie Merrill, an environmentalist who'd grown up in the nearby village of Stanley, saw the logic of it. "Oil and gas, generally, are relatively unknown in New Brunswick," she said. "That kind of culture wasn't instilled in people like it is in the western provinces." Merrill had been hired by the Conservation Council of New Brunswick, the province's leading environmental group, to work on water issues. She was drawn into the battle near her hometown. "People were like, 'Stephanie knows something about this. Let's get her to come and give a talk.'"

Before the shale gas battle, New Brunswick's small environmental movement had struggled against a bipartisan Liberal–PC consensus that supported large industrial development projects. Indigenous activists had focused on securing and exercising their constitutional rights to harvest trees and fish. But the two groups made common cause on fracking, pushing the opposition Liberal Party to endorse a moratorium. The Progressive Conservative government of David Alward framed his 2014 re-election campaign as a stark choice between Tory prosperity and Liberal nay-sayers. The PC slogan, "Say Yes," implied that the young opposition leader, Brian Gallant, opposed not only shale gas but Energy East, too.

Gallant's closeness to Justin Trudeau was fodder for the PC strategy. In 2013, Trudeau called the Energy East proposal "very interesting" but added that the diluted bitumen was "very toxic" and needed an environmental review—putting him at odds with Gallant's support for the pipeline. Stephanie Merrill told me that because the pipeline's footprint was smaller and narrower than shale exploration areas, it generated less opposition. "There's also a lot more localized pressure from industry, homegrown pressure," she said, citing Irving Oil's role. "SWN was coming from Texas. Maybe the government didn't feel as much need to appease that company."

Gallant also told me that there were differences, but not the ones Merrill perceived. Irving's roots in the province gave New Brunswickers a comfort level with oil, he said, while fracking was "relatively new." And the benefits and spinoffs from Energy East were clear, while shale gas deposits were mere estimates. "You're asking New Brunswickers to accept a procedure, hydraulic fracturing, about which they had concerns, for potentially no upside."

After winning the 2014 election, Gallant instituted the shale gas moratorium. But the PC campaign strategy resonated, and it still echoed in the Energy East debate. "New Brunswick is and always has been a resource-based economy," the mayor of the rural municipality of Upper Miramichi, Douglas Munn, told the National Energy Board in 2016. "We are slowly dying if something of economic value doesn't come our way." Lorne Amos, the president of a local business group, told the NEB that environmentalists were making "outlandish" statements about Energy East's risk to water. "Those statements are nothing but fear-mongering by people entrenched in the protest movement," he said. Alward's pro-pipeline government was gone, but his framing of the issue was very much alive.

From the Upper Miramichi, Energy East would pass through more forest, then around the top of Grand Lake at Cumberland Bay near the village of Chipman, where Irving has a large presence. A huge pile of logs stretched along Main Street in front of a J.D. Irving Ltd. sawmill with its leaf-green logo, and eighteen-wheelers were moving through the village streets where rail cars were loaded with boards bearing the Irving name.

Despite the activity, the Chipman area, like Plaster Rock, had a declining population. The village's only bank closed in 2016. "Most of our young people have gone west to the oil fields, or somewhere else," Dale Barton, who used to drive a truck for Irving, told me. "The mill is the only thing we have here now. It's not very good here and it's getting worse."

Barton lived in Cumberland Bay, where TransCanada would run the pipeline and build a pumping station. It was about twenty minutes outside Chipman's municipal limits—to the dismay of village officials. "They are quite put out because it will be in our area," said Barton. The station's property assessment would have represented a boon to the village's tiny budget. "Everybody's having trouble over tax base now," he said. "Oh, the squawking that's been going on. The village figured they'd have opportunities when it was handy to them."

Barton helped start a volunteer fire department in Cumberland Bay in 1987. He still went to meetings, and told me about the new fire hall recently built to house the trucks. TransCanada would put in money for extra training and equipment when the pump station was built, he said. And there were the jobs. "Hopefully some people from our area will be able to be involved in the work," he said. The possibility of a spill didn't concern him. "If everything is put there under regulation, I don't think there'll be any problem."

The Irving name validated Energy East for many New Brunswickers. "They're not perfect but they do create a lot of work in New Brunswick," said another Cumberland Bay man, Jerry Flowers, who welcomed Energy East. "I always say if you took the McCains and the Irvings out of New Brunswick, there wouldn't be much left." Dale Barton told me, though, that he favoured Energy East not because of the Irving connection but in spite of it. He didn't like the company's penny-pinching, its discouragement of friendly chit-chat between mill dispatchers and contract drivers, its use of government subsidies, and its outsized influence in New Brunswick. "They control just about everything when it comes right down to it," he said. "It might not be in their name, but they've got a hold on it."

The Irving empire was no longer monolithic. It began to splinter in 2005, with K.C. Irving's three sons carving up the conglomerate: J.K. and his heirs, who oversaw forestry and shipbuilding, divested from the oil company controlled by Arthur, who shed his family's stake in J.K.'s operations. A third brother, Jack, was aligned with Arthur. The fissure was not widely known in New Brunswick; the chain of daily newspapers the family owned hadn't reported it.

Despite the split, the Irving brothers remained each other's customers. The oil tankers that exploded in Lac-Mégantic in 2013 were to be hauled on the final leg of their journey to the Irving refinery on a J.D. Irving Ltd. railroad. And JDI, as it's known colloquially, supported Energy East at the NEB hearings in August 2016. The company's application to intervene said that it was "vitally concerned" with the "appropriateness" of the route through fifty-five parcels of Irving-owned woodlands and seventy kilometres of public forest Irving leased. But enthusiasm for large-scale industrial development was etched in the family DNA. "This investment in national energy infrastructure is not only important for the Canadian economy, it is critical for New Brunswick," David Soucy, JDI's vice-president of construction and equipment, told the board. "The extent of this opportunity to the New Brunswick workforce and our economy cannot be overstated."

After rounding Grand Lake, the proposed pipeline route cut straight south through more woods to the town of Hampton. There it crossed a four-lane highway and took a sharp turn right, doubling back westward toward Saint John and its final destination on the city's east side. It was an appropriate punctuation point: Saint John was New Brunswick's first city and its premier port, the one-time pounding heart of its seafaring, export-driven economy, a merchant capital, and a rough, gritty blue-collar hub. It was also the headquarters of the Irving family's corporate empire. Although they'd centralized their shipbuilding operations in Halifax in the nineties, moved increasingly into foreign markets, and kept billions of their wealth offshore in Bermuda, Saint John remained the Irvings' physical and rhetorical home.

The Tim Hortons on Bayside Drive, at one end of a causeway across Courtenay Bay on the eastern side of the harbour, was not an obvious vantage point from which to survey the family's holdings, but it offered a panorama of their dominance: JDI's paper mill sits just over the hill, fed by the family's extensive logging operations, while its wallboard plant, established at its former shipyard with the help of federal subsidies, is across the road from the mill. J.K. Irving's chain of newspapers, a near-monopoly in the province, is headquartered in the *Telegraph-Journal* building at the opposite end of the causeway.

Arthur Irving's holdings are in evidence, too: the oil refinery, Canada's largest, is tucked behind a hill, but across the road from the coffee shop are two extensions of its operations. A rail terminal was built there in 2013 to receive some western oil by train when it was relatively cheap—though most of the three hundred thousand barrels of crude the refinery processed each day still came from foreign suppliers. Next to the rail terminal was a marine terminal where refined gasoline, carried from the refinery in a short pipeline, departed in small tankers bound for the U.S. east coast. Irving accounted for three-quarters of Canada's gasoline exports to the U.S. and 19 percent of that country's gas imports.

Up the road from the two terminals was another monument, a $65 million highway interchange funded by governments in anticipation of increased traffic to a second Irving refinery announced in 2006; the project was cancelled following the global market crash. And far across the bay, atop the hill that is Saint John's urban core, a new eleven-storey tower to house Irving Oil's one thousand head-office employees was climbing into the sky. The city's heritage board approved the design even though it violated a bylaw; after a complaint, the city council retroactively amended the bylaw. "This is about making sure we get development in the city," the mayor, Mel Norton, told reporters. "It's not about any one developer."

The Irving family operates within the law—but it has a history of pushing the law to the limit, and seeking to change it when necessary. Ottawa once went to court to challenge Irving Oil's buying of foreign crude at wholesale prices using a Bermuda shell company. By reselling it to the Saint John refinery at a markup, most of the profits remained in tax-free Bermuda, reducing the New Brunswick corporation's margins and its domestic tax bill. The judge called it "a tax avoidance scheme" but ruled that it was perfectly legal. Bermuda was also home to K.C. Irving's offshore trust, also off-limits to Canadian taxation. And during a strike by refinery workers in the nineties,

Irving Oil persuaded New Brunswick's Liberal government to relax its emissions standards, arguing that there weren't enough staff to monitor them. In 1998, over the objections of public health officials, the same government approved a refinery expansion without an environmental impact assessment.

One of the most controversial concessions to Irving was approved in 2005. With its Spanish partner, Repsol, Irving Oil persuaded Saint John's city council to freeze the property assessment on Canaport LNG, their new liquefied natural gas terminal, for a quarter century. It deprived the cash-starved municipality of millions of dollars in annual revenue and sparked a rare public backlash against the city's leading employers. The tax freeze required provincial legislation, which was promptly passed. When Brian Gallant's Liberal government repealed it in 2016, consultants reassessed the terminal's value and reduced it by two-thirds, which cut Canaport LNG's "unfrozen" tax bill by $5 million.

Gordon Dalzell had followed all these developments during his two decades as Saint John's leading clean-air crusader. Inside the Tim's, Dalzell, a rumpled, avuncular man, leaned over and gently tapped the pages of my notebook to emphasize his points. He was one of Saint John's most vocal proponents of saying no to the Irvings, yet he insisted on giving them their due. "They've always treated me with great respect, and I've been respectful in my advocacy towards them," Dalzell said. "In fact I've often acknowledged the achievements that they've made. . . . I think we've actually done them a big favour over the years. I think they owe people like me and the air-quality advocates a thank-you. We were probably an annoyance to them, but in a sense it kept them focused."

In 1994, Dalzell was president of the home and school association at Champlain Heights School, near the refinery. He and other parents decided to do something about persistent air pollution affecting the children. "We'd notice it, the blue haze coming off the refinery," he said. Working with parents and asthma sufferers, the Citizens' Coalition for Clean Air scored early wins, including a provincial Clean Air Act and a sulphur dioxide emissions limit tougher than national rules. "This whole movement took on a life of its own," Dalzell said. "Gosh, we never stopped there for years."

When the citizens' coalition got started, the Irvings "were very insular, like a bunker mentality," Dalzell recalled. But when the oil company began expanding the refinery in 1998, it started to open up—forced into it by growing public scrutiny. "Give them their due," he said. "They have done a lot better and they know the public is engaged." Even so, Dalzell was a realist. After the principal at Champlain Heights ordered an evacuation one day because of a heavy odour wafting over from the refinery—a decision that made the news—Irving "started to be much more attentive and generous" to the school, Dalzell said, building a new playground and paying for high-tech interactive whiteboards in the classrooms. "I think it was quite frankly a way to appease them and keep them all happy," he added. "As soon as the media turned against them and they were exposed for their practices, they took an interest in the place. . . . I think that was part of their strategy."

That proved the value of constantly pressuring the company, Dalzell told me. "You had a group of malcontents, or cranks—I don't know what you want to call us, environmental advocates or activists—hovering around in the neighbourhood like we were," he recalled. "They paid attention, to give them credit, over the years, to their environmental performance." But only laws and regulations—and changing market demand—could force the company to adapt, he said. When Irving Oil began producing lower-emitting gasoline to sell in New England, "they did it for one reason: to satisfy the regulatory demands in the U.S. northeast."

When Arthur's son Kenneth took over as CEO, Irving Oil flirted with a greener direction. Kenneth built an electricity generation plant inside the refinery, fired by natural gas, to sell power to New England. He also explored the concept of tidal power turbines in the Bay of Fundy. The company needed to "get into other energy products" that Irving's competitors in the U.S. were offering, Kenneth once said. But the transmission line to New England was never built, and the tidal power project was scrapped, in part because of his father Arthur's interference. "He didn't hide his disdain for the path we were on," a source told *The Globe and Mail* for a lengthy profile of Kenneth in 2017. Another added: "His father never got out of the way, didn't really let Ken run the business, and that became a crisis in the end." Kenneth left the family company in 2010 and eventually started Luum, a "commute management platform" for companies trying to help employees get to work using more environmental forms of transportation. Irving Oil, meanwhile, turned its attention back to its core fossil fuel business with its embrace of Energy East.

The pipeline also became Gordon Dalzell's new preoccupation. TransCanada's twenty-two eight-storey storage tanks at the end of the line would have floating roofs, a common design in the industry because they allow venting and thus avoid the buildup of potentially explosive fumes. TransCanada told the National Energy Board that it would use "the most economically achievable control technology" for the tanks, but Dalzell said that fell short of even better, but costlier, systems. Irving had installed a "very top-notch" closed-loop system at the marine terminal to capture vapours before they could get into the air, he told me, reducing emissions at the site by 80 percent. "It can be done," he said. "Why doesn't TransCanada do the same thing?"

In east Saint John, levels of benzene and other volatile organic compounds—VOCs, in the shorthand of the industry—already exceeded Ontario's provincial standards, and Energy East tanks would more than double the eleven million barrels of oil Irving already stored at any given time. But New Brunswick hadn't established a binding benzene standard. The province included limits when it issued certificates of approval, but that didn't carry the same legal weight, Dalzell said. In the absence of regulations, TransCanada's consultant Albert Lees told the NEB, "we looked at air quality criteria that were available within each province for which the [Energy East] tank terminals actually exist, so that's Alberta, Saskatchewan . . . and also New Brunswick. As New Brunswick did not have a benzene criteria, we adopted the Alberta annual standard."

Dalzell said that the province should enact firm regulations using Ontario's much stricter standards. But, he added, officials were "under pressure" to accommodate TransCanada and not jeopardize the pipeline. After all of Dalzell's progress with Irving Oil in Saint John, a pipeline touted as linking the city to western Canada's far-flung fossil fuel prosperity was already connecting it another way—bringing Alberta's industry-friendly emissions rules all the way to New Brunswick.

And yet Dalzell was optimistic. In May 2017, the federal government issued a notice that it would begin regulating VOCs in the petroleum sector. "This is how Trudeau is going to kill these pipelines, or this one," Dalzell said. "They're dragging this out. This is all part of the strategy. Instead of saying no, we're just going to go slow." A few weeks after our interview, however, Dalzell discovered that the new rules exempted marine terminals and tank farms—the very facilities Energy East would build in Saint John, the ones that most concerned the veteran clean-air crusader. It was a win for TransCanada and its New Brunswick partner.

15

TIDEWATER

IN KING'S SQUARE, IN the heart of Saint John's historic uptown and under the shadow of Irving Oil's new corporate headquarters, stands a statue that symbolizes the city's—and New Brunswick's—competing commercial impulses. Samuel Leonard Tilley was a supporter of Confederation who struggled to persuade Saint John's merchants that John A. Macdonald's national vision was in their interest. Their markets were in New England, not the distant colonies of Upper and Lower Canada. Their business was on ships sailing south from the harbour, not with Macdonald's Intercolonial Railway. The city's business elite needed a rail link to New England, not the Canadas. Tilley prevailed, but for decades resentment would linger over Confederation's disruption of the city's natural trade ties. Canada's east–west axis and Saint John's north–south commercial impetus would remain in tension.

Frank McKenna understood that tension. As New Brunswick's Liberal premier in 1988, he broke ranks with his federal allies to support Brian Mulroney's free trade agreement with the U.S., which restored connections Confederation had broken. McKenna later saw the importance of the American relationship more profoundly as Prime Minister Paul Martin's ambassador to Washington. Arthur Irving also supported the free trade agreement, which simplified Irving Oil's expansion down the U.S. east coast. "The Maritimes are closer to New York and Boston than to Toronto," Irving once told an interviewer. "That is the natural way for us to go."

But in 2011, east–west trade suddenly became more appealing to McKenna and Irving in the form of Energy East.

McKenna was regarded as the intellectual father of the project, a perception he didn't discourage in media interviews.* He was still close to Arthur Irving, and was on the board of the oil sands giant Canadian Natural Resources Limited, making him a natural broker between Alberta's oil sands and New Brunswick's refinery. "He knows the industry inside out and knows everybody in Calgary," said Craig Leonard, the energy minister in the PC government of David Alward. "And as a former premier of New Brunswick, he knew the potential of Saint John. So he was definitely in the background, working both sides."

McKenna first publicized the idea in a November 2011 opinion piece for the *Financial Post*, arguing that delays to Keystone XL in Washington highlighted the need for Canada to end its dependence on the U.S. as its sole export market for oil. The American crude glut meant that Canadian oil was sold there for twenty-seven dollars less per barrel than it could fetch on on the world market, a "staggering" loss of potential revenue for Canada, McKenna wrote—$230 billion shaved from the country's GDP over a quarter century. Northern Gateway and Trans Mountain promised access to the Pacific coast and to Asian markets, he said, but "real diversity demands even more options." He called for a concerted effort to get oil moving, including by rail and through existing pipelines to Montreal—and through a new line linking Montreal to the Irving refinery in Saint John.

Irving stood to gain from such a pipeline. Its American competitors were profiting from cheaper Alberta oil, which Irving couldn't access in large

---

* McKenna refused, however, to be interviewed for this book.

quantities. Mike Ashar, a former Suncor executive recruited as Irving Oil's CEO, envisioned getting the crude to Saint John by sending it first by pipeline to the west coast and then onto tankers through the Panama Canal and up the eastern seaboard. He also established the rail yard to bring western oil by train. But a west–east pipe would make it even more lucrative: one estimate projected that Irving Oil would save $1.2 billion a year if it could buy discounted Alberta crude coming by pipeline. So when Ashar heard that TransCanada and Enbridge were talking about lines to Quebec, he and McKenna began working in tandem to get them to look even farther east. In a second opinion article in June 2012, McKenna made the explicit comparison to the CPR, focusing on an Alberta–New Brunswick link and arguing that moving oil to market should be "a nation-building exercise" and not "a corrosive debate pitting one region against another."

McKenna and Ashar approached David Alward, New Brunswick's Progressive Conservative premier. Supporting the project was a political risk: previous premiers had attached their names to promising energy megaprojects, such as a second Irving refinery or a new nuclear reactor, only to see them fall victim to market realities. But Alward instinctively liked the proposal. He had a son working in the oil patch. There was also a political upside, both for him and for Alison Redford in Alberta. "It kind of fit with both governments—two PC governments, New Brunswick desperate for the jobs, the activity, and able to play a role on the national stage, creating this link between Alberta and New Brunswick," Leonard said. "Right from the start, everybody recognized the potential of this fantastic political, economic story. Everybody started talking about 'the new railway.'"

The case became even more compelling in the summer of 2012, when it appeared that British Columbia was determined to block the Northern Gateway line to the Pacific. But Alberta's oil CEOs needed to be persuaded of the economics of going all the way to the east coast, so that autumn, a New Brunswick delegation quietly flew to Calgary to meet them. "You could tell at that point no one really cared where it ended up," Leonard said. "As long as you got it to a body of water, they were fine." Ashar's presentation explained how the deep, ice-free port on the Bay of Fundy would allow the largest tankers to load oil in such quantities that the economies of scale would eclipse those of export terminals in Montreal or Quebec City, which could accommodate only smaller ships. Ashar also pointed out that the sea route from Saint John to refineries on the coast of India, a market coveted by Alberta, was—counterintuitively—shorter than the one from British Columbia. "They started to put it all together," Leonard said. "From that point on, Saint John became a part of the discussion."

The New Brunswickers also met with the two big Calgary-based pipeline companies. Enbridge was planning the Line 9B reversal to Montreal while TransCanada saw Quebec City as its easternmost terminus, with a possible extension to Saint John to be explored later. But the New Brunswick crew made the point that if Saint John was the eventual goal, it had to be part of the plan from the outset; they argued that Quebec might block a subsequent extension once it had a secure new crude supply for its refineries. Another element of the pitch was that unlike British Columbia, New Brunswick had a broad political consensus that welcomed the pipeline. To underscore that point, in December 2012 the PC government and Liberal opposition in the New Brunswick legislature passed a unanimous resolution endorsing the pipeline. "It was unprecedented," one insider said, "to have all parties saying, 'Yes, we support pipelines,' against a backdrop of Keystone, a backdrop of B.C." TransCanada was persuaded, and said that it would test the market by seeking shipping commitments from producers.

Alward made his own trip to Alberta the following February, addressing the legislature, doing media interviews, and dining with oil patch executives at Calgary's exclusive Ranchmen's Club. Redford reciprocated four months later, a trip that included her visit to the Irving Oil refinery and her eyeballing of that buoy in the Bay of Fundy where tankers pumped foreign oil ashore— and where, she imagined, her oil could reach tidewater and thus the world.

What the public didn't see that day was that Irving's role in the project was suddenly in doubt. Arthur Irving didn't want to commit to buying a set number of barrels from the pipeline, preferring his usual practice of playing the market for the best price at any given time. Meanwhile, some of the Alberta producers feared that Irving would hold their oil hostage at the outlet to the ocean. "The oil companies were somewhat uncomfortable with the on-off switch ending at Irving Oil," one insider said. If a ship couldn't dock on one of Saint John's many foggy days, oil from the pipeline would have to be dumped—and that meant Irving, the only company with storage tanks in Saint John, could buy at a discount. "Irving is pretty secretive, and Alberta is slightly parochial," another insider told me, but the west–east culture clash was putting Alberta's connection to tidewater in jeopardy.

TransCanada was days away from the end of its open season, when oil producers would commit to how much oil they'd ship on the line—the final determinant of the project's viability. Alward's officials quietly prepared a Plan B, offering TransCanada a parcel of provincial land on the other side of Saint John's harbour so that it could build a terminal on its own. "This is bigger than Irving Oil," one provincial official remembered telling a TransCanada executive. "We're not going to lose this project because you can't get a deal with Irving Oil." When Arthur Irving learned that he might be cut out of the project, he went "completely crazy," according to an insider. "It got very, very, tense." Frank McKenna stepped in to broker a resolution that preserved Irving's role: Arthur agreed to take fifty thousand barrels a day from the pipeline for his refinery, and according to one report, TransCanada added the terminal at Cacouna to its route design to assure oil executives that Irving wouldn't have a chokehold on their exports.

They were just in time. Alberta oil producers had pledged to ship nine hundred thousand barrels a day through the pipeline, almost double what TransCanada required. A hundred thousand of those were from the Alberta government's own bitumen reserves, which it collected in lieu of royalties from oil sands producers—a commitment that would cost $4.6 billion over two decades, belying the claim that Energy East wasn't subsidized with public money.

But the deal was sealed. On August 1, 2013, TransCanada confirmed that it would apply to the National Energy Board to build Energy East. David Alward held a triumphant media event with Arthur Irving at the refinery under a bright blue summer sky. "If you think of behind-the-scenes calibration to make the pipeline happen," one insider told me, "it's not quite Pierre Berton and *The Last Spike*, but it had lots of obstacles, and many good Canadians did what they felt was right to make this happen."

A few blocks from the Tilley statue and the Irving Oil headquarters, the Atlantica Centre for Energy, a think tank–cum–lobby group, operates in donated space in the offices of a local engineering firm. Funded by energy companies, governments, and industrial players in the historic trading corridor between Atlantic Canada and New England, Atlantica describes itself as a "bridge" between the energy sector and the community. I contacted its president, Colleen Mitchell, because Irving Oil refused to respond to my interview requests—though Mitchell, a former marketing and communications executive with Irving, insisted she wasn't their proxy. Atlantica's sponsors included energy producers who profited when prices were high, but also manufacturers who were best off when energy prices were low. "We attempt as best as we're able to have a balanced approach," she said.

Since its inception, Atlantica had supported the proposed second Irving refinery, the refurbishment of New Brunswick's sole nuclear reactor, and shale gas development. "We change, depending on what's going on with governments, with industry, and with opportunities," Mitchell told me. The goal was "energy literacy" for the public: "There's so much information available to the public on the Internet, it's very difficult for them, not being immersed in it on a day-to-day basis, to determine what's factual and what's relevent to this region." She cited U.S. reports on shale gas that she said were germane only to the particular geology of those places. "We try and filter through a lot of the studies that are out there and select the ones that actually have relevance to New Brunswick, specifically, or Nova Scotia and PEI and the New England states."

Lately, Atlantica had been doing a lot of work on pipelines and their public acceptance. Mitchell described a conference she'd attended in Boston where one participant wondered if a new pipeline could ever again be built in a democratic country. Atlantica's role, she said, included rebutting the notion that a zero-carbon or low-carbon economy would be possible anytime soon. "Sometimes there's a disconnect between people saying, 'I don't want to use carbon fuels,' and then they hop in their SUV and drive home," she said. "They just don't understand. That's where our role comes in, trying to point out to people, sometimes, their own hypocrisy. They don't realize how dependent they are on carbon fuels and how long it will take to develop an alternative."

The future Mitchell preferred to envision was one in which Saint John's mix of liquefied natural gas, oil refining, nuclear power, electricity links to the U.S., and natural gas from Nova Scotia's offshore would transform it into an energy-trading hub. A visiting delegation of European Union ambassadors had been "blown away" by the city's energy assets, she said. "'In Europe we would kill for this opportunity,'" she paraphrased. "'You guys are sitting on this gold mine and nobody knows about it. Where are your cheerleaders?'" Somehow the energy sector, skilled at identifying and exploiting resources and markets, had overlooked Saint John, Mitchell suggested. "What we are is understated," she said. "We don't stand up on soapboxes and bring attention to ourselves."

This struck me as being at odds with a pattern in recent years of civic and business leaders striking a constant drumbeat of positivity about Saint John, using a succession of upbeat social media slogans such as "Renaissance City," "Live Life Uptown," and "Saint Awesome." Critics were labelled as negative and disloyal. When the mayor, Mel Norton, a skilled marketer, accepted a free flight on a corporate jet owned by Irving—a company he taxed and regulated—those who questioned his decision were castigated. And when *The*

Globe and Mail published a lengthy investigation of the Irving environmental record and divisions within the family, a former head of the Saint John Board of Trade, Bob Manning, lashed back on a business-friendly news website. "Let's not be so quick to complain, to seek out only negatives where there are plenty of positives," he wrote.

But a city that wanted to play in the energy big leagues had to expect more scrutiny. A pipeline the size of Energy East had continental, if not global, implications, and major energy players were looking for real information, not local boosterism. Bloomberg News revealed the last-minute clash between Irving and TransCanada, and Reuters journalists in Boston, where Irving sold a lot of gasoline, broke stories about operational problems at the refinery, air-quality complaints at the rail terminal, flaws with emissions controls at the marine terminal, and "environmental emergencies" not promptly reported to regulators.

Perhaps in response, Irving Oil shed some of its penchant for secrecy. Its executives granted interviews to select business journalists. Mark Sherman, a company vice-president, told the *Financial Post* that the pipeline would give the refinery more "optionality" in sourcing crude, which might allow for "other spin-off businesses" like petrochemical processing. Even Arthur Irving, notoriously media-shy, granted a rare interview to the *National Post*. "Nothing would please us more than to get Alberta oil in bigger quantities than we are getting now," he said. "There isn't a day that we don't think about that pipeline coming to Saint John, because guess what? It's got to come. Alberta needs it, Ottawa needs it, New Brunswick is all behind it, and Canada should be supporting it until we get it."

Liberal politicians learned how they were expected to support the pipeline: unequivocally. Weeks after becoming premier of New Brunswick, Brian Gallant said that the conditions Kathleen Wynne and Philippe Couillard had put on their support—including measuring the emissions impact—were "very reasonable and very achievable." He was promptly accused of jeopardizing the project. "It's a really slippery slope when you get into that," said Craig Leonard. "That changes the economics of the whole thing." Wynne and Couillard backed off on emissions after lobbying from Alberta, but Leonard told me that their comments "opened that door for those who are opposed to pipelines because it carries oil that would be produced in the oil sands." Gallant's support of Quebec's and Ontario's conditions also represented a crack in the new Alberta–New Brunswick partnership, he added. "The energy executives would look at that and say, 'Jesus Christ.'"

The same dynamic occurred during the 2015 federal election campaign. Any Liberal talk of NEB reform or new climate measures was attacked by Conservatives as insufficiently supportive. Justin Trudeau's refusal to endorse Energy East that summer—"because we are going through a process right now, [and] that process has been torqued and flawed"—came during a July radio interview in New Brunswick. "My phone, my Twitter, and everything just went crazy," said Wayne Long, then the Liberal candidate in Saint John. "It put me in a very, very difficult spot." Long told *The Globe and Mail* that he supported the project, which, he said, "put me in some hot water with the party." He understood that the subtleties of Trudeau's position—the NEB review was inadequate, but pre-empting its review would create larger problems—would be lost on voters. "My party would have preferred I took the same kind of stance, saying 'I can't say yes to Energy East because I don't know the outcome of the process,'" Long said. "I pushed back and said, 'No, no, no—I won't do that. I can't do that. I'm in favour of it. Period.'"

Trudeau's comments may explain the unusual scene the night of September 10, 2015, when the Irving Oil refinery hosted a federal Conservative campaign rally for Stephen Harper. In 1967, the Irvings had thrown their wealth into a provincial election to defeat a Liberal premier, Louis Robichaud, whose tax reforms affected their holdings. Robichaud won, but since then, PC and Liberal governments had quietly acceded to the family's wishes and the Irvings had avoided any signs of partisan preference. Yet there was Arthur Irving welcoming Harper to the refinery. While not exactly endorsing him, the octogenarian billionaire implied that he expected the Conservative leader to remain prime minister. "Come often," Irving said. "You're always welcome." Harper spoke of getting resources to market, but was careful to say that Energy East was subject to an "independent review" that should be "based on the facts."

The prime minister also took pains not to pre-empt the NEB. "If you look at Stephen Harper's words very carefully, he always said 'pending NEB review,'" Long pointed out—the same caveat Trudeau used. But two years after winning Saint John in the Trudeau wave, "I still will get, 'Well, if Stephen Harper had won, the pipeline would be here by now,'" Long said. "And I'm like, 'No. No.' In fact, we might be in the same position we are in. The process had to unfold."

Regardless, Long's own position had no nuance at all. "As an MP from Saint John–Rothesay, I'm staunchly in favour. I respect that the prime minister doesn't want to prejudice the process, but I've got a riding to look out for. He's got a country."

Orthodoxy may have taken hold in the political realm, but in the real world there were nuances, even in Saint John. With Cacouna cancelled, TransCanada had redesigned the Saint John export facility to handle more oil. TransCanada calculated that its infrastructure would be worth $3.7 million in property tax revenue for the city in 2016, but Saint John's new mayor, Don Darling—though a supporter—told the NEB there were risks that required extra emergency planning. "There are many questions that remain unanswered," Darling said. Even Irving Oil's partner in its Canaport LNG import terminal, the Spanish energy giant Repsol, said that there'd been "inadequate consultation" by TransCanada about coordinating its tanker traffic.

Pipelines were proving a complicated business. Colleen Mitchell lamented that a project could take a decade from conception to NEB approval. "The world is still moving during that entire ten-year period," she said. "It is very difficult to make a business decision on day one and hope that all the market dynamics haven't changed." Assume, as Andrew Leach had when I interviewed him in Edmonton, that producers would pay a shipping toll of nine dollars a barrel from Hardisty to Saint John. When the price differential between the U.S. and world benchmark prices, which was the motive to get Alberta oil to tidewater, was around twenty dollars a barrel in late 2012—and even greater when the discount on Western Canadian Select was applied—there was a clear after-toll profit for shippers. But by 2016 the gap was three dollars, making each barrel on Energy East a money loser. The domestic and world prices might "diverge again very quickly," the industry economist Ben Brunnen had told me. But then again, they might not.

With so much flux, Mitchell said, the National Energy Board shouldn't fiddle with the ground rules for its review. Atlantica opposed the board's May 2017 proposal to measure the pipeline's impact on upstream and downstream emissions, unless regulators applied it elsewhere. "If it's too difficult to get a pipeline built, or it doesn't get approved, because of emissions beyond the pipeline's control, how can you then just stick that product in a rail car?" she said. "We've just moved the problem from underground in a pipeline to over rail." (Transposing the climate impact was not, in fact, that straightforward, because rail was more expensive and required a higher barrel price to be viable.)

Irving Oil, in a letter to the NEB, also opposed the new criteria. Assessing downstream emissions was unnecessary because the amount of fuel its customers would burn would "remain relatively the same," it argued, regardless of whether the refinery got its crude from a pipeline or from ships. The source of its supply was irrelevant.

Where Irving Oil got its crude was anything but irrelevant to the most ardent supporters of Energy East. Terry Etam, writing in an online oil industry newsletter, said it was a "disconcerting shock" to learn that Irving imported crude from Saudi Arabia. The company had actually been doing so for a half century, since the early days of the refinery, but now Saudi oil was deemed unacceptable. The wrath wasn't directed at Irving, however, but at environmental opponents of Energy East, whose real target was the oil sands. "Where is the political outrage over oil imports from rogue nations with inferior environmental records and deplorable behaviours toward women, dissidents and minorities?" Claudia Cattaneo asked in the *Financial Post*. "Where are the beefed up regulatory reviews of Saudi Arabia's climate change impacts, or their dumping practices?" Irving imported from other countries, including Norway, the United Kingdom, Nigeria, Venezuela, and United States, but the Saudis were the most convenient whipping boys in the increasingly high-pitched, chest-thumping, nationalist push for Energy East.

TransCanada itself adopted the message. "Foreign oil isn't the solution for Canada," the company said in a typical tweet in April 2016. "Energy East is!" The project's media spokesperson, Tim Duboyce, told a New Brunswick newspaper that the pipeline "will end the need for refineries in Quebec and New Brunswick to import hundreds of thousands of barrels of foreign oil every day." Conservative politicians, ostensibly supporters of free trade, were also gripped by foreign-oil fever: Andrew Scheer, the federal Conservative leader, suggested that gas retailers be required to display pump stickers with the flags of the countries that supplied their oil, while Alberta Wildrose MLA Prasad Panda proposed banning "foreign dictator oil," a step that would violate international trade agreements. Politicians who usually urged governments to leave the oil sector alone were now advocating interfering in its business decisions.

Irving Oil was immune to such patriotic delirium. CEO Ian Whitcomb sounded the obligatory notes at a 2016 energy conference when he called Energy East "an opportunity to unite Canadians in a way that we haven't seen since the Trans-Canada Highway opened in 1962." But Whitcomb also told the *Financial Post* that the business case for Saudi oil would remain compelling with or without Energy East. Importing it on large tankers was a good deal, he said. "We will add Western Canadian crude to our portfolio as the economics dictate, but probably not at the expense of our Saudi barrels." Whitcomb also undermined the argument that Canada's oil was "ethical" because of the country's more rigorous environmental standards: he predicted that foreign suppliers would eventually align their policies. "Over time, things will come together," he said. "Over time, the environmental agenda is not a Canadian agenda or a U.S. agenda or a European agenda. It's a world agenda."

It was a candid and clarifying moment: for all the nation-building hype surrounding Energy East, the industry operated on supply and demand. If western bitumen was cheap, a pipeline made sense—but Saudi crude still made sense, too. "Any manufacturing facility wants this diversity of supply," Mitchell told me. "If you have the option to purchase from three or four different sources, it gives you that flexibility, and it helps with the viability of the facility. It just gives you another choice." Her comments steered clear of the flag-waving rhetoric: Alberta was just another potential supplier—if the price was right.

Duboyce, the TransCanada spokesperson, explained by email that when he said Energy East would "end the need" for foreign oil in eastern refineries, he was referring to the pipeline's overall capacity. "That said, I cannot speak to what refiners will choose to do in the future with the eventual option of receiving some or all of their oil from the pipeline." In fact, Irving's commitment to refine fifty thousand barrels a day from Energy East—a fraction of the 1.1 million the pipeline would move—was the maximum volume of heavy crude it could handle without installing an expensive coker to upgrade the oil.

That Irving saw past the overheated rhetoric about Canadian oil refined in Canada should have surprised no one. The company had lived the brutal dollars-and-cents logic of the oil business since its inception. In 1958, when the Diefenbaker-appointed Royal Commission on Energy studied whether eastern refineries should be forced to process Alberta oil exclusively, Arthur's father, K.C. Irving, appeared as a witness to oppose the idea. "Alberta prices were too high, out of line, and Irving wanted no part of them," his biographers wrote. "He argued that his refinery should not be compelled to purchase Canadian crude oil at prices higher than those for which imported crude was now available." Ottawa ended up applying the policy only as far east as the Ontario–Quebec border, leaving Irving free to import cheaper Middle East oil.

Whitcomb's candour about Saudi crude was a modern iteration of the same calculation. But it undermined the high-minded sloganeering orthodoxy around Energy East. It was a reminder that the route to Saint John wasn't really about Canada but the ocean beyond.

Forty-six hundred kilometres by pipeline route from Hardisty, Alberta, I was nearing the end of the line, where Energy East would reach the Bay of Fundy. After Alberta hill country and Saskatchewan grasslands, Manitoba lakes and the rocky Ontario expanse of the Canadian Shield, after the crossings of the Ottawa and St. Lawrence Rivers and the path into the Suncor refinery in Montreal, I was coming to the tidewater that was the rationale for the entire project.

Down Bayside Drive past the Irving paper mill and the hulking refinery, past the small offices and warehouses of suppliers, trucking firms, and equipment rental companies, Red Head Road ran along the shore of Saint John Harbour through a rural residential area mixed with forest and fields. Lynaya Astephen's modest yellow house sat close to the road, facing the shimmering harbour in the distance. Just across the road was the proposed site of TransCanada's tank terminal, where twenty-two large storage tanks would hold six hundred thousand barrels each of western oil.

Astephen drove me down to Anthony's Cove Road, which hugs the water around the opposite side of the TransCanada site. More houses dotted the narrow potholed road. To the right was a wide, rocky beach at low tide. Across the bay, the city was a broad, grey-blue panorama. "I love where I live," Astephen said. "I can walk to the beach. I can hear the waves late at night. Gorgeous sunsets." She'd bought the property in 2008. "I knew I wanted to buy my house before I even went inside. It was late February and I stood in the driveway and I looked out, and I could see the water and I could see this amazing sunset. It was just breathtaking, and I said, 'This is where I want to be.'"

Then, in March 2014, she received a letter from TransCanada about its plan to build its tank terminal near her home. Researching the company, she read online about the U.S. fight against Keystone XL, including the arrest of James Hansen, a NASA climate scientist, at a protest outside the White House. "I thought, 'There must be something going on if someone important like that got arrested.'" She decided that Energy East shouldn't proceed, for the sake of both her own little piece of paradise and the climate. "It's really sad," she said. "You move here and you expect things to stay the way you originally thought they would be, and some large corporations want to change that just to put money in their pockets and destroy the planet. I look out these windows every morning and I worry and I feel depressed."

TransCanada said in NEB filings that the "area of disturbance" across from Astephen's house was eighty-five hectares. The company would run two smaller lines from its twenty-two storage tanks there. One would carry the western crude to Irving's existing Canaport tanks on the bay, which now received imported oil from berthed tankers; from there some of it would be transferred, along with the foreign oil, to the refinery. Most of the bitumen, though, would travel through the second line to the marine export terminal, a jetty extending into the bay with two loading berths for large tankers.

Many of Astephen's neighbours also opposed Energy East. Gary Prosser, who lived on Anthony's Cove Road, asked the NEB hearings why the tank farm had to be close to his home. "While you're asked to make a decision in the best interest of Canada, my question to you is what price do I have to pay?" Prosser accused TransCanada officials of not fully answering his questions and those of his neighbours. John Van der Put, the company's vice-president for eastern oil projects, said they'd met Prosser many times and were "very willing to continue to have those discussions with him." But there was no hint of moving the tank farm.

Prosser already had a small pipeline on his land. Astephen pointed out the warning pole as she drove by. This line, belonging to Irving Oil, carried the company's imported oil the short distance from the Canaport storage tanks on the bay to the refinery. Alberta bitumen would move through it as well, but Prosser was told at the NEB hearings that because it already existed and belonged to Irving, it wasn't considered part of Energy East. That reassured him. "I will say up front, with the Irvings and their group of companies, I've had no problem whatsoever. They're part of the community and they understand it's important." He had "no comfort level" with TransCanada, he added, but Irving Oil had always given him "the very best cooperation."

Prosser was articulating a common Saint John sentiment: the Irvings cared about the local community because they were from here. Astephen wasn't as trusting. Unlike Gordon Dalzell, she didn't believe that you could negotiate with Irving Oil in good faith. "They have a lot of influence over the political system," she said. "They have a lot of control over how things are done." When she was growing up, her father ran an Irving service station, and she heard the stories about a benign K.C. Irving dropping in to check on how things were going. Now, as a climate activist, her view had changed. "A lot of people in this city have this impression that they're our saviours, but I think the opposite is true."

She did give Irving credit for candour. She read Whitcomb's comments about continuing to buy Saudi oil, contradicting the rhetoric about refining Canadian oil in Canada. "It was kind of funny that TransCanada was saying one line, and Irving was saying, 'That's not going to happen,'" she said. Down at the beach, three large tankers floated offshore, waiting to deliver loads of foreign oil to the company's Canaport tanks. There would be more ships in the bay if Energy East was built—an estimated 281 per year to cart away

Alberta bitumen. The original number was 115, but the cancellation of the Cacouna terminal meant that a lot more oil would need to be exported through Saint John. It worked out to five tankers a week, and almost three hundred million barrels of oil shipped out each year—about three-quarters of Energy East's total capacity.* "That's proof they're not going to be refining this here," Astephen said. "It's not going to be for use here on the east coast."

People in the west had told me that they didn't fear pipelines because they were part of the landscape—part of daily life. The little pipeline that Astephen pointed out to me, passing through Gary Prosser's property, was likewise part of the landscape here, and a revealing one. As the route through which foreign oil travelled to Irving Oil's refinery, it would remain vital to the company's business—more vital than Energy East.

From Lynaya Astephen's house, Red Head Road continued down to a point of land jutting into the Bay of Fundy. Two private roads led to the Canaport storage tanks. The tops of two tanks were visible behind some trees—giant vats of crude from Saudi Arabia and elsewhere. The smell of oil was in the air, something I hadn't detected in Hardisty, or at the entrance to the Suncor refinery in Montreal. Here it was unmistakable.

The water of the bay wasn't visible beyond the tops of the two tanks, but it was there, along with the buoy that had once fired Alison Redford's imagination. From that spit of land, she'd hoped, Alberta's bitumen would flow to an oil-hungry world, free of the constraints of inland Canada, free to pump

---

* This is my calculation based on TransCanada's forecast of 70 Aframax class tankers, 175 Suezmax class tankers, and 36 VLCC (very large crude carrier) tankers per year. Given each ship's maximum capacity, 299 million barrels would be exported per year—three-quarters of Energy East's annual capacity, based on 1.1 million barrels per day. Using TransCanada's assertion that it had shipping commitments of 995,000 barrels a day, or 363 million per year, the amount to be exported on those tankers is an even greater share of the total.

money back to Alberta, free to enrich the country through equalization, free to continue warming the planet.

That was the goal. But the sure thing, on that spit of land, was that foreign oil would continue to come ashore. The oily smell in the wind was the other essential truth about tidewater: it allowed Irving to cheaply import the Saudi crude that most helped its bottom line.

On the Bay of Fundy, the domestic, nationalist arguments for Energy East fell apart. It had always been based on an inherent contradiction: "We're going to provide lower-cost feedstock for eastern Canadian refineries; we're going to provide higher value for western Canadian producers," Andrew Leach said in Edmonton, paraphrasing the arguments. But, he said, "Irving's not going to run a western Canadian barrel for the sake of patriotism. They're going to run the cheapest barrel they can get their hands on. And western producers aren't going to sell to Irving for the sake of patriotism. They're going to maximize their value."

Energy East wasn't a nation-building exercise but a commercial venture designed to get oil to where it needed to be: where the best price was, regardless of country, border, sentiment, or slogan. That would prove to be its undoing.

EPILOGUE

"THE LAST THING OUT OF TOWN"

RUSS GIRLING, TRANSCANADA'S CEO, had his arms stiffly at his side. The pose, and his schoolboy brush cut, made him look like a nervous student standing before a mercurial principal. But the man behind the desk was the president of the United States, and with the stroke of a pen, he was about to give Girling the passing grade he'd been seeking for years.

It was March 24, 2017, and Girling was in the Oval Office, listening to Donald Trump utter the words he had so longed to hear: Keystone XL was approved. "It's gonna be an incredible pipeline, greatest technology known to man, or woman, and frankly we're very proud of it," Trump said, seated at his desk. Two cabinet secretaries, some trade union leaders, and other officials stood behind him. So did Girling. "Russ," Trump said, half-turning his head, "you've been waiting for a long, long time, and I hope you don't pay your consultants anything, because they had nothing to do with the approval." The men surrounding the president chuckled. Having given himself all the credit, Trump rattled off some statistics, including the eight hundred thousand barrels of oil Keystone XL would deliver from Alberta to the Gulf Coast— "That's some big pipeline"—and invited Girling to say a few words.

The CEO from Calgary haltingly delivered the same message he'd delivered for years: pipelines were "the safest and most reliable way to move our products to market," and "there's thousands of people ready and itching to get to work." Trump seized on this, mentioning the blue-collar workers who'd voted for him because of Keystone XL. "They appreciated it very much, Russ, at the polls, as you probably noticed." The president tried to sum up: "So the bottom line—Keystone. Finished," he said with a flourish, turning back to Girling. "They're going to start construction when?"

"Well," Girling said, dampening the mood a notch, "we've got some work to do in Nebraska, to get our permits there—"

"Nebraska?" Trump cut in. "I'll call Nebraska."

Girling stammered through a quick explanation of the state approval process. Trump waved it off, promising to contact the Republican governor. "I'll call him today." With that, he ended the little ceremony, a signature Trump tableau, shamelessly self-aggrandizing and unintentionally comedic.

No one had mentioned the other pipeline Russ Girling was trying to get approved, the one his company was selling back home as a Canadian epic, a patriotic nation-building exercise. In the Oval Office, such parochial pitches wouldn't register. Keystone XL would carry Alberta crude to refineries on the Gulf Coast of Texas. Oil had to get to market and Trump was ensuring it would. That spelled serious trouble for Energy East.

In 2013 Energy East felt like the only chance to get Alberta bitumen to tidewater. Now it was suddenly the last project in the queue, bringing up the rear in the race to lay pipe and reach buyers. In once-recalcitrant British Columbia, Premier Christy Clark had endorsed Kinder Morgan's Trans Mountain pipeline from Edmonton to the Pacific after the company agreed to fund $25 million a year in environmental projects. The NEB recommended the project in May 2016, and Justin Trudeau's government gave its approval six months later, at an announcement where the prime minister declared that the Alberta NDP's climate policies had made pipelines politically palatable. It appeared his balancing act would now take physical form in eleven hundred kilometres of steel.

The following year, Clark lost power to an NDP–Green Party coalition opposed to Trans Mountain, and Indigenous activists warned investors in the pipeline that they might never see a profit. The company itself cautioned shareholders that the project, and their returns, could be jeopardized if climate policies, the growth of renewable energy, and public opinion led to "an overall decrease in the global demand for hydrocarbons." But CEO Ian Anderson said he was confident the pipeline would be completed, as was Rachel Notley. "Mark my words—that pipeline will be built," she said. "The decisions have been made."

Even with construction not yet underway, two approvals for two pipelines appeared to be two too many for Energy East. Political obstacles to a Pacific route in 2012 and 2013, coupled with Obama's stalling in the U.S., had forced TransCanada to look east in the first place. But at the time, forecast growth in oil sands production warranted "three Keystones," as Russ Girling put it then. After the 2014 price crash, however, projections showed barely enough production to justify two. The *Wall Street Journal* reported that TransCanada was even "struggling" to lock up enough shipping commitments to make Keystone XL viable. Producers were hesitant to book space "on a pipeline they may not need," the *Journal* reported, and Girling told investors that the drop in oil prices globally "complicates the negotiation" because refineries were reluctant to sign long-term contracts for Alberta crude. Six months after Trump's permit, TransCanada extended the deadline, citing Hurricane Harvey's impact on Gulf Coast refineries. But that wouldn't have been an issue had producers rushed to snap up capacity. One analyst said Texas refiners worried that Alberta producers were more interested in selling to Asia through Trans Mountain.

Even so, Keystone had crossed the regulatory finish line; so had Trans Mountain. Randy Boissonault, a Liberal MP from Edmonton, would later reveal that Girling told him and other Alberta Liberals in May "that if

Keystone XL was approved in addition to TMX, there wouldn't be an economic reason to build Energy East." The world of 2013—when too much oil had too few routes to market—had been turned upside down. With prices mired around fifty dollars a barrel for most of 2017, the complex and messy oil sands extraction process no longer offered a reliable return on investment for the world's largest energy companies. ExxonMobil wrote down more than three billion barrels of its reserves in northern Alberta, declaring them unrecoverable. Shell unloaded its Albian oil sands mine and other assets. Norway's Statoil ASA, Total SA of France, and Houston-based ConocoPhillips all pulled back from the oil sands to focus on lower-cost extraction elsewhere; Statoil CEO Eldar Saetre told Reuters that the company wanted "the most carbon-efficient barrels," and that heavier oil "will have to stay in the ground."

Canadian firms bought some of the assets unloaded by global players, and other indicators—drilling activity, shipments of oil by rail—were ticking up, but long-term prospects were in doubt. "It remains unclear," one analyst wrote, "whether reducing project size and deferring projects will be sufficient to keep the oilsands as an expanding production domain." At a Senate hearing in Ottawa, Gary Houston, a TransCanada vice-president, said that shippers "continue to show a great interest in Energy East," noting they had signed twenty-year contracts to use the pipeline. But another vice-president, Louis Bergeron, acknowledged that the combined capacity of proposed pipelines now exceeded the forecast supply. "The industry will have to look at that."

Another blow to the project's business case had been apparent since 2014. While Alberta producers were still forced to accept a discount when they sold into the U.S., the gap between the U.S. West Texas Intermediate benchmark and the world Brent price, tantalizingly high in 2012 and 2013, had narrowed dramatically. It was almost nothing by 2016, eliminating most of the potential premium that oil sands producers would gain if they reached a TransCanada export terminal on the Bay of Fundy. Energy East "no longer exploits the large discount" between the two prices, said an internal memorandum from the Department of Finance in Ottawa.

The global momentum for climate action, and its implications for fossil fuel markets, was another profound challenge for Energy East. Even Trump's withdrawal from the Paris agreement was widely viewed as a rearguard action and a temporary setback. In the United States, energy consumption fell in the first decade of the twenty-first century—for the first time in the country's history. The fastest growth in energy demand in 2016 was for solar power. "Even leaders in the oil and gas sector have been forced to confront an existential question," wrote the *Financial Times*. "Will the 21st century be the last one for fossil fuels?" Another writer described ExxonMobil's endorsement of the once-heretical concept of a carbon tax as "big oil's opening bid in what promises to be a long and contentious negotiation over the terms of surrender."

Dieter Helm, a renowned Oxford University economist, said there was "still a dominant zeitgeist within the oil majors that there is one last hoorah to come. I don't think there is." Shell's chief financial officer speculated that demand for oil might peak as early as 2021 and then decline. This was what Steven Guilbeault of Equiterre meant when he told me that "time is our friend." The longer Energy East was delayed, the more clearly markets could see a different world—and the more pessimistic the outlook for the pipeline's viability.

Early in 2017, Justin Trudeau held a series of town hall meetings across the country. They revealed that his quest for the middle ground on oil, climate, and energy remained unfulfilled. In Peterborough, Ontario, Trudeau spoke of phasing out the oil sands someday. Two weeks later, in Calgary, a participant shouted at him, "You cannot come to this province and attack the single-biggest employer." Trudeau responded that his goal was to get resources to market. Then, in Winnipeg, anti-pipeline activists accused him of kowtowing to the industry. "Climate leaders don't build pipelines," they yelled. The prime minister's critics on the right said that those voices, and the advent of the anti-pipeline NDP–Green coalition government in British Columbia, demonstrated that his environmental policies had been for naught. "Justin has poured billions of dollars into all kinds of green funds around the world. He has signed on to Paris, he has given speeches about the importance of it," said Lisa Raitt, Stephen Harper's former natural resources minister. "He's done more than what was needed, and still, people who don't want to have pipelines don't want to have pipelines."

Environmentalists squabbled, meanwhile, over whether Trudeau had done enough. Bill McKibben, the well-known American activist, declared the prime minister "a stunning hypocrite" for approving Trans Mountain and called his rhetoric "meaningless." Quoting Trudeau's comment that "no country would find 173 billion barrels of oil in the ground and just leave them there," McKibben noted that that amount, if fully exploited, would burn 30 percent of the earth's remaining carbon budget, the amount that would take the planet past the 1.5 degree warming goal in the Paris treaty.

But Tzeporah Berman, the former Greenpeace climate change director, rebutted McKibben, saying that Canada had made "enormous gains" with Trudeau's climate plan. Berman opposed new pipelines but had joined the advisory group drafting details of Rachel Notley's emissions cap; she argued that it was better to work with governments putting in place "building blocks" for more robust climate action in the future. Trudeau's and Notley's policies weren't enough to meet the Paris goals, she acknowledged, but "does that mean that we shouldn't do all of the climate policy that is being proposed, and we shouldn't acknowledge when government does that? I don't think so."

One of those building blocks was Trudeau's overhaul of the National Energy Board. In May 2017, an independent commission called for longer timelines for complex reviews, looser criteria on who could intervene, and a broader definition of what projects needed reviews—essentially an undoing of Harper's Bill C-38. But the Liberals wouldn't introduce the legislation for another year. In the interim, the NEB was still grappling with Energy East.

On August 23, 2017, the board's new panel for the project confirmed what it had proposed in May: it would assess upstream and downstream emissions, and would analyze whether "supply and demand scenarios" result-ing from government climate policies would affect the business case for the pipeline. TransCanada had argued that the new criteria were redundant given that the government would be assessing upstream emissions as part of its own interim pipeline review process once the NEB's work was done; Jim Carr, the federal natural resources minister, had even signed a memorandum of agree-ment with the board to that effect. The new panel's adoption of the addi-tional emissions criteria, TransCanada's lawyers said, was "a violation" of that agreement. The NEB needed to demonstrate "continuity, consistency and a degree of predictability," they argued, warning that they might challenge the new criteria in court.

Instead, TransCanada suspended its application on September 7 and said it would spend thirty days pondering what these "significant changes to the regulatory process" meant. Facing the potential collapse of an economic life-line, New Brunswick's premier, Brian Gallant, accused the NEB of "changing some of the criteria midway through" and lobbied Ottawa to pay for the emissions assessment. Carr quickly agreed, but this conflated two different issues: the cost of the climate analysis and the impact of its findings. On a $15 billion pipeline project, the cost of an emissions review was hardly fatal. What it might conclude could be far more consequential.

Another eleventh-hour plea came from a surprising quarter: Carry the Kettle First Nation. TransCanada had nurtured a relationship with the Saskatchewan band, putting $18 million on the table to win support for Energy East. Chief Elsie Jack had told me that Enbridge, whose Line 3 crossed the band's former Long Lodge reserve, hadn't been nearly as accom-modating; when federal officials conducted additional Indigenous consulta-tions on Line 3, they refused to consider the "cumulative impacts" of the project on the band, she alleged.

So on September 29—nine days before the end of the review period TransCanada had given itself—Carry the Kettle wrote to Ottawa to argue that the additional NEB criteria for Energy East were "unfair and inequitable" because they applied only to TransCanada and not to Enbridge. The board was "creating market inequities between pipeline companies," said the submission, authored by the band's consultant, James Tanner. Tanner told me that when Chief Elsie Jack expressed hesitations about Energy East in 2016, she was "responding quite appropriately to the concern in her community," but the band had ultimately decided that pipelines were better than rail. "You want a pipeline to ship your oil, if you're going to ship oil," Tanner said.

The plea was too late. On October 5, TransCanada confirmed what everyone now knew to be inevitable. In a letter to the NEB, the company said that despite Gallant's success in persuading Ottawa to fund the emissions assessment, "there remains substantial uncertainty around the scope, timing and cost" of the review. Given "the existing and likely future delays" caused by the process, the potential cost, "and the increasingly challenging issues and obstacles" facing the pipeline, TransCanada said, it was formally withdrawing its application.

Energy East—once called an essential piece of national infrastructure—was dead. TransCanada's letter was full of dry corporate and legal jargon, but the impact was nonetheless profound: Canada's regional and ideological divisions over energy and climate were ripped open once more.

There was a rare consensus among the project's most vehement supporters and opponents: the new NEB rules had killed it. "Today is a result of the disastrous energy policies promoted by Justin Trudeau and his failure to champion the Canadian energy sector," Conservative MP Lisa Raitt said in Ottawa. In Saskatchewan, Brad Wall blamed the Liberals for "a lack of interest and leadership—or worse, intentional decisions and policies" that had proven fatal. Environmentalists also attributed the decision to the NEB—and cheered. "The downfall of this project is due in large part to the recent changes to include climate change and emissions in the Energy East review," Teika Newton said. Steven Guilbeault told the CBC that the board had shown "more determination to do a decent evaluation of the project and not just rubber stamp it." Ecojustice, an environmental law firm, said that TransCanada "didn't want the ugly truth about its pipeline's full climate implications to be a factor in the government's decision-making."

The NEB itself, in its August 23 notice, had said it was taking its cues from Trudeau, attributing the new criteria to "the federal government's stated interest in assessing upstream GHG emissions associated with major pipe-lines." But both sides in the debate had other motives for blaming, or credit-ing, the new rules. For Conservatives, it was a partisan opportunity to bash the prime minister; for environmentalists, it was proof that their long cam-paign had yielded results. But Trudeau's government denied responsibility: although Carr acknowledged that the NEB criteria likely "played into" TransCanada's decision, the main cause, he said, was that the 2013 business case for Energy East no longer existed: "Conditions have changed. There's additional capacity that's been built or is currently under construction [and] commodity prices are not what they were then." He insisted that Trudeau's cabinet would have treated the pipeline like any other when deciding to accept or overrule the NEB's eventual recommendations, but "there is nothing a government can do to control a business decision that is entirely in the hands of the shareholders and those who are responsible to the shareholders."

Trudeau's provincial allies shifted their messages to align with his. Brian Gallant, who had lamented "a lot of twists and turns" in the NEB process, said that he'd spoken a second time to Girling and was "given assurances" that the "market conditions and demand" had doomed the project. "Obviously we recognize there have been other pipelines that have been approved," Gallant said. Alberta's energy minister had decried the new NEB criteria as "historic overreach" in September, but a month later, Rachel Notley said the final deci-sion was "driven by a broad range of factors that any responsible business must consider." Neutral observers agreed: Andrew Leach, the economist, tweeted sarcastically that the prime minister's anti-oil agenda was so devious that "it led to massive price drops a whole year before he was elected." Business columnist Terence Corcoran chided climate activists for taking credit and said that Energy East "grew out of a set of circumstances that were temporary." It was hard to imagine the new NEB criteria being fatal had oil still been trading at a hundred dollars per barrel.

Dennis McConaghy, a former TransCanada executive and no fan of Trudeau's policies, speculated that the company was pushing oil shippers to book capacity on Keystone XL by telling them "that we are closing this [Energy East] thing down and KXL is the last thing out of town"—the last pipeline TransCanada might build to tidewater. Oil producers sign long-term, binding contracts for pipeline capacity, and to ensure a line's viability, regulations require that they pay tolls whether they use it or not. Leach argued that given TransCanada's difficulty in lining up bookings for Keystone XL, the company would have wanted some of the producers with Energy East contracts to shift those commitments to Keystone—but they could escape their Energy East toll obligations only if that project were cancelled. "Was TransCanada making a business decision when they cancelled Energy East?" Leach asked. "Of course. It was a decision that will likely allow them to save Keystone XL."

In November, TransCanada declared that it was "encouraged" by Keystone XL bookings. But it remained silent on Energy East as the rhetorical storm continued over the cancellation: none of the company's executives granted interviews to explain how much of the decision was the NEB and how much was market conditions. The company's only comment was its October 5 letter to the board citing "likely future delays resulting from the regulatory process" but also "the increasingly challenging issues and obstacles." Responding to a question from an analyst at an investor conference in January 2018, Girling said that the company had other opportunities "far less complex, far more real, and far more doable" than Energy East. "And we had to make a hard decision. I still believe that Energy East is a great idea for this nation, but it didn't appear that we could get all the pieces put together that were necessary." It was a maddeningly ambiguous answer that might have been referring to the

NEB—but that might also encompass everything from low oil prices to the uncertain outlook for the oil sands, from Indigenous protests to the Paris climate treaty.*

The answer had consequences. Trudeau's Conservative critics weren't grappling with the logical ramifications of their own arguments: if the new NEB criteria killed the project, why didn't they apportion some blame to Jean Charest, their erstwhile political ally, for his secret meeting with board members? If not for that disastrous error, the review—under the board's old, more forgiving criteria—would have been nearing its end in the fall of 2017. More profoundly, if the simple existence of an emissions assessment was enough to kill Energy East, how strong was the case for the pipeline in a world of climate treaties and carbon prices?

And in a period that saw the southern United States struck by two catastrophic hurricanes, those who attacked stricter climate regulations did not speak of emissions reductions as a worthy goal—and nor did they offer serious alternative proposals for how Canada should adapt to a changing world.

Environmentalists who claimed credit for the demise of Energy East also had to confront the implications of their purported victory. Killing the pipeline had taken five years, but compared to actually lowering emissions, it had been relatively easy, a triumph more symbolic than enduring—the short-term, feel-good activist equivalent of fast food. The independent federal environmental commissioner concluded in a 2017 report that Trudeau's government had taken "little or no action" and had "come up short" on reducing emissions. Canada remained on track to blow past its Paris climate targets for emissions, and even if it succeeded in meeting them, the Paris accord itself wouldn't be enough to keep the world from warming too much.

---

*   TransCanada was also silent on whether it would pay Carry the Kettle First Nation the $3 million it had promised, under its agreement with the band, if the pipeline did not go ahead. The band's consultant, Jim Tanner, told me in early 2018 that the company had quietly agreed to forward the payment. In April, Chief Elsie Jack was defeated in band elections.

The demise of one pipeline wasn't going to move that needle. Not even close. Yet for the better part of a decade many activists had focused not on this broader reality but on Energy East and its counterparts, Keystone XL, Trans Mountain, and Northern Gateway.

Two days after the cancellation, an Alberta company called Chaleur Terminals said it would explore shipping crude by train to the New Brunswick port of Belledune. Oil prices were inching up in 2017, not enough to make the oil sands boom again, but enough for producers take a second look at oil-by-rail, at least until Keystone XL and Trans Mountain were operating. "We're starting to see more and more indications of barrels getting on the rails," one analyst said. "It's slowly trending in that direction." By early 2018, there was still no construction announcement for Keystone XL, even after Rachel Notley committed some of the Alberta government's own oil reserves—once destined for Energy East—to strengthen its business case. At the same time, British Columbia threatened to block shipments of bitumen through the province on Trans Mountain. Pipeline uncertainty heightened the impetus for oil-by-rail: the shipping bottleneck to the U.S. was opening the price gap again, hurting Alberta producers, and there was no longer a backup pipeline for those two projects—no Plan C to ship oil east. If tanker cars of crude oil began moving again in large numbers, Energy East's demise would prove a pyrrhic victory for environmentalists: the fossil fuel they loathed would be transported in increasing volumes with no emissions tests whatsoever. Travelling by rail, it would play its role in warming the planet virtually unchecked.

The same week Energy East was cancelled, the International Energy Agency issued a bullish report on renewable energy. "The era of expensive renewables is over," declared the IEA's executive director, Fatih Birol. The agency forecast that demand for oil would continue to rise in the coming decades, but at a declining rate. Britain and France said they would ban new gas-fuelled cars starting in 2040, and China, the world's largest market, hinted it might do the same. Shell announced it would install electric vehicle chargers at all twenty-five thousand of its gas stations worldwide. And Irving Oil, always quick to respond to market demand, allowed New Brunswick's electric utility to install charging stations at seven of its locations in the province.

In that environment, it was possible to see the new NEB criteria and world market conditions not as mutually exclusive theories of a pipeline's demise, but as two manifestations of the same reality—that oil's status as the most vital, defining commodity on earth was now in question. The new rules reflected the reality of climate change and the possibility of peak demand, and were nudging Canada to adapt.

Whether Trudeau's Liberals were willing to say so publicly—whether they even realized it themselves—their policies, and the NEB's adoption of new criteria, reflected a turn toward the ideas of the 2016 report by Policy Horizons, the internal government think tank: that oil was at risk of losing its value in a global market shifting to renewables, that a pipeline premised on thirty years of oil shipments "could be at high risk of becoming economically unviable"—and that Canada faced a choice.

Ottawa, the report said, could resist the trend and risk increasingly negative perceptions of the country's oil—and might even be forced to bail out wrongheaded fossil fuel investments. Or it could lead the transition to a clean-energy future by shifting away from the oil sands to less expensive and less dirty conventional crude—a "niche market" product in this imagined future—and by spurring renewables to help shape a "carbon-constrained global economy."

Seen through that prism, Trudeau's climate framework, and the NEB criteria it had inspired, looked like the second path, an attempt to heed the signals the world was sending—to establish a new set of assumptions and ground rules, then let the market sort out which individual projects could withstand climate scrutiny. It was, perhaps, a clumsy attempt. A too narrowly focused attempt. Given that emissions were forecast to keep growing, it may even have been a wholly inadequate attempt. But it was an attempt.

Back when I was following the Energy East route across Saskatchewan, a year before the project's cancellation, I whizzed past a team of about a dozen cyclists pedalling east on the Trans-Canada Highway outside the town of Herbert. They were clad in serious-looking red-and-black gear and were riding serious-looking bicycles. TransCanada's right-of-way passed about twelve kilometres north of Herbert, while the CP rail line cut right through the town.

Herbert had a CPR museum housed in its old train station, which was dwarfed by a nearby grain terminal. An old red freight car and a bright yellow CP caboose were linked by wooden walkways so that visitors could walk between them and the museum. But it was Sunday, and everything was closed.

In the parking lot, two men were packing a tent awning and folding chairs into a rented cube van. They were the support team for the cyclists I'd passed, part of the National Kids Cancer Ride. The cross-Canada fundraising relay had started on the Pacific Ocean in White Rock, British Columbia, and would end on the Atlantic at Halifax. A light rain was falling. They'd decided to cancel a rest stop in Herbert and keep pushing east.

Jim Lahay had retired after forty-five years as a trucker, "so I've seen a lot of this country"; he'd signed up as a volunteer driver in part because he enjoyed the journey for its own sake. "I love Canada from coast to coast," he said. He'd done the cancer ride twice and had also taken his granddaughter on a drive from London, Ontario, to Victoria and back. They'd driven east to the Maritimes, too. "So yes, we've seen the country, and love it."

I asked Lahay about the Energy East debate. "I think I can maybe speak for different parts of the country and how I understand them," he said. "Alberta and Saskatchewan definitely need it to get their product to market, a market other than the U.S.—the international market. But going through Ontario and Quebec, I also see where they're very concerned about where it's going to cross the water, and what that may do if a break happens in the pipeline. And I also see New Brunswick could use the jobs to support themselves down there. So I see all sides of it. I understand all sides of it."

If there was an average, even-handed, well-informed Canadian take on Energy East, it was Jim Lahay's. He appreciated that shipping oil by rail "has its own hazards," he went on. But he also took a longer view, wondering if there would even be a demand for oil when the pipeline was finished. "I think in five to ten years' time, we're going to see a great transition to alternative energy, be it solar, be it wind," he said. "I think the cars are getting progressively more hybrid, more electric. I think over the next ten years, it's not going to serve its full lifetime use."

The other driver started the engine on the cube van. I asked Lahay whether he thought a consensus on Energy East was possible across the vast landscape we were travelling. "Of course I do," he said. "We're Canada. We've come together on so many things over the years. Yes, we have our different ideas, but when it comes to the good of the country, this country has always come together. We are Canadian."

The cancellation of Energy East left the nation with an uneasy status quo in the short term. Alberta was back to where it had been when the project was conceived: fighting to get pipelines built, except now the province's carbon economy faced a more uncertain future. Quebec got its way—again—but found itself in its old role as the object of western resentment. New Brunswick had pinned its hopes on another megaproject only to see it evaporate like the others, but the relentlessly optimistic business leaders in Saint John who had deemed the pipeline essential now asserted that the city was "no longer a one-engine or one-project" town and would muddle through somehow.

The long-term picture was more troubling. The project's demise may have been an indicator of a less carbon-intensive future, but politically, it was no catharsis. The same competing impulses Jim Lahay had described were on display again when British Columbia's premier, John Horgan, said he would consider using provincial regulations to stop Kinder Morgan's Trans Mountain expansion—despite the federal government's jurisdiction over the project.

Historically, Canada's crises have been resolved with grand bargains and compromises, from the Quebec Act of 1774 to the patriation of the Constitution in 1982. British Columbia's gambit jeopardized Justin Trudeau's bargain: Horgan was "putting at risk the entire national climate change plan," delicately constructed with Rachel Notley, Trudeau declared. "Alberta will not be able to stay on if the Kinder Morgan pipeline doesn't go through. We will not have them fighting to reach their carbon targets." But the prime minister's strategy of trade-offs was losing its lustre. When he suggested that Ottawa would force through Trans Mountain, Tzeporah Berman, the former Greenpeace leader who had sought consensus with Suncor and defended Trudeau's incrementalism, warned that "conflict"—in the form of activists physically impeding construction—was "looking necessary." In March, protestors, including Green Party leader Elizabeth May, were arrested after they blocked access to Kinder Morgan's work site in Burnaby.

Trudeau's carbon-tax plan and the interim NEB process he had put in place for Trans Mountain, with additional Indigenous and environmental consultations, had not persuaded its most ardent opponents. It was incumbent on the federal government to defend its regulatory regime and the subsequent cabinet approval, but the prime minister's calculus was premised on pipelines now in return for lower emissions in the future—a promise environmentalists had heard before. And on a given pipeline project, no middle ground was possible: it would be built, or it would not.

In April Kinder Morgan issued an ultimatum. The company announced it could not commit the approximately $300 million per month it needed during construction season without "clarity." Horgan had cannily threatened restrictions—thus spooking investors—without actually taking any concrete action Ottawa could challenge in court. British Columbia's objections were "neither validated nor quashed," said Kinder Morgan's CEO, Steve Kean. "A company cannot litigate its way to an in-service pipeline amidst jurisdictional differences between governments." Without a resolution by the end of May, he warned, "it is difficult to conceive of any scenario in which we would proceed with the project."

The existential questions posed by Energy East flared back to life. Oil prices might continue to recover from the 2014 crash, but a return to boom times in Alberta—and to easy regulatory approval of pipelines—couldn't be taken for granted. And the transition to a lower-carbon economy, if it happened, would not be neat and tidy. The day TransCanada cancelled Energy East, Brad Wall wrote that the decision, and the policies he said led to it, "may well have some westerners wondering if this country really values western Canada, the resources we have, and the things we do to contribute to the national economy and to quality of life for all." One might think from his ominous messages that Trudeau hadn't said yes to two pipelines, or that a prairie-based, pipeline-friendly federal government hadn't been in power for a decade before that. But his larger point was undeniable—and was later underscored by the Trans Mountain confrontation. If Canada was going to put climate action on an equal footing with its oil economy, if Energy East's demise heralded a turning point in national priorities, if pipeline opponents could fight even a legally approved project to a stalemate, the risk to the economic fundamentals of Alberta and Saskatchewan would pose a profound test for the future of the country.

Two days before Kinder Morgan's deadline, the Trudeau government announced it would nationalize Trans Mountain, sweeping away the jitters of shareholders. The goal was to build the project then sell it back to the private sector—roughly the same solution the St. Laurent government used in 1955 to push through TransCanada's first gas line. Pipeline politics in Canada had come full circle: the construction of a major oil-sands line was now impossible without state intervention.

In the midst of the Trans Mountain drama, a few scattered voices, mainly Conservative politicians, called for Trudeau to revive Energy East, as if a government acquisition of one pipeline suddenly rendered viable a second, more expensive, more politically arduous proposal. But the market conditions that killed Energy East had not changed. In a world in which deeper emissions reductions were inevitable domestically and globally, Trans Mountain was winning the race to transport a commodity for which future demand was uncertain—a race to become perhaps the last major oil pipeline built in Canada.

Two sales pitches had been made for Energy East, and both had failed. In one, it was a simple steel tube built to carry a product that would otherwise move through other means, and was thus unfreighted with climate implications—an untenable proposition as activists, frustrated with a lack of action on climate, marshalled opposition. So politicians adopted a second argument, that it was a nation-building project, like the CPR. But making Energy East a political objective invited an equally political response—and that made the broader battle about oil, energy, and climate inevitable.

Of course, nationalist rhetoric was never a good fit for any oil pipeline, even Energy East: most of its crude would have left Canada, and Arthur Irving would have continued importing Saudi oil. The new line would have accepted U.S. oil through the Cromer lateral, and the conversion in eastern Ontario would have hinged on importing more American gas to replace Alberta's. Underscoring this continental reality was how readily the industry rushed back to its Plan A, Keystone XL's high-speed link to the U.S. Gulf Coast, when it was suddenly on offer again.

A pipeline that was supposed to unite the country instead became a different national metaphor, highlighting regional divisions and then falling victim to the same global economic forces, and the same north–south gravity, that had always bedevilled Canada. Marketed as a national dream, Energy East was subjected to the most polarizing and onerous debate the nation could muster.

And by the standards that its most vocal supporters had themselves set— as a tool of supply and demand, then as a measure of patriotism—it was a failure even before it began, little more than a pipe dream.

NOTES

Most of the interviews for this book took place during two trips along the Energy East route. The first was from Hardisty, Alberta, to Thunder Bay, Ontario, in September 2016. The second was from North Bay, Ontario, to Plaster Rock, New Brunswick, in May 2017. I also visited Calgary and Edmonton ahead of my visit to Hardisty, and made short trips to Saint John and Cumberland Bay, New Brunswick, in June 2017. Some other interviews were done by telephone or in person at other times. Quotations that don't come from my interviews are indicated in these notes or in the text.

Besides the sources mentioned in the chapter notes below, several books helped my research or shaped my thinking in a more overarching way: *Let the Eastern Bastards Freeze in the Dark* by Mary Janigan (Vintage Canada, 2012), *Stupid to the Last Drop* by William Mardsen (Knopf Canada, 2007), *Pipeline* by William Kilbourn (Clarke, Irwin and Company, 1970), *The Prize* by Daniel Yergen (Free Press, 2009), *Private Empire* by Steve Coll (Penguin, 2012), *The Patch* by Chris Turner (Simon and Schuster, 2017), and *The Carbon Bubble* by Jeff Rubin (Random House Canada, 2015). The book that moved me to tackle a project about the environment and climate change was *The Sixth Extinction* by Elizabeth Kolbert (Henry Holt and Company, 2014).

I was disappointed that none of the major Alberta oil sands companies that planned to ship on Energy East were willing to grant me interviews. The companies operating the three refineries that would have received oil from the pipeline—Suncor, Valero, and Irving Oil—also did not respond to my requests for interviews or refinery visits. Most particularly, I regret that TransCanada chose not to cooperate. The company's spokesperson for Energy East, Tim Duboyce, responded helpfully (though not always fully) to my factual questions by email, but the refusal of interviews prevented me from telling the stories of the executives, engineers, and technicians who conceive, build, and operate the company's pipelines.

As reticent as TransCanada was about talking to me, the company could not avoid the regulatory requirements of the National Energy Board, including an obligation to file a massive volume of documents as part of its pipeline application. The NEB, for all the criticism of its approach to pipelines, maintains an exhaustive online archive of filings, an invaluable tool for my research. I relied on two documents in particular, both from the Energy East application, Vol. 14, Project and Assessment Overview (May 2016): section two, "Project Description," and section four, "Alternative Means of Carrying Out the Project." The latter document is a 138-page explanation of how the company made its decisions on routing for the new sections of the pipeline. I use it frequently in the narrative. I also found many of the people I interviewed along the route by consulting applications to intervene in the Energy East hearings, filed on the NEB website.

PROLOGUE

Rebecca Penty of Bloomberg News described the context for the west–east pipeline in an early story, "TransCanada Looks East Amid Keystone Pipeline Delay," on February 7, 2013. The March 3, 2016, Policy Horizons Canada document, "Canada in a Changing Global Energy Landscape," was reported by Robson Fletcher of CBC News on May 30, 2016, and a copy of the document was posted with the online story. Adam Huras's long article "Pipeline: Birth of the Plan," New Brunswick *Telegraph-Journal*, August 24, 2013, was a vital source. Divya Reddy was quoted in Kyle Bakx, "Keystone XL Could Be Canada's Last Big Oil Export Pipeline," CBC News, January 25, 2017.

CHAPTER ONE

Luiza Ch. Savage's "The Untold Story of Keystone" in *Maclean's*, January 27, 2014, recounts the battle in Nebraska, while a story by a team of Bloomberg reporters, Edward Greenspon, Andrew Mayeda, Rebecca Penty, and Theophilos Argitis, described the Harper–Obama dynamic in rich detail in "How Obama Shocked Harper as Keystone's Frustrator-in-Chief," April 26, 2014. For Dennis McConaghy's comments, see Kyle Bakx, "The Card Canada Never Played to Get Keystone XL Approved," CBC News, December 20, 2016. The growth of oil-by-rail was investigated by Grant Roberston and Jacquie McNish, "Inside the Oil-Shipping Free-for-All That Brought Disaster to Lac-Mégantic," *The Globe and Mail*, December 2, 2013.

CHAPTER TWO

Information about the sharp-tailed grouse is from a March 2010 brochure by the Alberta Conservation Association. Calgary's office tower woes were reported by Katia Dmitrieva and Rebecca Penty, "'It Is a Bloodbath': Calgary Office Towers Are About to Feel the Full Force of the Oil Crash," Bloomberg News, November 10, 2015, and by Jeff Lewis and Kelly Cryderman, "Cenovus Shows Office Space Amid Glut," *The Globe and Mail*, June 18, 2016. The Kilbourn, Turner, and Marsden books were valuable in this chapter, as was Chris Varcoe, "When the Oil Sands Hit Pay Dirt," *Calgary Herald*, September 26, 2017.

CHAPTER THREE

Marcella Munro's comments are from Don Braid, "NDP's New Calgary Hand Declares Love for Oilsands and her BMW," *Calgary Herald*, September 14, 2015. The argument about Alberta's "captured" political system was made by Kevin Taft, "Captured State: How the Oil Industry Still Runs Alberta," *Alberta Views*, September 20, 2017. The entire conversation between Steve Williams and Tzeporah Berman is available on YouTube at https://youtu.be/huVVxujh6ZY, and the divisions within the industry were reported in Carl Meyer, "Civil War in the Oil Patch," *National Observer*, May 25, 2017, and Geoffrey Morgan, "'The Splinters Are Showing': Conventional Producers Quit CAPP Amid Rifts Over Carbon Tax," *Financial Post*, June 21, 2017. Justin Trudeau's comments on Alberta's climate plan are from James Wood and Chris Varcoe, "Trudeau Green-Lights Trans Mountain Expansion, Enbridge Line 3, but Rejects Northern Gateway," *Calgary Herald*, November 29, 2016, and Rachel Notley's assertion that climate and pipelines had been "delinked" was made on CBC Radio's *The House* on December 3, 2016. The geographical coordinates for all the pump stations were included in TransCanada's regulatory documents filed publicly with the National Energy Board. See also Zane Schwartz, "Did Climate Change Contribute to the Fort McMurray Fire?" in *Maclean's*, May 4, 2016.

CHAPTER FOUR

Bill and Janet Albrecht of Burstall, Saskatchewan, helped me by phone with some last-minute fact-checking about the Empress gas plants. Louise Crop Eared Wolf's comment on the Great Sand Hills is from Energy East project submissions, Vol. 16: Socio-Economic Effects Assessment—Part B: Saskatchewan and Manitoba, appendix 5A: Aboriginal Community Profiles and Literature Review—Saskatchewan; Pat Provost's is from the transcript of the NEB's Energy East Aboriginal consultations. *The Great Sand Hills: A Prairie Oasis*, by Rebecca Grambo and Branimir Gjetvaj (Nature Saskatchewan,

2007), is a loving description of this unique ecosystem. John Nilson's "dead in the water" comment is from Hansard, Legislative Assembly of Saskatchewan, Standing Committee on the Economy, April 5, 2011. Geoff Leo of CBC News reported key details about the Husky spill in "Husky Oil Spill Began When Pumping Resumed Through Pipeline Expansion Project," CBC News, July 28, 2016.

CHAPTER FIVE

Frank McKenna's op-ed, "Let's Build a Canadian Oil Pipeline from Coast to Coast," appeared in *The Globe and Mail*, June 18, 2012. Brad Wall's CPR comparison is from his remarks to journalists covering the East Coast Energy Connection conference in Saint John, New Brunswick, on June 15, 2016. Mark Scholz, "Pipelines Are the Nation-Building Opportunity of Our Time," was published in the *Calgary Herald*, July 1, 2016. For the CPR as national myth, I drew on E.J. Pratt, *Towards the Last Spike* (MacMillan, 1952), F.R. Scott, "All the Spikes But the Last" (Representative Poetry Online, University of Toronto), and three books by Pierre Berton: *The Last Spike: The Great Railway 1881–1885* (McClelland and Stewart, 1971), *The Joy of Writing* (Doubleday Canada, 2003), and *My Times: Living with History, 1947–1995* (Doubleday Canada, 1995), as well as A.B. McKillop, *Pierre Berton: A Biography* (McClelland and Stewart, 2008).

The federal government's text of Treaty Four is available at www.aadnc-aandc .gc.ca/eng/1100100028689/1100100028690, but see also Blair Stonechild, "Treaty Four," *Encyclopedia of Saskatchewan* (University of Regina and Canadian Plains Research Centre). The tragic history of Carry the Kettle First Nation is told in the Indian Claims Commission report, "Carry the Kettle First Nation Inquiry: Cypress Hills Claim," Ottawa, July 2000. Candace Savage's *A Geography of Blood* (Greystone Books, 2012) was also helpful. The account of the pictograph's journey back to Fort Qu'Appelle is from Ashley Robinson, "Historical Pictograph Tells Story of Treaty 4 Signing," *Regina Leader-Post*, January 6, 2017.

Jorge Barrera's story "Nakota Chief Says TransCanada Used 'Conniving Tactics' to Secure Energy East Deal Ahead of Band Vote" was published by APTN News on March 10, 2016. The online story included a PDF copy of the agreement.

CHAPTER SIX

Figures on Saskatchewan's oil and natural gas revenue are from the provincial Department of Finance. The two *New York Times* stories on Boundary Dam were Henry Fountain, "Corralling Carbon Before It Belches from Stack," July 22, 2014, and Ian Austin, "Technology to Make Clean Energy from Coal Is Stumbling in Practice," March 29, 2016. Reporting on Boundary Dam's financial woes includes Stefani Langenegger, "Sask. Carbon Capture Plant Doubles the Price of Power," CBC News, June 17, 2016; D.C. Fraser, "Sask. Energy Minister Says Residents Already Paying Carbon Tax," *Regina Leader-Post*, May 11, 2017, and Kyle Bakx, "Brad Wall and the Elusive Goal of Carbon Capture and Storage," CBC News, December 3, 2015. See also Robson Fletcher, "Canada's Oil Industry 'In the Middle of a Battle,' Brad Wall Tells Calgary Petroleum Club," CBC Calgary, June 8, 2016. Wall's 2008 Empire Club speech can be found at https://youtu.be/rPoX7G8xCqQ. The 2016 sequel is at http://vvcnetwork.ca /empireclub/20160614. Other key interviews with Wall are Max Fawcett, "The Full Alberta Oil Interview with Saskatchewan Premier Brad Wall," *Alberta Oil*, September 2, 2015, and John Ivison, "NEP 2.0: 'Another Trudeau's' Environmental Rules Sow Seeds of Unity Crisis, Critics Say," *National Post*, August 7, 2017. Information about Boundary Dam's performance is from SaskPower's web blog devoted to the project, and the utility's reluctance to build more carbon-capture units was reported by Stefani Langenegger, "SaskPower 'Highly Unlikely' to Recommend Further Carbon Capture Projects," CBC News, November 3, 2017.

CHAPTER SEVEN

The differing figures on the Upland pipeline are from a TransCanada fact sheet, "Proposed Project: Upland Pipeline Project," December 2015, and Brian Zinchuk, "Getting the Skinny on TransCanada Pipeline Projects," *Pipeline News*, June 4, 2015. See also Claudia Cattaneo, "TransCanada Corp Moves Forward with Upland Pipeline Amid 'Extraordinarily Difficult' Keystone Process," *Financial Post*, February 13, 2015. Zinchuk's article is also the source for John Soini's subsequent comments about activists. The description of the protest at the Phil Fontaine speech is from a video included with Connie Walker's story, "Protest During Phil Fontaine's Speech Sparks Online Debate," CBC News, January 23, 2014; Fontaine's defence of his TransCanada role is from Shawn McCarthy, "First Nations Leader Phil Fontaine: An Angry Radical Embraces Compromise," *The Globe and Mail*, May 16, 2014.

Colby Richardson's comment on fossil fuels is from Sean Silcoff's profile of the family, "Growing Up Richardson," *Report on Business* magazine, November 2017. The *Financial Post*'s catalogue of blocked energy projects is available at http://business.financialpost.com/features/arrested-development, while Vivian Krause wrote about "The Cash Pipeline Opposing Canadian Oil Pipelines" in the *Financial Post*, October 3, 2016. Her full list for 2015 is at http://fairquestions.typepad.com/rethink_campaigns/2016/12/anti -pipeline-groups-funded-by-tides-in-2015.html. How the divestment debate in the U.S. shifted mainstream opinion on climate action is described in David Roberts, "The McKibben Effect: A Case Study in How Radical Environmentalism Can Work," Vox.com, September 29, 2017. Abacus Data's polling on energy and climate is available on the company's website.

CHAPTER EIGHT

For research on whether dilbit sinks or floats, see Jason Markusoff, "Does Spilled Pipeline Bitumen Sink or Float?" in *Maclean's*, January 7, 2017. For the hydroelectric power needed to run Energy East pump stations, see Will

Braun, "2014 Big Step Back for Manitoba Power," *Winnipeg Free Press*, January 5, 2015. Dennis LeNeveu's report, "Potential Impacts of the Energy East Pipeline on the City of Winnipeg" (Manitoba Energy Justice Coalition, 2015), includes discussion of the impact on Shoal Lake No. 40. See as well Richard Bolton, *Being Out on the Lake: Iskatewizaagegan Anishinaabeg Perspectives on Contemporary Fishing Practice and Well-Being* (Natural Resources Institute, University of Manitoba, 2012). The city's response to concerns about the water in Shoal Lake is available at www.winnipeg.ca/waterandwaste/water/shoalLake.stm. Dan Levin, "A Museum About Rights, and a Legacy of Uncomfortable Truths," *The New York Times*, October 5, 2016, noted the sad irony of the Canadian Human Rights Museum using water drawn from Shoal Lake.

CHAPTER NINE

Kenora's history is recounted in Florence Mead (ed.), *Through the Kenora Gateway* (Kenora Centennial Committee, 1981). Wab Kinew's description of anti-Indigenous racism in the city is from his memoir, *The Reason You Walk* (Viking Canada, 2015). The CBC archives page includes several reports on the Berger inquiry, including "Berger on Native Land Claims, Now Settled," September 6, 1988. See also "Thomas Berger: My Idea of Canada," June 2, 2005, on the Citizens for Public Justice website. Teika Newton posted her audio recording of the April 19, 2016, Kenora council meeting at https://soundcloud.com/user259276247/20160419a, with Dave Canfield's reference to the Calgary trip audible at the 23:30 mark. Reporting on Edelman's advice to TransCanada includes Shawn McCarthy, "Greenpeace Sees 'Dirty Tricks' in PR Firm's TransCanada Plan," *The Globe and Mail*, November 17, 2014, and Margo McDiarmid, "Energy East Pipeline 'Advocates' Targeted in TransCanada PR Move," CBC News, November 18, 2014. For background on the "Last Spike at Feist Lake" plaque, see Ontario Heritage Trust, Featured Plaque of the Month, June 2009. I also cite Northwestern Ontario Municipalities Association, "Presentation to

Ontario Energy Board re: Energy East Project," January 2015, and KBM Resources Group, "Developing a Northwestern Ontario Definition of Significant Water Crossings," report for Common Voice Northwest, June 20, 2017.

CHAPTER TEN

For Black River–Matheson's reliance on TransCanada, including Mayor Mike Milinkovich's comments, see Township of Black River–Matheson, "TCPL Energy East Pipeline OEB Presentation," April 1, 2014. For other elements of the debate in North Bay, see Trout Lake Conservation Association, "Concerns for Potential Energy East Impacts to Trout Lake and Its Watershed," draft version, March 2016; "Former Fire Chief Throws Support Behind Energy East Pipeline," BayToday.ca, October 15, 2016; Marina von Stackelberg, "TransCanada Removes Energy East Video After Controversial Appearance of North Bay Fire Chief," CBC News, November 7, 2016, and "Appearing in TransCanada Energy East Video Was OK with Former Fire Chief," CBC News, November 8, 2016.

Coverage of Kathleen Wynne's approach to Energy East included Adrian Morrow, "Wynne Drops Main Climate Change Requirement in Considering Energy East Pipeline," *The Globe and Mail*, December 3, 2014, and James Wood, "Notley's Pipeline Advocacy Wins Support from Wynne, Trudeau," *Calgary Herald*, January 22, 2016. See also Office of the Auditor General of Ontario: Oakville Power Plant Cancellation Costs (report), October 2013. Comprehensive indictments of Wynne's green energy policies cited are Terence Corcoran, "Boondoggle: How Ontario's Pursuit of Renewable Energy Broke the Province's Electricity System," *Financial Post*, October 6, 2016, and Tom Adams, "Ontario's Renewable Energy 'Disaster' Is What Drives Up the Cost of Your Hydro," InsideToronto.com, March 9, 2017.

CHAPTER ELEVEN

A persuasive and entertaining debunking of the idea that the astrolabe found in the Ottawa Valley was Champlain's is Douglas Hunter, "The Mystery of Champlain's Astrolabe," *The Beaver*, December 2004–January 2005. Stephen Harper's lack of climate action is examined in George Hoberg, "Unsustainable Development: Energy and Environment in the Harper Decade," in *The Harper Factor: Assessing a Prime Minister's Policy Legacy*, Jennifer Ditchburn and Graham Fox (eds.), McGill-Queen's Press, 2016. The Bruce Heyman–Frank McKenna discussion of Keystone XL is available at https://vimeo.com/97233500. Catherine McKenna's rationale for keeping Energy East under existing NEB rules is from CBC's *The House*, January 30, 2016. Susan Delacourt's subsequent comments on the pipeline as unity crisis were from the same episode.

Russ Girling's view of an emissions test is from Tracy Johnson, "TransCanada CEO Says Don't Blame Pipelines for Climate Change," CBC News, March 1, 2016, and his comments about the failure to win over opponents are from Claudia Cattaneo, "Policy Doesn't Sway Pipeline Opponents," *National Post*, July 29, 2016. The fateful Jean Charest–NEB meeting was revealed in Mike DeSouza, "Canadian Pipeline Panel Apologizes, Releases Records on Meeting with Charest," *National Observer*, August 4, 2016; the scoop on Harper's postdated NEB appointments was by Elizabeth Thompson, "Doomed Harper Government Made 49 'Future' Patronage Appointments," *iPolitics*, November 23, 2015. The links between climate change and the Ottawa River flooding of 2017 are from Ivan Semeniuk, "Anatomy of a Deluge," *The Globe and Mail*, May 10, 2017. Sophie Brochu's speaking notes from her October 14, 2014, speech are on the Gaz Métro website.

CHAPTER TWELVE

The Entec study, "Étude de faisabilité préliminaire de traverse par FDH, Québec: Rivière des Outaouais," Calgary, June 11, 2014, which had disappeared from the NEB's online archive, was obtained by the activist group

Les Citoyens du Courant and resubmitted to the board on April 1, 2017. TransCanada's letter promising "an expanded approach" to the river crossing is from the NEB archive and is dated June 29, 2016. A joint report by two groups, Environmental Defence and Equiterre, "Application Incomplete," June 2017, describes their concerns about several river crossings. Daniel Cloutier's comments are from proceedings of the House of Commons committee on Natural Resources, May 9, 2013. The Deloitte study on refinery savings is "Energy East: The Economic Benefits of TransCanada's Canadian Mainline Conversion Project," September 2013. For the Diefenbaker-created oil border between Ontario and Quebec, see Tammy Nemeth, "Consolidating the Continental Drift: American Influence on Diefenbaker's National Oil Policy," *Journal of the Canadian Historical Association*, vol. 13, no. 1, 2002, and "A Tale of Two Canadas," *Alberta Oil* magazine, March 20, 2017. I also consulted Transportation Safety Board of Canada, "Railway Investigation Report R13D0054: Runaway and Main-Track Derailment," August 19, 2014.

Coverage of the Marois government's dealings with pipelines include Geneviève Lajoie, "Pétrole des sables bitumineux: Daniel Breton s'oppose," Agence QMI, November 14, 2012; Robert Dutrisac, "Marois entrouvre la porte au pétrole albertain," *Le Devoir*, November 23, 2012; Alexandre Shields, "Québec se voit comme 'partenaire' des pétrolières," *Le Devoir*, May 23, 2013; and Jean-Marc Salvet, "Oléoducs: Le gouvernement Marois divisé," *Le Soleil*, August 29, 2013. The 2015 National Film Board documentary *Pipelines, Power and Democracy* (Olivier D. Asselin, director) followed Daniel Breton's post-ministerial wrestling with the pipeline question. The anti-pipeline speech by interim PQ leader Stéphane Bédard is at https://pq.org/videos/allocution-du-chef-de-lopposition-officielle-steph.

CHAPTER THIRTEEN

Jeffrey Simpson wrote about Equiterre's co-founder in "Steven Who? Steven Guilbeault. Remember the Name," *The Globe and Mail*, September 11, 2010.

Coverage of Energy East in Quebec included Gabriel Delisle, "Yves Lévesque en faveur de la construction d'une station de pompage à Trois-Rivières," *Le Nouvelliste*, April 10, 2015, and Michel Corbeil, "Pipeline Énergie Est: Traversée 'à haute risque' à Saint-Augustin," *Le Soleil*, November 6, 2014. The report for TransCanada was Golder Associates, "Energy East Pipeline (New-Build Portion), Hydrotechnical Hazards Phase II Assessment," March 12, 2015. For Cacouna, see Diane Tremblay, "Cacouna essentiel au project," *Journal du Québec*, October 19, 2014, and Marc-Antoine Paquin, "Une année emotive pour Ghislaine Daris," *Infodimanche Rivière-du-Loup*, January 5, 2016. Louis Bergeron's comments are from Nicolas Van Praet, "TransCanada Tasks Its New Quebec Pitchman with Selling Energy East," *The Globe and Mail*, February 8, 2016. See also Appendix I to National Energy Board letter, "Draft List of Issues," May 10, 2017, for the board's proposal to assess upstream and downstream emissions.

CHAPTER FOURTEEN

I relied on research for my previous book, *Irving vs. Irving* (Penguin Random House Canada, 2014) for this chapter and the next one. For the Plaster Rock derailment, see Shawn Berry, "Evacuees Returning Home," *New Brunswick Telegraph-Journal*, January 13, 2014. Figures on Irving Oil's U.S. exports are from Claudia Cattaneo, "Playing the Piper," *Financial Post*, June 9, 2016, and Arthur Irving's description of the company's New England orientation is from John DeMont, *Citizens Irving* (Doubleday Canada, 1991).

CHAPTER FIFTEEN

Another key story by Bloomberg News is an account of the early days of Energy East, including the near-collapse of talks between Irving and TransCanada, by Rebecca Penty, Hugo Miller, Andrew Mayed, and Edward Greenspon, "Keystone Be Darned: Canada Finds Oil Route Around Obama," Bloomberg

News, October 8, 2014. Richard Valdmanis and Dave Sherwood, "A Family Plan to Pump Canada's Oil," Reuters, March 27, 2014, is another comprehensive account. The suggestion that a second terminal was added at Cacouna to placate Irving-wary producers is from Cattaneo, "Playing the Piper." The Alberta government's commitment to ship oil on Energy East is from Josh Wingrove, "TransCanada Wants Alberta Government to Buy Capacity in Keystone XL Pipeline," Bloomberg News, November 2, 2017. Bob Manning's ode to the billionaire industrialists, "Let's Celebrate the Irving Family, Not Criticize Them," appeared in *Huddle Today*, April 12, 2012. Reuters coverage of Irving's environmental record by Dave Sherwood and Richard Valdmanis included "Air Quality Problems Dog Irving's Oil-by-Rail Terminal," August 29, 2014; "Gatekeeper of Canada's Energy East Pipeline Has Mixed Environmental Record," April 22, 2015; "Partner in Canada's Energy East Struggled with Pollution Controls," November 11, 2015; and "Irving Oil Pollution Raises Environmental Concerns in Saint John," June 10, 2016.

On Irving's purchase of Saudi oil, see Terry Etam, "Saudi Oil at a New Brunswick Refinery—What Kind of a Domestic Energy Policy Is That?" *The Boe Report*, January 25, 2016, and Claudia Cattaneo, "As Oilsands Punished, Tanker Loads of Cheap Saudi Oil Sail into Canadian Exports Daily," *Financial Post*, February 9, 2016. Tim Duboyce's comment that the pipeline would "end the need" for foreign oil is from Chris Morris, "Energy East 'Critical,'" New Brunswick *Telegraph-Journal*, January 4, 2017. Ian Whitcomb's key comments that Saudi imports would continue are from Claudia Cattaneo, "Irving Oil's President Says It Would Keep Saudi Imports Even if Energy East Goes Ahead," *Financial Post*, April 12, 2016. The account of K.C. Irving resisting a federal requirement to buy Alberta oil is from Douglas How and Ralph Costello, *K.C.: The Biography of K.C. Irving* (Key Porter Books, 1993).

EPILOGUE

Information about the Trans Mountain pipeline is from Peter O'Neil, "Pipeline Politics: What's Next for B.C.?" *Vancouver Sun*, January 12, 2017, and Keith Stewart, "Kinder Morgan Investors Should Be Prepared to Lose Their Shirts," Greenpeace Canada blog post, May 29, 2017. On Energy East becoming unnecessary, see Jacques Poitras, "Trumped? Energy East Faces New Obstacle," CBC News, January 27, 2017, and on industry reluctance on Keystone XL, I cite Christopher M. Matthews and Bradley Olson, "New Problem for Keystone XL: Oil Companies Don't Want It," *The Wall Street Journal*, June 29, 2017, and Shawn McCarthy, "TransCanada Extends KXL Process Amid Fears of Excess Pipeline Capacity," *The Globe and Mail*, September 6, 2017. See also Shawn McCarthy and Kelly Cryderman, "TransCanada Affirms Commitment to Energy East Pipeline," *The Globe and Mail*, January 31, 2017. The shrinking of the tidewater differential was described in a memorandum from Jean-François Perrault to Paul Rochon, Department of Finance, Ottawa, December 10, 2015, obtained through the Access to Information Act.

Throughout 2017, there were too many articles speculating about "peak demand" or "the end of oil" to cite here, but among the most relevant were Amy Myers Jaffe, "How Does Canada Respond to Stranded Asset Risk?" Canadian Global Affairs Institute, April 2017; Liam Denning, "The Energy Revolution Will Be Optimized," Bloomberg View, August 16, 2017; Pilita Clark, "The Big Green Bang: How Renewable Energy Became Unstoppable," *Financial Times*, May 18, 2017; Jillian Ambrose, "Down Forever, No Last Hoorah: Why the Market for Fossil Fuels Is All Burnt Out," *Financial Post*, April 19, 2017; and David Roberts, "Exxon's Support for a Carbon Tax Is the First Step in Big Oil's Long, Negotiated Surrender," Vox News, June 27, 2017. For Statoil's comments on the shift away from heavy oil, see Nerijus Adomaitis and Ron Bousso, "Statoil Plants Flag in Big Oil's Race for 'Cleaner' Crude," Reuters, November 21, 2017.

Differing takes on Justin Trudeau by environmentalists were Bill McKibben, "Stop Swooning Over Justin Trudeau. The Man Is a Disaster for the Planet,"

The Guardian, April 17, 2017, and Tzeporah Berman, "Just How Environmental Are Canada's Environmental Policies?" *The Real News*, April 29, 2017. Jim Carr's comments on Energy East were on CBC's *The House* on October 7, 2017. Analyses of Energy East's demise include Claudia Cattaneo, "Trudeau's Sad Legacy: Billions in Energy Infrastructure Spending, Scuttled on His Watch," *Financial Post*, September 8, 2017; Terence Corcoran, "Economics Killed the Energy East Pipe Dream—and That's Good," *Financial Post*, October 5, 2017; and Andrew Leach, "How Donald Trump Killed the Energy East Pipeline," *The Globe and Mail*, October 9, 2017. Russ Girling's comments at the investor conference were reported by Chris Varcoe, "After 'Bruises' of Past, TransCanada Vows to Carefully Move Ahead with Keystone XL," *Calgary Herald*, January 26, 2018.

Justin Trudeau's comments about British Columbia's attempts to block Trans Mountain are from Elizabeth McSheffrey, "Trudeau Spills on Kinder Morgan Pipeline," *National Observer*, February 14, 2018. See also Chris Varcoe, "Despite Alberta's Climate Efforts, Tzeporah Berman Says Pipeline to Coast Not Acceptable," *Calgary Herald*, February 15, 2018. Other sources include Kyle Bakx, "Costlier and More Dangerous Crude by Rail Set to Rise Again as Production Swells," CBC News, October 31, 2017; Anmar Frangoul, "New Era of Solar Power Is Now Upon Us, IEA Says," CNBC, October 4, 2017; and Barbara Simpson, "Saint John Businesses 'Regrouping' After Energy East News," *New Brunswick Telegraph-Journal*, October 6, 2017.

ACKNOWLEDGMENTS

A trip along a proposed 4600-kilometre pipeline route can't be organized alone. I relied on many friends and colleagues for assistance with the logistics of the journey.

CBC colleagues Paul Haavardsrud and Kyle Bakx in Calgary, Michelle Bellefontaine in Edmonton, Stefani Langenegger in Regina, and Angelica Montgomery and Catou MacKinnon in Quebec City provided suggestions and insights. Bloomberg's Rebecca Penty let me draw on her expertise in the oil industry, which was particularly valuable. Thanks to all of them.

For accommodations along the way, my gratitude—and an offer to reciprocate at any time—goes to Sean Prpick and Maud Beaulieu in Regina; Mark Reid and family in Winnipeg; and John Ruttle and Celia Armitage, and Peter Simpson and Jennifer Campbell, in Ottawa. Thanks as well to the staff of the Legislative Library in Edmonton, and of municipal libraries in Moose Jaw, Kenora, and Stittsville.

I am in debt to the people along the Energy East route who agreed to talk to me about their views on pipelines, energy, and climate change, especially those whom I approached at random, without warning. They were, to a person, generous and insightful. This is their story.

Although the point of the trip was to speak to these "ordinary Canadians," politicians are an important part of this story, too. Marcella Munro greased the wheels for my conversation with Shannon Phillips, Stefan Baranski helped me contact Alison Redford, and Josée Jutras arranged my interview with Pauline Marois. These conversations added important context to the book.

Thanks to Louise Robertson for help with my visit to the Treaty Four commemoration ceremony in Fort Qu'Appelle, Jim Tanner for connecting me with Chief Elsie Jack, and Cuyler Cotton for setting me up with Daryl Redsky at Shoal Lake No. 40.

Tim Duboyce, TransCanada's lead spokesperson on Energy East in eastern Canada, patiently fielded dozens of questions I sent him by email. Tim wasn't always able to provide me with all the answers I wanted, but I appreciate his efforts and his good-natured approach. Sarah Kiley from the National Energy Board also responded helpfully to many, many e-mailed questions.

At CBC New Brunswick, I am fortunate to work with a crack team of journalists who enrich my day job immeasurably. They show interest in my book projects, provide help when I ask for it, and listen patiently when I rattle on about seemingly pedantic details about pipelines. Rachel Cave helped me reflect Brad Wall's visit to Saint John, and Terry Seguin provided tips on his hometown of North Bay. Mary-Pat Schutta, Darrow MacIntyre, and Denise Wilson gave me permission to work on this book on the side. I continue to be grateful to the University of New Brunswick Department of English for conferring on me the status of honorary research associate, which grants me borrowing privileges at the Harriet Irving Library—a boon to any researcher. I also want to acknowledge Janet North of Westminster Books in Fredericton for her continued support for New Brunswick authors.

This book was copyedited by Karen Alliston, whose sure hand improved my writing considerably. She deleted countless repetitive words, insisted that I clarify several poorly explained concepts, and caught a few potentially embarrassing errors. Any that remain are mine.

There are three women without whom this project would not have been possible. My agent, Hilary McMahon, helped me hone the idea into an appealing pitch and went to bat for the project. Diane Turbide at Penguin Random House Canada saw the potential in the story. Her green light—and her flexibility with the advance—allowed me to travel across large parts of my country that I otherwise would never have seen up close. Diane also helped refine the themes when the book's primary subject, Energy East, was abruptly killed in October 2017. It was a humbling and enriching experience to work with her and the supremely talented team at Penguin Random House who saw this book through to completion.

Lastly, my wife, Giselle Goguen, stood by me, and this book, with unwavering support. She provided advice and feedback rooted in, and worthy of, her own impressive journalistic track record, sharp intellect, and incisive writing. My debt to her is one I can never really repay, though I will continue to try every day. Whatever route I find myself on, it always leads back to her.

INDEX